THE PRIVATE CITY

Philadelphia in Three Periods of Its Growth

SAM BASS WARNER, JR.

THE PRIVATE CITY

Philadelphia in Three Periods of Its Growth

upp

PHILADELPHIA, UNIVERSITY OF PENNSYLVANIA PRESS

To my Mother and Father

First *Pennsylvania Paperback* edition 1971
Revised paperback edition 1987

Part and chapter illustrations by John Maass. Part opening
illustrations courtesy of Free Library of Philadelphia (Parts
One and Two) and Philadelphia Department of Records (Part Three)

Maps by Liam Dunne.

Library of Congress Cataloging-in-Publication Data

Warner, Sam Bass, 1928–
    The private city.

    Bibliography: p.
    Includes index.
    1. Philadelphia (Pa.)—History. I. Title.
F158.3.W18   1987   974.8'11   86–25124
ISBN 0–8122–8061–X
ISBN 0–8122–1243–6 (pbk.)

Contents

Acknowledgments

The most helpful gift a scholar can be given is time, time to learn, time to do research, and time to write. I received very generous grants of time from the M.I.T.-Harvard Joint Center for Urban Studies and from the Washington University Institute for Urban and Regional Studies. Without the support of these two institutions this book would not have been possible.

The presentation of the statistical data in the book takes a somewhat novel form for a history because of an opportunity created by the Washington University Computer Facilities through its National Science Foundation grant G-22296. The basic statistical tabulations were made on I.B.M. cards and thus I could omit the usual appendix of figures which is generally too scant for the research scholar to use and too detailed for the ordinary reader to comprehend. Instead, any scholar who wishes to rework the basic material of this study for his own purposes may secure punched cards from the Inter-University Consortium for Political Research, Box 1248, Ann Arbor, Michigan 48104.

Many people have helped me in collecting data. My former student, Roger Wolf, and his roommates at George Washington Law School spent days copying the 1860 Census schedules at the National Archives. The late Harlan G. Loomer of Philadelphia lent me numerous items from his collection of twentieth-century Philadelphia materials, including unpublished U.S. Census tract data for 1930. In addition he offered his wisdom and experience in city planning research. The libraries of the University of Pennsylvania, the Pennsylvania Historical Society, the Pennsylvania Historical and Museum Commission, and the Free Library of Philadelphia were generous with time and materials. I especially want to thank John Daly of the Department of Records of the City of Philadelphia, and Marjorie Karlson and her fellow reference librarians of the Washington University Library for their repeated thoughtful service.

Over the years several research assistants have contributed enormously to this study as well as to other projects of mine. My thanks go to Diane V. Friebert, Naomi S. Waldstein, Marilyn Walterman, and Henry D. McClure. It was Henry McClure who conceived of the method of analyzing the eighteenth-century tax lists and then carried out the tabulations.

Several scholars at the University of Pennsylvania showed me many kindnesses—Neil Leonard, Anthony N. B. Garvan, Everett S. Lee, and Anne R. Miller. I am indebted to Robert H. Levy, whose perceptive research while at the University of Pennsylvania contributed to the accuracy of ward boundaries and descriptions of riots in Philadelphia from sources that were inaccessible to a St. Louis scholar. My former colleagues and students at Washington University also helped in many ways—Rowland T. Berthoff, Barry D. Karl, Ralph R. Morrow, Charles L. Leven, and Joseph R. Passonneau.

Finally, I want to thank two friends for their generous and thoughtful criticism. My former colleague Gilbert Shapiro spurred me on during the early stages, and my former editor Max R. Hall struggled through a first draft.

Sam Bass Warner, Jr.

Introduction to the Revised Edition

This book is about the unfolding of the American tradition of city building and city living. It does not treat what was unique about Philadelphia, but presents the city as a resonant example of the major cities that have given form to the culture and society of the United States: New York, Los Angeles, Chicago, Philadelphia, Detroit, San Francisco, Dallas, Houston, Boston, Miami, Atlanta, Minneapolis, Cleveland, St. Louis, and the like.

Ours is not a nation dominated by its capital city, the way France is by Paris; instead it functions as a confederacy of regional metropolises. Each city is at once the competitor and the partner of all the others. I chose Philadelphia because industrialism has defined our cities and Philadelphia is the oldest of the industrial cities. In the history of Philadelphia we observe first the setting of the American urban tradition during the years of the Revolution, and then the triumphs and failures of that tradition as the successive stages of industrialization and urbanization unfold. Philadelphia is not, like London, a mother of cities, but she is the eldest of the sisters.

At the time this book was written, during the early and mid-1960's, American cities were experiencing one of their periodic moments of explosive change. There were, as on previous occasions, explosions of expectations, explosions of populations, and explosions in city building. After decades of economic depression and world war there were fresh hopes for family life, a marriage boom and a baby boom. Millions of Americans expressed their pent-up hopes for clean, comfortable new houses and neighborhoods in the purchase of detached suburban houses with new electrical appliances, family rooms, and yards. On the job front there were expectations that the harsh times of the twenties and thirties were over and that union and management cooperation, new machines, new processes, and new products could simultaneously raise wages, profits, and working conditions. On this wave of rising expectations for comfort and decency came the beginnings of the Civil Rights movement with its insistent demands that

Afro-American citizens be no longer excluded from the refashioned society.

These were boom times, the years when the federal government laid down the superhighways, and the old dense central cities and their close-in suburbs spilled out over miles and miles of nearby villages and towns to transform the industrial city into its present dispersed metropolitan patterns. These were the years of the shopping mall, the industrial and office park, and the regional high school with the majority of its students bound for college.

A sense of optimism pervaded many people's lives and work. A feeling that old prejudices could be ignored, and old ways forgotten, freed people's hopes. Even as the center city emptied out, and boarded up shops and houses and vacant lots dotted formerly busy streets, many believed that the center could be rebuilt so that it would be pleasanter and more habitable than what existed before. These were also the years of federally sponsored urban renewal.

This history, first published in 1968, speaks in two voices: a voice of optimism and a voice of warning. First, it shares the optimism of its decade and the heightened sense of fresh possibilities. It uses that optimism as its measure of the past. If during the 1960's good city planning and good private and public management could simultaneously renew the center city and build a whole new metropolis on the suburban fringes, then surely modern standards of habitability were the correct tests by which to evaluate past municipal performance. To speak of the past in such a way does not mean to castigate eighteenth-century Philadelphians for not chlorinating their well water, or to attack the Philadelphia row house for its absence of cross ventilation. Rather it means to speak of the contrasts between present expectations for a healthy life, civic peace, and open expression, and the varying approximations to these goals that have been achieved in both the past and the present.

Second, the book was written as a warning, as an urban historian's companion to Michael Harrington's influential *The Other America, Poverty in the United States* (New York: Macmillan, 1962). At the time of my Philadelphia research I was a historian attached to a school of architecture and an urban studies center at Washington University. As I listened to my colleagues who were then actively involved in urban design and urban policy analysis, and as I observed what was happening around me in St. Louis, I saw history being re-enacted. It seemed to me that neither the general public, nor the mayors and the administrators, nor the citizen members of the advisory committees, were aware of the tradition that governed their actions. Ignorant of the past experience of the American city these optimistic and well-meaning citizens were applying a mistaken set of values and attitudes to their urban constructions and reconstructions. I feared that their cultural consensus would choke off the abundant promise of the times, narrow family and neighborhood life, hobble private building, and cripple public planning. The sense of unease brought on by my St. Louis experiences became, as I studied the history of Philadelphia, an awareness of the depth and power of the America urban tradition. It is a tradition that has brought and still brings many successes, but it also causes the repeated failures of our cities and metropolises.

In this book I gave the American urban tradition the name "privatism." I so relabeled liberal capitalism because I wanted to encourage my readers to start by examining their own personal values and commitments and then to think in outgoing circles of awareness of the many aspects of city life which that tradition has drawn upon and influenced. I feared that if I used the term capitalism many readers might mistakenly interpret the history of the city as a narrow tale of the working out of open price-setting markets. This economist's abstraction is an extremely useful analytical concept, but if this abstraction of the market is mistaken for the totality of an urban society then the actual workings of a city will be lost.

The urban renewal mayor, Joseph Clark, used the term capitalism in its narrow sense when he said a few years ago that "two hundred and sixty-eight years of laissez-faire economics had left the city in a hell of a mess." Just as he knew that the revival of the city depended on combined public and private efforts, so Philadelphia's history must be organized according to the many urban dimensions in which liberal capitalism has manifested itself here in America.[1]

Privatism was given its modern American meaning by the Revolutionary generation and was codified by the constitutions and charters of the United States, of Pennsylvania, and of Philadelphia. As a tradition it gives value and direction to individuals, families, organizations, and governments. For men it suggested Benjamin Franklin's

1. Stanley Newman, ed., *The Politics of Utopia: Toward America's Third Century* (Lecture Series, April 28–May 23, 1975, Temple University, Political Science Department, Philadelphia, 1975, pages by lecture only), Clark 3.

model for a life course: a youth of self-discipline and hard work devoted to the accumulation of personal wealth, followed by a more
leisurely middle age of comfort, public honor, and community service. For women it implied marriage, homemaking, and childrearing
for such a husband, with the hoped-for later life of a comfortable
home, well-settled children, and a community of family and friends.

As a human settlement pattern the tradition suggested a city
where the men would cooperate most easily in public tasks that
promised mutual material benefit, and where philanthropy would
flourish among the wealthy. Given such values it also promised extreme difficulties should any group of individuals seek to alter the settled distribution of wealth, income, or political advantage. Likewise,
projects that required continuing investments without near-term
economic rewards, or undertakings that addressed the right to an
equality of being for disadvantaged or poor citizens, would experience
repeated difficulties.

As I look back over the history of Philadelphia today, even after
all the transformations of modern family life, business, and government, the concept of privatism is still an excellent tool for organizing
the millions of Philadelphia lives and for interpreting the workings
of the city's institutions. Philadelphia has enjoyed an extraordinary
success as a hive of money-makers and money-makers' families. Even
today most children are admonished to work hard, to make money;
and even today the housekeeping and child-raising falls to women in
Philadelphia's families. Many of the city's philanthropies in medicine,
art, music, and learning are outstanding. Its private businesses are no
more rapacious than those elsewhere, and many of the wealthy citizens
continue in active civic roles. Although the close links between state
and local politics have given Philadelphia a special municipal history,
a balance sheet of the municipality's successes and failures shows that
it stands comfortably in the middle of the nation's metropolises.

Of course no tradition can endure unless it changes with the
times, and the hold which privatism has upon the hearts of Americans
is in part explained by its adaptability. As a set of values and a moral
code it still makes distinctions between behavior within the family
and behavior towards customers and fellow employees. Its attitude
towards a child's hoard of coins and towards the accounts of an oil re-
finery strongly differentiates the varieties of private property.

Privatism is a cultural consensus whose meanings have followed the growth of the city from the years of sailors, slaves, laborers, servants, shopkeepers, and merchants to the present times of machine operators, salesmen, attendants, nurses, corporate executives, and government administrators. During the nineteenth century the great thrust of private and public effort was to organize an atomized city into reliable and effective social units: the private manufacturing corporation, the labor union, the political machine, and the railroad were its achievements. Now that the metropolis has been reconstructed as a region of networks of closely interacting institutions the task for the future has shifted. Ways must be found to admit the vast army of Philadelphia's poor citizens into these organizations and their prosperous economy. At the same time for the benefit of those already inside, and for the health of the region as a whole, ways must be found to release the power and creativity of the many who are trapped within those organizations which are unjust, ill-managed, or ossified.[2]

There are many themes that can be used to organize the complicated histories of cities: the history of the municipal corporation; changes in technology; the progress of the arts; experiences of different racial, ethnic, or religious groups; or the history of a particular institution, a business, a union, a college, a hospital or the like. Since this history of Philadelphia was first published in 1968 many such books have been written; indeed Philadelphia has become a leading center of urban history. A list of these titles is given in the Bibliography at the end of this new edition, so that those interested in either the history of the American city, or that of the city of Philadelphia itself, can find additional material.

Were I to undertake another history of Philadelphia, I would extend the time covered to 1950 and I would give much more attention to the various ways in which Philadelphians spoke of, imagined, and thereby understood their city.

The reason for extending the third era of this book, the period of the Industrial Metropolis of 1920, down to 1950 would be to make clear the distinction between Philadelphia in the 1920's and today. To someone like me, whose childhood was spent in the urban stagnation of the Great Depression and World War II, the twenties seemed

2. Theodore Hershberg et al., "A Tale of Three Cities: Blacks, Immigrants, and Opportunity in Philadelphia, 1850–1880, 1930, 1970," in Theodore Hershberg ed., *Philadelphia, Work, Space, Family, and Group Experience in the Nineteenth Century* (New York, 1981), 461–491.

to be the decade when the modern American city came into being: big business, highly mechanized industrial production, automobiles, and suburbs. That was true, but as I was doing my research during the 1960's I did not appreciate the force of the decentralization I saw going on around me. The process differed both quantitatively and qualitatively from the suburbanization of the 1920's or earlier.

A new period in Philadelphia's history began during the 1950's. The changes set in motion then permeated as many aspects of urban life as had the previous century's factory industrialization. During the years since 1950 America's big cities have been transformed from their old industrial metropolitan form into new dispersed urban regions. They had been giant dense center cities surrounded by a few small satellite industrial cities and some residential suburbs. Now they have become regions fifty miles across, peppered with a multiplicity of specialized clusters and commercial strips, and centered on a less dense, less all-encompassing inner core.

The briefest survey of the population in and around Philadelphia reveals the sudden shift in settlement pattern. Until 1950 the history of the Philadelphia region could still be told in terms of the Philadelphia municipality, an institution with the same boundaries as Philadelphia County: in population it constituted 59.8% of the two-state region in 1860, 58.7% in 1930, and still 53.1% in 1950. By 1980, however, the U. S. Census reported Philadelphia's sudden decline to only 33.6% of the same region.

These simple percentages summarize major social changes. During the early decades of the twentieth century Philadelphia's industry boomed, and as it did it spread itself along the established axis of the Delaware River and the parallel north-south rail lines which ran from New York towards Baltimore and the South. Trenton (Mercer County), North Philadelphia, Camden, and Chester (Delaware County) were the prime locations of the industrial metropolis (compare Table 1, 1860 to 1930).

At the center stood the downtown of offices, stores, services, and wholesaling. Although the first decades of the twentieth century were the years when every American family tried to buy an automobile, and many families succeeded, most residents of the industrial metropolis still travelled on public transit: in streetcars, subways, the new motor busses, and commuter railroads. Consequently the city's resi-

TABLE I

METROPOLITAN PHILADELPHIA

Percent of the Region's Population

County	1860	1930	1950	1980
Pennsylvania				
Philadelphia	59.8	58.7	53.1	33.6
Bucks	6.8	2.9	3.7	10.0
Chester	7.9	3.8	4.1	6.3
Delaware	3.3	8.4	10.6	11.0
Montgomery	7.5	8.0	9.0	12.8
New Jersey				
Burlington	5.3	2.8	3.5	7.2
Camden	3.6	7.6	7.7	9.4
Gloucester	1.9	2.1	2.4	4.0
Mercer	3.9	5.6	5.9	6.1

Total Population of Metropolitan Philadelphia

	944,821	3,324,183	3,900,892	5,024,681

Population of the City of Philadelphia

	565,529	1,950,961	2,071,605	1,688,210

Sources: Joseph Oberman and Stephen Kozakowski, *History of Development in the Delaware Valley Region* (Year 2000 Plan Report No. 1, Delaware Valley Regional Planning Commission, Philadelphia, September, 1976), 53, 69; U.S. Bureau of the Census, *U.S. Census of Population: 1950*, Volume One, *Number of Inhabitants* (Washington, D.C., 1952) , Table 5; *U.S. Census of Population: 1980*, Volume One, *Characteristics of the Population: Pennsylvania* and *New Jersey* (Washington, D.C., 1982; PC 80–1–B40, Pa; PC 80–1–B32, N.J.), Table 14.

dential growth followed the established street patterns and rail align-ments which had been laid down prior to the Civil War.

When the suburban boom returned after the hiatus of World War I Philadelphia's area of residential fashion continued to advance along the rail commuting lines. It reached outward in spokes from Elkins Park on the north to Bryn Mawr and Upper Darby on the west. Despite this push, however, most of the new houses built in the Phila-delphia region prior to the end of World War II were located within the municipal boundaries of the city. The dense pattern of row house construction and the availability of 20,000 acres of farm land within the city limits allowed the industrial metropolis to carry on in its familiar pattern.[3]

Since 1950 the region has grown along entirely different lines. The construction of interstate highways and arterial streets has broken the street railway and rail transportation organization. Industries, offices, and stores spread out over the entire region to a radius of twenty-five miles from Philadelphia's City Hall. In doing so, they did not merely repeat the past in a widely dispersed fashion; rather both the pattern of settlement and many of its physical elements were new. The great suburban constructions in King of Prussia are not fresh versions of old satellite cities like Chester or Trenton. Instead they form a new low-density configuration of offices, factories, warehouses, stores, and hotels which do not have a single center—something like a small downtown—but instead form a network of interstate highway interchanges, wide roads, and parking lots. Yet such an arrangement is so popular in today's ways of doing business that industrial space in King of Prussia rents for more than comparable space in Philadelphia, and retail rents are only exceeded by peaks at the Philadelphia downtown core and on Chestnut Street.[4]

Similarly, the Oxford Valley Mall, an everyday, albeit giant seventy-million dollar shopping center in the northeast part of the region, is neither a suburban reconstruction of Market Street, nor is it Gimbel's or Wanamaker's department store enlarged. It is a new kind of place. Although it is decorated like a department store, its ownership has shifted from family proprietorships to corporate branches and franchises, its merchandise from American to international, and the governance of its walkways and paved areas from municipal to private management. The only important continuity with the past is that it remains predominantly a place of women.[5]

These new settlement patterns and building types were constructions of a highly elaborate process which transformed the society and

3. Joseph Oberman and Stephen Kozakowski, *History of Development in the Delaware Valley Region* (Year 2000 Plan Report No. 1, Delaware Valley Regional Planning Commission, Philadelphia, September, 1976), 58–75.

4. Urban Land Institute, *Philadelphia, Pennsylvania, Metropolitan Area . . . Today* (Washington, D. C., 1981), xix; Peter O. Muller, *Contemporary Suburban America* (Englewood Cliffs, 1981), 156–157, 163–166.

5. Urban Land Institute, *Philadelphia Metropolitan Area Today*, 145; Sam Bass Warner, Jr., "The Liberal City," *Design Quarterly #129: Skyways* (1985): 16–19.

economy of Philadelphia. In 1950 it still made sense to harken back to the old characterization of the region as the "Workshop of the World": machine shops, foundries, locomotive plants, shipyards, textile mills, garment shops, coal wharves, and railroads dominated the daily experience of Philadelphians. Such things also probably dominated residents' imaginative cityscapes. In the national media there were jokes about the dullness of the city, jokes which, in fact, were comments on the narrowness of the institutions and routines demanded by industrial work. Whatever their cultural richness, neither old Philadelphia nor new Detroit were entertaining cities. The mill city exacts a heavy price from both public and private lives. By the mid-1980's, however, the proportion of the region's workers employed in manufacturing establishments had fallen by half: it fell to twenty percent of the region's employed.[6]

Because we have yet to capture the social and cultural meanings of the new era, it is still commonly labeled by a name taken from the economist's tabulation of products: the "service economy." The term calls attention to economic outputs other than manufacturing, mining, or farming. It embraces the activities of finance, commerce, business, and home and personal services. When one translates these product categories into names for the jobs people do, the listing becomes more concrete.

Thus Philadelphia's bankers and insurance men, real estate agents, lawyers, and accountants are old breeds who are multiplying, while the region's civil and mechanical engineers must give up their former high standing to mathematicians and computer scientists. Philadelphia's physicians are now tied to biology laboratories and very specialized institutions of medical service. Patients must make their way through the labyrinth of advanced medical care, a network requiring an enormous staff of technicians, nurses, cleaners, and washers who try to care for the human beings connected with the machinery and the drugs. Programmers and temporary secretaries are new occupations, but the old roles of waiter, bartender, cook, and dishwasher also characterize the 1980's service economy. The door-to-door carpet washer and the vinyl siding salesman have replaced the cleaning lady and the house painter; downtown, the city planner and

6. Anita A. Summers and Thomas F. Luce, *Economic Report on the Philadelphia Metropolitan Area, 1985* (Philadelphia, 1985), 6–10.

the Internal Revenue Service agent are embodiments of the ubiquity of government in the new Philadelphia.[7]

Because the Philadelphia region is so richly supplied with natural, financial, and human resources it accomplished its transition from an old manufacturing center to a new mixed region of services and manufacturing with comparative ease. A decade or so of economic stagnation from 1970 to the early 1980's, a time when steel mills, machine builders, and foundries closed, and textiles and garments moved overseas, sufficed to close out the old activities and to shift the labor force into new lines of work. All the while the port of Philadelphia, the oil refineries, the banks and insurance companies, the big retailers, and the electrical, drug, and chemical industries carried on successfully. Because of these resources, and because of the region's central position in the giant northeastern United States market, Philadelphia did not have to undergo the long depression that Boston went through from 1921 to 1960. Its diversity also protected it from suffering like one-industry Detroit.

A recent listing of the leading local employers records the transition from the old workshop to the new mixed economy. In 1980 the region's largest employer was, fittingly enough, devoted to talk and gossip, Bell Telephone of Pennsylvania: 18,000 employees. The phone company's leadership nicely reflects Philadelphia's increasing attention to human services and commerce. Next on the list came the famous national retailer, Sears Roebuck, with 13,000. Close behind this old firm stood a newly giant employer, the University of Pennsylvania, with almost 13,000 employees. The next two institutions were long-established ones: the retailer Strawbridge and Clothier with 12,000 and Philadelphia Electric with 10,000. These were followed by United States Steel and Temple University, both with 8,700. The balance of the list of the region's fifteen largest employers mixed activities from the old economy like Campbell's Soup, Sun Oil, and John Wanamaker with the newer manufacturing activities of General Electric, General Motors, and the food retailer, Acme Markets. The city's former specialty in rail transportation was now expressed as public institutions that were the aftermath of private bankruptcies: the federal government's Conrail, and the region's SEPTA (South East Pennsylvania Transportation Authority).[8]

7. Summers and Luce, *Economic Report*, 73–75.
8. Urban Land Institute, *Philadelphia Metropolitan Area Today*, xxi.

The economist's report is clear enough. The machines of advanced industrialization no longer require, as they did a century ago, the tending hands and straining backs of most of the city's workers. Machine-tending has turned out to be only a phase in the unfolding history of industrial urbanization. Philadelphians have returned more and more to the ancient city activities of buying and selling, lending money, talking, eating, drinking, entertaining, teaching, nursing, and politics. The ways in which these timeless urban activities are carried out, however, are now so different from in the past that we are all at a loss to describe and evaluate our regional cities. They are as much a surprise and a mystery to us today as their predecessors were to our great-grandparents.

At present, Philadelphians use two very different languages to describe their new city. One language, that of regional science, tries to comprehend the size and complexity of the metropolitan region by drawing upon the familiar images of business and the abstract terms of economics and social science. The other language seeks concretion and personalization by imagining the region to be a clustering of small social cells, of communities. Its imagery is not the abstractions of the social sciences but stories of family life, neighboring, and local politics. One language is abstract and often mathematical; the other is detailed and often narrative.

The regional science language accepts the vast expanse of a dispersed Philadelphia, and attempts to give meaning to a society composed of 5,025,000 inhabitants by focusing on its economic life. The economic reports and the regional plans are, like all abstractions, ways of discussing a limited set of concerns. The issues are far-reaching social patterns.

As a regionalist you notice such surprises as the fact that there are more acres of office space outside Philadelphia's downtown than inside it. You try to comprehend the new scale of buying and selling which is expanding to be an ever-lengthening list of overseas products. At the same time more and more Philadelphia firms and institutions sell their goods and services to national and international customers. You notice, too, that despite the reach of electronic communications and the speed and flexibility of air transportation, the metropolitan density of messages and goods is such that there is intense competition for the attention, space, and time of listeners, viewers, and buyers. You can no longer place an advertisement in the *Phila-*

delphia Inquirer, or put a novelty in a downtown store window, with the expectation that it will sell. Instead, to market a new product now usually takes more effort and capital than it does to invent one.

Similarly, from the regional stance you notice that although the new high-technology economy draws its strength from the innovations of men and women who sit in offices and laboratories and who spend their day thinking, that thinking rests upon an extraordinarily elaborated physical structure of pipes, wires, roads, bridges, buildings, and houses. It also rests upon long-sustained and vastly expensive investments in schools, libraries, colleges, and universities, all of which seem necessary to the work of the thinkers, but little of which are charged to either the thinker or his or her employer. Such overlapping events and indirect social dependencies are the puzzles that concern the regionalists.[9]

Although this language includes residential life, it does so only indirectly, through the abstractions of employment, income, retail sales, traffic counts, journey-to-work tabulations, and the statistics of demography. What makes today's regional language so comfortable to us is its combination of social science with the traditional American view that a city is a gathering place of money-makers. Thus, despite its abstractions and mathematics it is familiar discourse.

Yet like the nineteenth-century words of paid-in capital, horse-powers, mill hands, and tons of iron, the regional language abstracts but a small fraction of urban life. It records the stages of life—birth, school, employment, marriage, change-of-address, homeownership, divorce, death—but it confines the meaning of these events to their economic import. To give some more concreteness to the details of daily living in the modern metropolis the language of community has now come back into vogue. By this convention you examine the metropolitan region as if it were composed of hundreds of small villages. You seek out the place names—Frankford, Fishtown, Society Hill, Overbrook, Chester, Jenkintown—and the institutions which support those names, and you try to form a picture of representative lives be-

9. For example, Center for Greater Philadelphia, University of Pennsylvania, *Southeastern Pennsylvania State Legislator's Conference: Toward a Shared Delaware Valley Agenda* (Conference May 29–30, 1986, Radnor, Pa.); or an older geographical summary of the region, Peter O. Muller, Kenneth C. Meyer, and Roman A. Cybriwsky, *Philadelphia: A Study of Conflicts and Social Cleavages* (Cambridge, 1976), 35–64.

ing carried on beneath the umbrella of the named places.[10] The inter-view, the photograph, the oral history, the study of local institutions are the prime methods of this approach. Whereas in the regional language the author and the reader share social science concepts, in this language they share the actualities of individual lives. The one is based on economics, the other on anthropology. The great merit of the community approach lies in its drawing out the details of settled family life. It tries to find the meanings of the city in terms of the daily routines of families, and to order these activities so as to make a pattern which can be called the community's way of life. Families make communities, and communities make up the metropolitan region.

A former University of Pennsylvania sociologist, Herbert J. Gans, carried out the best of these community studies during the late 1950's and early 1960's. In 1958 Gans purchased a new Cape Cod style house in Levittown, then being built at Willingboro, New Jersey. Willingboro was a township of truck farms and orchards situated at the outer edge of the Philadelphia metropolis, seventeen miles from downtown. A famous firm of developers who had already executed massproduced settlements in Long Island, N. Y., and Bucks County, Pa., proposed to erect 12,000 inexpensive houses. The design of the streets and lots conformed to a neighborhood unit plan: every 1,200 houses were grouped around a park which contained an elementary school. Such a physical layout was thought to promote sociability and to encourage the formation of a sense of community. The home purchasers were mostly families moving out from old inner city locations; about one quarter were working class and three quarters were lower middle class.[11]

As a participant-observer living in Levittown, Gans sought the answers to two questions that are keys to understanding the living patterns of the modern metropolis. First, did the spatial patterns of houses and streets predict the patterns of sociability? Second, did a community-wide way of living develop in Levittown, or were its ways

10. There is a popular guide to Philadelphia which published a map with the place names for the city, but not for the region: Richard Saul Wurman, *Man-Made Philadephia: A Guide to Its Physical and Cultural Environment* (Cambridge, 1972), 70.

11. Herbert J. Gans, *The Levittowners, Ways of Life and Politics in a New Suburban Community* (New York, 1967), xxvii-xxi, 4–12.

multiple and determined by events outside the new residential area?

Gans's report was a mixed one. Suburban Philadelphians were not helpless molecules caught in the powerful magnetic fields of economic markets. Neither did they live as if within some encompassing country town or urban ethnic village. Except for the political institutions of Levittown, there were no boundaries that marked the edge of a place, nor any single center that drew everyone at regular intervals. The units of sociability varied a great deal from family to family, and they were never defined physically.[12]

Residents followed common paths to work, on errands, for child care, and visiting, but these paths varied with sex, age, income, and the habits and needs of particular individuals and families. There was a good deal of visiting back and forth with relatives, though less than among the inner city working class. Unlike the Philadelphia of 1900 or 1930, relatives lived far away. Mothers and daughters tried to remain close, but they talked on the telephone, they could no longer go to market together. And now, twenty years after Gans's report, both are apt to be working in paid employment! Children, through play and school, promoted neighborhood contacts, but the degree to which these acquaintanceships matured into either friendships or organized activities like PTA's or the Girl Scouts, depended a good deal on the class of the families.

Although 38% of Willingboro's citizens are now Afro-Americans, the community's politics remains what it has always been: a few activists and the paid professionals manage the township's affairs. Levittown, N. J. was settled by hardworking, independent families who go their own way. Its residents are still the same sort of people. They come together as a community in times of crisis when there is need for them to organize themselves. For the rest of the time they are as privatist as all their fellow Americans. These are the patterns and tendencies that Gans reported in 1967 and they have continued to appear in metropolitan community studies. For most Philadelphians, as for most Americans, there is no nesting set of social pathways, personal indentifications, and family obligations and responsibilities that together form an urban village. There is not one Levittown, Frankford, or Society Hill, there are many.[13]

In the United States the language of community, like the lan-

12. Gans, *Levittowners*, 173–174.
13. Gans, *Levittowners*, 24–29, 172–181; Gans, *Levittowners* (New York, 1982), v-xvi.

guage of economics, has always been highly politicized. Beneath the concepts of economics and social science lies the politics of privatism, and beneath the named communities lies the politics of exclusion.[14] These buried foundations of attitude and value matter a great deal to the life of a city because the politics of community is often at odds with the goal of openness that is the ideal of the liberal capitalist city.[15]

The smallest cells of urban living are the families, and families can only exist if their members draw sharp boundaries between those included and those outside, between those within the circle of mutual obligations, the relatives, and all others. The politics of exclusion are thus the inescapable politics of families, and families are often active promoters of such a use of power.

So too with religion. Since ancient times ministers, priests, and rabbis have been exhorting their flocks to draw together so that they may preserve their faith against the erosion of outside influences. Politicians have reinforced such outlooks because it is efficacious for them to deal with voters in blocks and stereotypes; such boundaries also divide the electorate against itself and give the politician the powers of the bargain striker. Storekeepers, newspapers, and local radio stations also like to promote the names and images of a place in an attempt to secure customer loyalty. Together all these actors, the clustering families, the congregations, the local politicians, the store-keepers, and the media can cover the social pathways of people with strong place labels. In some aspects of our urban living these labels give us a sense of who and where we are. They seem, however, most powerful in defensive mobilizations, to preserve what is now, to keep out unwelcome newcomers.

During the late nineteenth century many observers of the indus-trial city were appalled by the rapid turnover in poor and working class neighborhoods, by the sheer volume of flow of people seeking jobs and cheap rents. They feared the city was becoming an atomized mass of drifting individuals. As a remedy, reformers created a special local institution, the settlement house, to promote sociability and to teach American ways. Although the settlement house was a phil-

14. Muller, *Contemporary Suburban America*, 66–71.
15. See in this connection Seymour J. Mandelbaum's articles asking what sorts of communities Philadelphia might be: "What is Philadelphia? The City as Polity," *Cities* (February, 1984): 274–285; "Cities and Communication, the Limits of Community," *Telecommunications Policy* (June, 1986): 132–140.

anthropic community agency of the middle class, designed to assist the
working class and the poor, its rationale held strong appeal for the
middle classes as well. Commuter suburbs in the late nineteenth
century began to be designed like villages gathered round their railroad stations. Whereas prosperous post-Civil War West Philadelphia
marched along the old city street grid, the later, more distant house-
builders of Chestnut Hill experimented with country clubs and cluster development.[16]

During the 1920's the idea of neighborhood unit planning, the
conscious layout of new subdivisions to create bounded and centered
residential communities, became the norm of good suburban design.
After World War II the inexpensive Levittowns followed the fashion,
and so today does the latest up-market subdivision in Valley Forge:
the Chesterbrook settlement being built on Alexander J. Cassatt's
former country estate.[17]

There is much that is useful in the community approach to cities.
As a literary, social science, and artistic tradition it encourages the
examination of the details of ordinary living, the study of small areas,
the tracing of the patterns of different classes, ethnic, and racial
groups. As a city planning idea it certainly enhanced the amenities of
suburbs and encouraged a good deal of fine domestic architecture. Yet
the celebration and reinforcement of the symbols of inclusion, and
the physical concentration of closed institutions, always run the
danger of promoting the politics of exclusion.

At issue is not mere snobbishness, or the class and racial nastiness
of adolescents. At issue is the basic value of the liberal city itself. A
city is nothing if it is not a place for strangers to trade, to work together, and to share ideas and experiences. The test of a successful city
is not the cohesion of its congregations and its neighborhoods, but the
manner in which it treats strangers.

Cities have always been composed of all sorts of communities: extended families, immigrant groups, parishes, guilds, political machines, and corporations of many kinds. These communities have
often tried to dominate the city for their own interests. In the medi-
eval city, however, it was the guarantee of safe passage and fair dealing
in the public market that enabled the towns to flourish. Since then

16. John Andrew Gallery, ed., *Philadelphia Architecture, A Guide to the City* (Cambridge, 1984), 162.
17. Urban Land Institute, *Philadelphia Metropolitan Area Today*, 111–115.

centuries of political effort have been required to expand the areas of safe passage, civil peace, and fair dealing. Philadelphia is one of the landmarks in that progress. William Penn established his town as an open settlement, free to all faiths.

Today in Philadelphia, as in the rest of the United States, the major barriers to strangers are residential and institutional—the inability of whites to live near Afro-Americans, and the unwillingness of whites to train Afro-American school children and to employ Afro-American citizens as their fellow workers. From the strong barriers of race rise the worst disorders of the new regional metropolis: bad schools, dangerous neighborhoods, poverty, unemployment, and crime. Roger Lane of Haverford College has published a fine book about the history of the exclusion of blacks from the economic and political institutions of Philadelphia during the years subsequent to the Civil War. The harvest of this exclusion has been today's problems. It could have been, instead, the gift of new citizens for Penn's open city.[18]

The Philadelphia Social History Project documented the uniqueness of the experience of the city's black citizens. During the twentieth century their segregation has been increasing while the distance of their homes from places of employment has been lengthening. With the post World War II suburbanization of white Philadelphians a wholly new kind of city neighborhood appeared—the all-residential, all-Afro-American blocks—the ghetto.[19]

Poverty automatically makes you a stranger in many neighborhoods, and a dark skin and poverty together make you a stranger in many more. Despite the impressive gains in civil rights, politics, and employment made by Philadelphia's Afro-Americans, a majority of these citizens remain behind in poverty. They seem socially and politically invisible in their old Philadelphia ghettoes. They are strangers within the new metropolitan Philadelphia. Yet it is by our relations to these citizen strangers, most black, but many white also, that the progress of the new city must be judged. Neither the language of regionalism nor the language of the community revival deals with this issue. The regional language merely records the segregation; the community language is rooted in the politics of exclusion.

18. Roger Lane, *Roots of Violence in Black Philadelphia 1860–1900* (Cambridge, 1986); and William Labov, "Zone Questionnaire 2," *Zone*, 1 & 2 (1986): 426–431.
19. Theodore Hershberg et al., "A Tale of Three Cities," 480–482.

In my own work I have always found the position of curious ignorance to be the most useful stance from which to contemplate the city. My goal is to seek out what lies beyond or beneath the familiar. It is clear that since 1950 a whole new city has been built outside and on top of the previous Philadelphias. It is also clear that the meanings of the new city escape us. As in former times of rapid change, the situation calls out for artists, writers, architects, and city planners to supply us with fresh images for organizing our experience and making the new city comprehensible to us. It is my hope that this present history, which organizes the past of Philadelphia according to one major theme, will stimulate others to explore and explain the many Philadelphias—those that are now and those that have flourished in the past.

SAM BASS WARNER, JR.
Boston
September 1986

Part One

THE EIGHTEENTH-CENTURY TOWN

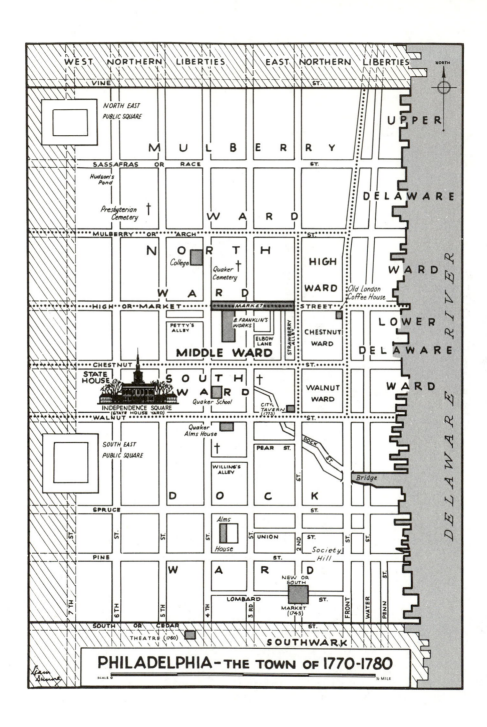

WEST NORTHERN LIBERTIES   EAST NORTHERN LIBERTIES

NORTH

VINE   ST.

NORTH EAST PUBLIC SQUARE

M U L B E R R Y   ST.

UPPER

SASSAFRAS OR RACE   ST.

Hudson's Pond

DELAWARE

Presbyterian Cemetery †

W A R D

MULBERRY OR ARCH   ST.

N O R T H

College

Quaker Cemetery †

HIGH WARD

Old London Coffee House

WARD

W A R D

HIGH OR MARKET   STREET

MARKET

& FRANKLIN'S WORKS

PETTY'S ALLEY

ELBOW LANE

STRAWBERRY ALLEY

CHESTNUT WARD

LOWER DELAWARE

MIDDLE WARD

CHESTNUT   ST.

STATE HOUSE

S O U T H

W A R D †

Quaker School

CITY TAVERN (1773)

WALNUT WARD

WARD

INDEPENDENCE SQUARE (STATE HOUSE YARD)

WALNUT   ST.

SOUTH EAST PUBLIC SQUARE

Quaker Alms House †

PEAR ST.

DOCK ST.

Bridge

WILLING'S ALLEY

D O C K   ST.

SPRUCE   ST.

Alms House

UNION

2ND ST.

Society Hill

PINE   ST.

W A R D

NEW OR SOUTH ST.

LOMBARD

MARKET (1745)

FRONT

WATER

PENN ST.

7TH   6TH   5TH   4TH   3RD ST.

SOUTH OR CEDAR   ST.

THEATRE (1760)

SOUTHWARK

D E L A W A R E   R I V E R

PHILADELPHIA — THE TOWN OF 1770-1780

SCALE 0   ½ MILE

1

The Environment of
Private Opportunity

American cities have grown with the general culture of the nation, not apart from it. Late eighteenth-century Philadelphia was no exception. Its citizens, formerly the first wave of a Holy Experiment, had been swept up in the tides of secularization and borne on by steady prosperity to a modern view of the world. Like the Puritans of Massachusetts and Connecticut, the Quakers of Pennsylvania had proved unable to sustain the primacy of religion against the solvents of cheap land and private opportunity. Quaker, Anglican, Presbyterian, Methodist, Pietist—each label had its social and political implications—but all congregations shared in the general American secular culture of privatism.[1]

Already by the time of the Revolution privatism had become the American tradition. Its essence lay in its concentration upon the individual and the individual's search for wealth. Psychologically, privatism meant that the individual should seek happiness in personal independence and in the search for wealth; socially, privatism meant that the individual should see his first loyalty as his immedi-

1. Quaker historians agree that the Holy Experiment died from materialism and secularization during the eighteenth century, Frederick B. Tolles, *Meeting House and Counting House* (Chapel Hill, 1948), 240-243; Sydney V. James, *A People Among Peoples* (Cambridge,1963), 37-43, 211-215; and see the charges against his contemporaries in John Woolman, *The Journal of John Woolman* (F. B. Tolles, Introduction, New York, 1961).

ate family, and that a community should be a union of such money-making, accumulating families; politically, privatism meant that the community should keep the peace among individual money-makers, and, if possible, help to create an open and thriving setting where each citizen would have some substantial opportunity to prosper.

To describe the American tradition of privatism is not to summarize the entire American cultural tradition. Privatism lies at the core of many modern cultures; privatism alone will not distinguish the experience of America from that of other nations. The tradition of privatism is, however, the most important element of our culture for understanding the development of cities. The tradition of privatism has always meant that the cities of the United States depended for their wages, employment, and general prosperity upon the aggregate successes and failures of thousands of individual enterprises, not upon community action. It has also meant that the physical forms of American cities, their lots, houses, factories, and streets have been the outcome of a real estate market of profit-seeking builders, land speculators, and large investors. Finally, the tradition of privatism has meant that the local politics of American cities have depended for their actors, and for a good deal of their subject matter, on the changing focus of men's private economic activities.[2]

In the eighteenth century the tradition of privatism and the social and economic environment of colonial towns nicely complemented each other. Later as towns grew to big cities, and big cities grew to metropolises, the tradition became more and more ill-suited to the realities of urban life. The tradition assumed that there would be no major conflict between private interest, honestly and liberally viewed, and the public welfare. The modes of eighteenth-century town life encouraged this expectation that if each man would look to his own prosperity the entire town would prosper. And so it had.

Founded in 1682 under William Penn's liberal instructions, and settled first with Quaker artisans and a few Quaker merchants, the town had since prospered as the capital of a thriving colony.[3] By

---

2. Howard Mumford Jones, *O Strange New World* (New York, 1964), 194-272, treats with this tradition as a blend of Christian and classical ideas.

3. Tolles, *Meeting House*, 41.

1720 Philadelphia was said to have 10,000 inhabitants; by 1775 it had more than doubled to 23,700.[4] The townsite bordered the Delaware and Schuylkill rivers, both of which tapped rich forests and excellent farm lands. The line of north-south trade ran nearby, and Philadelphia also lay within reach of the Susquehanna and Potomac rivers openings to the west. Philadelphia, thus, soon excelled in most of the staples of colonial trade, exporting furs, lumber, staves, iron, wheat, and flour, and importing rum, sugar, wine, and English manufactures.

Conditions outside the colony encouraged a heavy immigration of new settlers. Because Pennsylvania had been founded late, by comparison to other Atlantic colonies, west-bound space abounded on ships sailing from Great Britain and the Low Countries. Quakers, of course, fleeing persecution in England came to the colony in large numbers, but by the early eighteenth century their group came to be rivaled by Scotch-Irish and German immigrants. The Act of Union joining Scotland to England opened up the entire British Empire to poor Scots, while Irish wars and famines, and rack-renting landlords drove their fellow Presbyterians from Ulster. On the continent west German peasants fled the destruction of Louis XIV's repeated wars. Finally, in America the Indian control of upstate New York deflected the flow of westward settlers south to Pennsylvania. The result of all these outside events was a boom in the colony and the town; Pennsylvania and Philadelphia had everything, settlers, natural resources, capital, religious freedom, and comparatively little government.[5]

Within the town three conditions confirmed its privatism—its individualized structure of work, its general prosperity, and its open society and economy. When eighteenth-century Philadelphians spoke of the individual and his search for wealth as the goal of government they were simply basing their political arguments on the common place facts of town life. The core element of the town economy was the one-man shop. Most Philadelphians labored alone,

4. Carl Bridenbaugh, *Cities in the Wilderness* (N.Y. 1938), 303; and see notes to Table I. Also, James T. Lemon, "Urbanization of the Development of Eighteenth Century Southeastern Pennsylvania," *William and Mary Quarterly*, XXIV (Oct., 1967), 502-542; Hannah B. Roach, "The Planning of Philadelphia," *Pennsylvania Magazine*, XCII (January and April, 1968).

5. Marcus L. Hansen, *Atlantic Migration* (Cambridge, 1940), Ch. II.

some with a helper or two. A storekeeper tended his shop by himself or with the aid of his family or a servant. Craftsmen often worked with an apprentice, or more rarely with another skilled man.[6]

More than at later times, this Philadelphia was a town of entrepreneurs. Artisans sewed shoes, made wagons, boiled soap, or laid bricks for customers who had already placed an order. Workers did not labor under the close price and time disciplines of manufacture for large-scale inventories or big speculative wholesale markets. Most Philadelphians were either independent contractors hiring out on a job-by-job basis, or they were artisan shopkeepers retailing the products of their work. Even the establishment of a large merchant more resembled a small store than a modern wholesale house. Such a merchant frequently had a partner and the two partners carried on the business with the aid of a full-time clerk and an apprentice or servant to help with errands.[7] When a cargo arrived at the pier the partners would hire some laborers to unload the goods and move them to the storehouse. Thus, a very large proportion of the town's men—artisans, shopkeepers, and merchants—shared the common experience of the individual entrepreneur.

In later years the work groups of factories, offices, stores, and construction crews would have enormous significance for the discipline, acculturation, and education of Philadelphia's residents. Such groups were almost entirely absent from the eighteenth-century town. Shipyard, ropewalk, and distillery workers labored in groups of five and even ten, but theirs were exceptionally large urban production units. In the colonial era the plantation, whether for agriculture or manufacture, was the characteristic place of large work gangs.[8] In 1775, associated with Philadelphia's general run of family enterprises were only about 900 indentured servants, 600 slaves, and perhaps 200 hired servants who lived with their employers.[9] These helpers shared the discipline of family life and work; they did not live by the modes of the work gang. Taken all together

6. Comments suggesting an individualized or family work structure, Carl Bridenbaugh, *The Colonial Craftsman* (New York, 1950), 126-129, 136-139, 141-143.

7. Harry D. Berg, "The Organization of Business in Colonial Philadelphia," *Pennsylvania History*, X (July, 1943), 157-177; Arthur H. Cole, "The Tempo of Mercantile Life in Colonial America," *Business History Review*, XXXIII (Autumn, 1959), 277-299.

8. Richard B. Morris, *Government and Labor in Early America* (New York, 1946), 38-40.

9. Indentured servants and slaves, Table I. The reconstruction of the Middle Ward as of April 8, 1773 showed seventeen hired servants in residence there. On this basis two hundred such servants were guessed for the city, see notes to Table III.

the eighteenth-century exceptions to the entrepreneurial role had but little significance for the functioning of the town's society.

A German visitor of 1750 wrote: "Pennsylvania is heaven for farmers, paradise for artisans, and hell for officials and preachers."[10] By the same token, Philadelphia on the eve of the Revolution was a town of freedom and abundance for the common man. For young persons there was a great demand for apprentices in all lines of work. An unskilled laborer without connections could find work with board and wages to begin accumulating a little money for tools. An artisan who wanted to carry a few shopkeeping goods in his shop, or a storekeeper with a good reputation, could get his stock from the merchant and settle for his advance a year later.

The ordinary artisan or shopkeeper, if his health was good, could be assured of a comfortable, if frugal, living. To be sure, houses were small and rents high, and furnishings were spare compared to later levels of living: no carpets, no upholstered furniture, a sand-scrubbed floor, and whitewashed walls. Stoves and fireplaces only partially heated drafty rooms, and in severe winters the cost of firewood or imported coal was a major item of family expense. Nevertheless, at the city's markets food was cheap and plentiful. The earnings of the ordinary artisan and shopkeeper could support a wife and children without their having to take outside employment. The rapid growth of the town and its trade meant regular work and good earnings for artisans and easy business, if not wealth, for shopkeepers.[11]

Although the customary hours of work were long, sunrise to sunset, the pace of work was often easy and varied with the season. Those who worked outside their homes, like men in the building trades, took an hour for breakfast, a break in the middle of the day, and an hour for dinner in the afternoon. Coopers, shoemakers, smiths, and men who practiced their craft in their own houses and yards must have stopped work as customers and friends came in, and a trip or two to the local tavern must also have been usual. Although there were no formal vacations, the traditional English holidays and frequent *ad hoc* town celebrations provided about twenty days off each year.

10. Gottlieb Mittelberger, *Journey to Pennsylvania* (Oscar Handlin and John Clive, eds., Cambridge, 1960), 48.

11. Jackson Turner Main, *The Social Structure of Revolutionary America* (Princeton, 1965), 74-83, 115-163; Chapter IV; Mittelberger, *Journey*, 48-51, 74-75.

Franklin's *Autobiography* abounds with injunctions for regular habits, and the reputation for diligence he established by staying at his bench for the entire formal working day suggests that his was an extraordinary pace. For most workers rush seasons of hard work and long hours alternated with slack times. These variations meant days for fishing or spare moments for gossip on the streets and visits to the tavern.

Such a commonplace prosperity, generous at least by eighteenth-century standards, confirmed the privatism of the town and its age. As important a confirmation came from the openness of its economy and society. The failure of the craft guilds to control the trades of the town gave newcomers and resident artisans alike an occupational freedom unknown in Europe. Shopkeepers and artisans—and often one man was both—could take up any craft or open any line of business they wished. Although Philadelphia had inherited English regulations favoring the "freemen" of the town, established artisans could not maintain their control of the town's businesses against newcomers. The carpenters and cordwainers managed to form associations to set prices for their work, but failed when they attempted to close the membership of their trades. In Philadelphia men added trades and lines of goods as they thought demand justified. Although this freedom undoubtedly produced a great deal of incompetent craftsmanship, the importance to the individual artisan or shopkeeper of open trades and plentiful work cannot be overestimated. It meant for the common man that there was always a chance for a fresh start. This chance for a new beginning was the urban equivalent of the contemporary farmer's chance to pick up and try again in the West.[12]

Already in these years the American pattern of social mobility by property obtained. No invidious distinction between land and trade favored some occupations over others. As eighteenth-century Philadelphians grew rich they kept their original occupations, whether they were carpenters, distillers, printers, or lawyers. Whatever a man's occupation, there were only a few channels for investment open to the rising man. Since there were no banks, private money lending was the most important investment opportunity in the town. Houses and land were also a favorite way of using savings

<hr>

12. Morris, *Government and Labor in Early America*, 2-3, 141-143; the American jack-of-all-trades tradition, Mittelberger, *Journey*, 42-3; artisans' associations, Bridenbaugh, *Colonial Craftsman*, 141-143.

both among the rich and those with a little capital. Only 19 percent
of the families of Philadelphia owned their houses and therefore
home rentals offered a safe investment. Other opportunities were
shares in voyages, marine insurance, and, of course, land and farms
outside the town.[13]

The prosperity and abundant opportunity of the town should
not be confused with an even distribution of wealth. According to
the published tax list for 1774 the upper tenth of the taxpaying
households owned 89 percent of the taxable property. In this respect
late eighteenth-century Philadelphia resembled the later Philadelphias—it was a pyramid of wealth in which about five hundred men
guided the town's economic life. Its unique quality lay in the general prosperity of the common artisan and shopkeeper and the
widely shared entrepreneurial experience and goals of the artisan,
shopkeeper, and merchant.[14]

The wealthy presided over a municipal regime of little government. Both in form and function the town's government advertised
the lack of concern for public management of the community. The
municipal corporation of Philadelphia, copied from the forms of an
old English borough, counted for little. Its only important functions
in the late eighteenth-century were the management of the markets
and the holding of the Recorder's Court. A closed corporation,
choosing its members by co-option, it had become a club of wealthy
merchants, without much purse, power, or popularity.

By modern standards the town was hardly governed at all. The

13. Wilbur C. Plummer, "Consumer Credit in Colonial Philadelphia," *Pennsylvania
Magazine*, LXVI (October, 1942), 385-409. The homeownership percentage was calculated from the number of homeowners and renters listed in the manuscript version of
the Seventeenth Eighteen Penny Provincial Tax of April 8, 1774 (in possession of the
Pennsylvania Historical and Museum Commission, Harrisburg). A reconstruction of the
Middle Ward as of April 8, 1774 shows holdings of land and houses in small lots, and
pairs of structures, not big tracts. Rich men, like Israel Pemeberton, and men of few
investments, both participated in the housing market (see notes to Table III).

14. The published version of the Seventeenth Eighteen Penny Provincial Tax, *Pennsylvania Archives, 3rd Series*, XIV (Harrisburg, 1897), 223-445, was used for a quick
calculation of the distribution of taxable wealth. The taxpayers on this published list
were arranged in order of the size of their published "assessment." The top ten
percent, or 498 names, accounted for 89 percent of the 86,100 pounds of assessment
given for Philadelphia, the Northern Liberties, and Southwark. This published list is
not a sufficient guide to the distribution of wealth since the tax was largely a real
property tax to which a head tax and a few personalty items were added. The very
important property of stock-in-trade and money-on-loan went untaxed and hence
unlisted. Also, the compilers of the published list mixed in many cases the taxes-paid
entries with the assessment entries thereby distorting even the assessment distribution.

constable in each ward and a few watchmen provided an ineffective police, the safety of the house and shop being secured by citizens' helping each other to drive away intruders or pursue thieves.[15] Most streets went unpaved, the public wharves little repaired. There were no public schools, no public water, and at best thin charity.

The enduring contribution of the colonial era to Philadelphia government lay in its inauguration of the committee system of municipal government. This system, if system it may be called in the eighteenth century, consisted of placing the administration of specific tasks in the hands of independent committees, or commissions. The Pennsylvania Provincial Assembly, lacking faith in the municipal corporation, created a number of commissions. First came the Board of Assessors established to raise money to pay the debts of the corporation and to require that wharves and streets be repaired and a workhouse erected. Then came separate street commissioners, next the City Wardens to manage the night watch and the lighting of the streets, and, still later, a Board of Overseers of the Poor. None of these commissions' performance would satisfy modern municipal standards. The commissioners were elected officials, chosen under the colonial fifty-pound, freehold qualification by the voters of Philadelphia. Like the town's fire companies, lending libraries, and tavern clubs these commissions helped train Philadelphians to the habits of committee government, a form of management they would have to call upon when creating a new independent government during the Revolution. Like many of the laws and forms of the colonial era which passed into the usage of the subsequent Commonwealth of Pennsylvania, the committee system of government was the legacy of colonial municipal life to later Philadelphias.[16]

The real secret of the peace and order of the eighteenth-century town lay not in its government but in the informal structure of its

15. There are charming accounts of private policing in Henry D. Biddle, ed., *Extracts from the Journal of Elizabeth Drinker* (Philadelphia, 1889), robbery in her alley, Dec. 15, 1777; insane soldier wanders into the house June 30, 1778; "saucy Ann" and her soldier, Nov. 25, 26, Dec. 2, 1777, Jan. 4, 1778. A call for more considerate treatment of the town watchmen, Advertisement, *Pennsylvania Gazette,* Jan. 20, 1779.

16. For a description of the colonial government of Philadelphia, Judith M. Diamondstone, "Philadelphia's Municipal Corporation, 1701-1776," *Pennsylvania Magazine,* XC (April, 1966), 183-201; Edward P. Allinson & Boise Penrose, "The City Government of Philadelphia," *Johns Hopkins Studies in Historical and Political Science,* V (Baltimore, 1887), 14-33.

community. Unlike later and larger Philadelphias, the eighteenth-century town was a community. Graded by wealth and divided by distinctions of class though it was, it functioned as a single community. The community had been created out of a remarkably inclusive network of business and economic relationships and it was maintained by the daily interactions of trade and sociability. Because it was small and because every rank and occupation lived jumbled together in a narrow compass the town suffered none of the communications problems of later Philadelphias.

At most, 23,700 people lived in Philadelphia on the eve of the Revolution, 16,500 in the city proper, 7,000 in the adjacent districts of Northern Liberties and Southwark (Table I). The town crowded next to its shore. Its wharves and warehouses stretched a mile and a half along the Delaware river, but the built-up blocks of houses at their deepest point, along Market street, reached back from the river at most half a mile to about Seventh Street.[17]

The settlement pattern of the town combined two opposing social tendencies. The clustering of marine trades and merchants next to the Delaware suggested the beginnings of the specialized industrial quarters then characteristic of European cities. On the other hand, the rummage of classes and occupations found in many Philadelphia blocks continued the old tradition of mixed work and residence characteristic of American and English country towns.

Ship carpenters, ship joiners, ship smiths, and sail makers lived and worked along the Delaware river shore. Sailors and stevedores dwelt among the yards and wharves along the entire shore, but they gathered especially on the south side of town (Dock Ward and Southwark). Mixed among them were many of the houses and shops of the merchants which were concentrated one block back from the riverfront. Together the shipbuilders, the marine trades, and the merchants pre-empted the narrow strip of frontage between the river and Second street.[18]

17. The tax records and constables' returns of 1774 and 1775 show dense settlement to end and Seventh Street with but a few families living on scattered farms west from this point to the Schuylkill river (see notes to Middle Ward, Table III). A map made by John Reed of the City and Liberties of Philadelphia, supposed to have been made in 1774 (now in the possession of the American Philosophical Society) was shaded to show dense settlement to Tenth street.

18. Evidence of these concentrations was gathered from the tabulations made to construct Table II, Index of Dissimilarity.

TABLE I

POPULATION OF URBAN PHILADELPHIA 1775

Ward	Maximum Population			Indentured Servants			Slaves			Free	
	Adults	Children	Total	Adults	Children	Total	Adults	Children	Total	Adults	Children
Dock	2,064	1,985	4,049	90	179	269	63	105	168	1,911	1,701
Walnut	268	218	486	16	6	22	30	7	37	222	205
South	432	315	747	18	27	45	19	15	34	395	273
Middle	945	740	1,685	41	61	102	49	22	71	855	657
Chestnut	337	248	585	10	32	42	23	7	30	304	209
Lower Delaware	312	304	616	17	33	50	35	19	54	260	252
High Street	391	391	782	12	29	41	22	14	36	357	348
North	947	829	1,776	37	63	100	60	16	76	850	750
Mulberry	2,699	2,087	4,786	81	101	182	44	32	76	2,574	1,954
Upper Delaware	574	474	1,048	20	33	53	18	12	30	536	429
Sub Total, City of Philadelphia	8,969	7,591	16,560	342	564	906	363	249	612	8,264	6,778
East Northern Liberties			2,340								
West Northern Liberties			1,758								
Southwark			3,081								
Total Urban Philadelphia			23,739								

The crowding of marine trades and commerce next to the port also influenced the location of other Philadelphians. Tailors, hatters, tinsmiths, and silversmiths clustered in the central wards of town (Walnut, Lower Delaware, and Middle Wards) to be near, if not in, the portside concentration of customers. Conversely, those who needed large lots, or those who could not afford expensive land, drifted toward the edge of town. Here on the fringes the building trades, weavers, dyers, tanners, distillers, and laborers dwelt in more than normal proportions.

The differential pricing of land seems to have affected the laborers more than any other occupational group in the colonial town (Table II). Surprisingly enough, they were more segregated in this period than in the mid-nineteenth century, when the immigrant laborer was such a prominent element of the city. In 1774 the special locations of the laborers were the northern and southern edges

TABLE II

INDEX OF DISSIMILARITY

INDUSTRIAL GROUPINGS AND SOME ADDITIONAL CATEGORIES
PHILADELPHIA, NORTHERN LIBERTIES, AND SOUTHWARK,
1774; PHILADELPHIA COUNTY, 1860

1774	Index	1860	Index
Laborers	37.2	Negro, free, native born	47.3
Metalworking, ex. iron, steel	32.5	Miscellaneous textiles	40.3
Iron, steel, shipbuilding	29.4	Germany, foreign born	34.1
Paper & printing	29.4	Bakeries	30.7
Transport, ex. rail, transit	24.7	Iron, steel, shipbuilding	29.0
Misc. textiles	24.3	Hotels, laundries, domestic	25.9
Clothing	22.3	Metalworking, ex. iron, steel	25.6
Building trades	21.2	Professional, ex. entertainment	25.4
Wholesale & retail	20.5	Laborers	21.9
German surnames	19.7	Clothing	21.8
Professional, ex. entertainment	19.7	Ireland, N S, for. born	19.8
Bakeries	16.7	Transport, ex. rail, transit	19.6
Hotels, laundries, domestic	15.1	Paper & printing	19.0
Homeowners	6.1	Britain, ex. Ireland, for. born	17.5
		Building trades	16.4
		Pennsylvania, native born	10.1
		Wholesale & retail	9.6

of town—the Northern Liberties and adjacent parts of the Mulberry Ward, and Southwark.

A slight ethnic clustering also existed in eighteenth-century Philadelphia, but by no means of the same intensity as later twentieth-century ethnic and racial ghettos. German immigrants and their descendants had concentrated north of Market Street, over half of them living in the North, High, and Mulberry wards of Philadelphia and in the adjacent Northern Liberties Districts. This was also the Quaker side of town. Such ethnic and religious clusters, however, did not seem to have important effects upon the functioning of the town.

One can get some idea of the quality of urban life imposed by this settlement pattern by looking at one ward in a little detail. The Constable in making his enumeration of the residents of the Middle Ward left notes on his list showing when he turned the corner of a street. This record, plus some material from tax ledgers make it possible to reconstruct the settlement pattern of this ward in 1774.

As its name suggests, the Middle Ward lay in the center of town, bounded on the north by Market Street, then the highway connecting Philadelphia to Chester and the south and to Lancaster and the west. The ward also was next to the market traffic. The sheds of the farmers' market in these years stretched up Market Street from the Delaware River only as far as Fourth Street. The Middle Ward was not a crowded dockside ward, but began just behind the dockside wards at Second Street. Its well-filled section covered five blocks to Seventh Street, Market to Chestnut. Beyond these blocks of houses the farms of the ward extended all the way west to the Schuylkill River.

Many famous Philadelphians lived within the ward. The old-fashioned Quaker radical, Anthony Benezet, the Proprietors John and Richard Penn, two opponents of the British who later turned Tory, Joseph Galloway, and James Allen, and the steadfast revolutionaries Benjamin Franklin and Daniel Clymer all lived in the center of the ward. The State House Yard (now Independence Square) stood across Chestnut Street between Fifth and Sixth streets. Such distinction, however, did not create the solid blocks of *haut bourgeois* fashion that they would today; rather it embroidered the commonplace fabric which was the revolutionary town. In 1774 the Middle Ward was the home of at least 1,401 men, women,

and children of every degree and condition from Proprietor to slave
(Table III).

The physical arrangements of the ward reflected the high cost
of eighteenth-century housing and the crowding of Philadelphians
near their port. Each of the Middle Ward's five settled blocks contained slightly less than five acres of land. On the first block of the
ward (between Second and Third streets, the area nearest the Delaware River) there stood 137 dwellings, on the next 65, on the next
67, on the next 29, and on westernmost 39. To accommodate so

TABLE III

THE MIDDLE WARD OF PHILADELPHIA, APRIL 8, 1774

Free Adults (346 households x 2 for wives)	692
Children	469
Negro Slaves	78
Bound Servants in Residence	65
Hired Servants in Residence	17
Inmates (other free adults living in households)	80
Population	1,401
Homeowners	80
Houserenters	266
Taxpayers living with other families	102
Total Taxpayers	448

---

many families in so little space some of the blocks of the ward had
been cut by alleys so that little houses might be crowded onto the
back lots of the houses facing the main streets. Strawberry Alley and
Elbow Lane cut through the first block, Petty's Alley divided the
third block, and Benjamin Franklin had begun the alley process
with his house lot off Market Street in the second block of the ward.
He had built a row of three houses on Market Street, thereby turning his home yard into an interior lot. His son-in-law Richard
Bache, a merchant, rented one of the new row houses, Eden Hay-
dock, a plumber, rented another, and Frederick Stonemetz, a
cooper, took the third. In the early nineteenth century Franklin's
home parcel became Franklin Court, an alley lot which opened up
the interior of the block.[19]

19. Edward M. Riley, "Franklin's Home," *Historic Philadelphia* (American Philosophical Society, *Transactions*, XLIII, 1953), 148-160.

Such density of housing and such methods of land division had by 1774 destroyed the hopes of Penn and his surveyor for a "Green Town."[20] The practice of subdividing blocks with alleys and jamming tiny houses on vacant rear yards continued strongly for the next ninety years. By 1860 the density of population in Philadelphia's inner wards reached its all-time peak.[21] Then, in the second half of the nineteenth century the street railway opened up vast tracts of cheap suburban land and thereby destroyed the market for new alley construction. The old alleys with their dark and cramped houses, however, did not disappear at once. Rather they remained standing for years, giving discomfort to Philadelphia's poor for many generations, and the history of some alleys is not yet closed.

Already in the 1770's the crowding of the land exceeded the sanitary capabilities of the town. The streets and alleys reeked of garbage, manure, and night soil, and some private and public wells must have been dangerously polluted. Every few years an epidemic swept through the town. In the 1790's the city would pay a terrible price in deaths from recurring yellow fever.[22]

Though dangerous to health the eighteenth-century pattern of settlement guaranteed every citizen a knowledge of town life. At such density and small scale no generation could be raised ignorant of the other side of town, of the ways of life of the working class, or of the manners of the *haut bourgeois*. Within the Middle Ward at least 346 families with 469 children, 17 hired servants, 65 indentured servants, 78 Negro slaves, and 80 tenants share the settled 25 acres (Table III). Those who left a record carried on seventy different occupations (Table IV).[23]

20. Anthony N. B. Garvan, "Proprietary Philadelphia as Artifact," *The Historian and the City* (Oscar Handlin and John Burchard, ed., Cambridge, 1964). 177-201.

21. Philadelphia City Planning Commission Map, "Year of Population Peak, Philadelphia, by Wards," dated August, 1949.

22. Bad conditions in alley "huts" of the poor, presumably one-story houses with a sleeping attic reached by a ladder as in the typical rural one-room cabin, Benjamin Rush, *Autobiography of Benjamin Rush* (American Philosophical Society, *Memoirs*, XXV, 1948), 83-84; cellar of a drunken, perhaps insane woman oyster seller, *Journal of Elizabeth Drinker*, Sept. 2, 1793; eighteenth century epidemics, small pox, yellow fever, dysentery or typhoid, John Duffy, *Epidemics in Colonial America* (Baton Rouge, 1953), 78-100, 142-161, 220-230, and Struthers Burt, *Philadelphia Holy Experiment* (New York, 1946), 159.

23. No authority tells to what extent eighteenth century artisans worked at home as opposed to working outside. With the exception of the building and marine trades

Although merchants and shopkeepers, hatters, innkeepers, and tavernkeepers concentrated more heavily in this ward than in most others, variety best characterizes the occupational structure of the ward as it did all the other wards of the first Philadelphia. The Proprietors, the merchants, and the doctors shared the narrow compass of the Middle Ward with such ungenteel occupations as laborer, porter, carter, skinner, watchman, crier, paver, grazier, and even goatkeeper. The outer three blocks of the ward also housed several breweries and a distillery, and every one of the five blocks contained one or more of those notorious enemies of sweet residential air—the stable.[24]

One cannot, at this late date, reconstruct in detail the communications patterns of eighteenth-century Philadelphia, but the crowded living of the age encouraged a street and tavern life which more resembled the social habits of the later nineteenth and early twentieth-century immigrant ghettos than the isolated private family life of today's working class and middle class.

The high cost of building kept houses small, cramped, and in short supply. The common artisan's or shopkeeper's house was a narrow structure, about seventeen feet wide and twenty-five feet deep. A story-and-a-half high, it offered about eight hundred square feet of floor space on its ground floor and attic. Most often the owner plied his trade in the largest front room. The Middle Ward records show that although some families had five to seven children, most had few. The average number of children per household was 1.3, and counting servants and slaves the average household was four persons. The small houses, thus, were cramped but not severely crowded. If the artisan or shopkeeper prospered he would add a kitchen ell or more likely move to a house of similar proportion with a kitchen ell at the rear. The house of an ordinary merchant or even a craftsman who had grown rich, would be like the artisan's house with the ell, but would be two and one-half stories instead of

---

most artisans are supposed to have worked at home. This supposition gets some indirect confirmation from the general agreement that most men labored alone and that most businesses in the city were family businesses. Neither Bridenbaugh in his *Colonial Craftsman* nor Morris in his *Government and Labor* tell of many urban establishments which might have employed many workers outside of their own homes.

24. A good sense of what the mixed settlement pattern of the city meant is given by Alexander Graydon, *Memoirs of a Life, Chiefly Passed in Pennsylvania* (Harrisburg, 1811), 34-35.

TABLE IV

275 PERSONS WHOSE OCCUPATIONS CAN BE IDENTIFIED
MIDDLE WARD, APRIL 8, 1774

23	Shopkeepers	2	Druggists
19	Merchants	2	Livery stables
17	Laborers	2	Silversmiths
15	Cordwainers	2	Stablekeepers
13	Hatters	2	Staymakers
13	Tailors	2	Stockingweavers
13	Tavernkeepers	2	Tobacconists
11	Innkeepers	1	Boatbuilder
10	Bakers	1	Breechesmaker
10	Carpenters	1	Cheesemonger
7	Joiners	1	Crier
7	Saddlemakers	1	Distiller
6	Coopers	1	Engraver
5	Colonial Officers	1	Ferryman
5	Schoolmasters	1	Goatkeeper
4	Brewers	1	Grazier
4	Hucksters	1	Grocer
4	Porters	1	Harnessmaker
4	Skinners	1	Heelmaker
3	Barbers	1	Lawyer
3	Blacksmiths	1	Minister
3	Carvers	1	Painter
3	Coppersmiths	1	Paver
3	Curriers	1	Plumber
3	Mariners	1	Printer
3	Potters	1	Reedmaker
3	Smiths	1	Ropemaker
3	Tinkers	1	Scrivener
3	Watchmen	1	Sheriff
2	Bookbinders	1	Snuffmaker
2	Brushmakers	1	Threadmaker
2	Butchers	1	Upholder
2	Carters	1	Watchmaker
2	Chaisemakers	1	Wheelwright
2	Cutters	1	Workhouse keeper
2	Doctors		

Source:
    See appendix for Table II

one and one-half. Such houses of the prosperous also possessed deep lots for gardens, a shed for a cow and some chickens, and perhaps a horse.[25]

A town of small houses, where most houses also served as stores, offices and workshops, encouraged people to live out upon the streets. Moreover, the pace of work, most of it governed by the seasons or advance orders from customers, was irregular, what one would call today a rural pace. Both the physical structure of the town and the pace of its work thus encouraged a more public, gossipy style of life than could later be sustained when a steady pace of work and larger interiors drove people into sharply defined spaces for work and residence.

The ordinary housewife shopped daily, going to the baker's for her bread, and taking her meat and pies to the baker's oven to be cooked. Street peddlers called her out for fish, eggs, and produce, and twice a week the farmers of Philadelphia County held a full market at the public stalls. As in the nineteenth century with its dark tenements and crowded row houses, sunlight must have been a great source of pleasure for women sewing and spinning and many must have worked at these and other household chores out on their doorsteps, as their tenement sisters did years later.

For the husband the eighteenth-century custom of men's gossip at the tavern provided the first Philadelphia's basic cells of community life. Every ward in the city had its inns and taverns. The 1774 tax list recorded 93 tavernkeepers and 72 innkeepers in the city of Philadelphia, Southwark, and the Northern Liberties, approximately one neighborhood drinking place for every 140 persons in the city (23,000/165). The Middle Ward, alone, held 18 inns and taverns. Some must have served purely a neighborhood custom; others, like the London Coffee House or the City Tavern served as central communications nodes for the entire city.

Then, as now, each one had its own crowd of regulars and thus each constituted an informal community cell of the city. Out of the

25. The tax records of 1774 give evidence of a colonial housing shortage, for the ratio of occupied to unoccupied dwellings did not exceed two percent that year. Artisans' houses, Grant M. Simon, "Houses and Early Life in Philadelphia," *Historic Philadelphia,* 282-3; typical house for the prosperous, Advertisement, *Pennsylvania Gazette,* March 17, 1779.

meetings of the regulars at the neighborhood tavern or inn came much of the commonplace community development which preceded the Revolution and proved later to be essential to the governance of the city and the management of the ward. Regular meetings of friends, or men of common occupations, led to clubs of all kinds and of every degree of formality from regular billiard sessions to fire companies and political juntos. Benjamin Franklin and the many community innovations of his junto showed the potential of these informal tavern groups. They provided the underlying social fabric of the town and when the Revolution began made it possible to quickly gather militia companies, to form effective committees of correspondence and of inspection, and to organize and to manage mass town meetings.

At the center of the town's communications system stood the merchants' coffee houses. On the eve of the Revolution Philadelphia had two such major meeting places—the old London Coffee House (established 1754), run by William Bradford, the newspaper publisher, and the new City Tavern (established 1773), just founded by a syndicate of merchants. The London Coffee House, located at Front and Market streets, adjacent to the town's principal market stalls and overlooking the Delaware, had been for many years the place where merchants gathered every noon to read incoming newspapers, to discuss prices, and to arrange for cargoes and marine insurance. These noon meetings in time ripened into the specialized institutions of exchanges, banks, and insurance companies. As yet, Philadelphia had but one insurance company and its merchants' business depended on the variety of functions of these daily tavern gatherings. For many years ship captains and travelers first stopped at the London Coffee House when they arrived in town, messages were left, auction notices posted and auctions held. Frequently on market days, after a parade through the streets, horses were auctioned in front of the tavern doors. Slaves and indentured servants stood before the same block.

As the town grew the importing merchants no longer had a need to be near the market dealers. The merchant community split into at least two parts. The new City Tavern surpassed the old London Coffee House as a place of fashion with the importing merchants, though its function remained that of its competitor. On May 19, 1774, Paul Revere brought his news of the closing of the

Port of Boston to the City Tavern, and here numerous Revolutionary committees gathered. The still extant Philadelphia Assemblies were held at this new tavern, as was the endless series of banquets and balls which served the town with high entertainment.[26]

Because the merchants' tavern was a public place in a small town it escaped the limitations of later Philadelphia merchant centers—the exchanges, the Chamber of Commerce, and the gentlemen's clubs. These later gatherings were either meeting places of specialists and thereby encouraged only the brokers' or downtown merchants' view of the city, or they were closed organizations which directed their members' attention inward toward the sociability of the group. The eighteenth-century tavern, however, opened out to all the life of the street and it did not shield the leaders of the town from contact with the life that surrounded them.[27]

It was the unity of everyday life, from tavern, to street, to workplace, to housing, which held the town and its leaders together in the eighteenth century. This unity made it possible for the minority of Revolutionary merchants, artisans, and shopkeepers to hold together, run the town, and manage a share of the war against England, even in the face of Quaker neutrality and Tory opposition.

26. The name "coffee house," which had been imported from England, merely designated a genteel tavern. Coffee, tea, lemonade, and beer were served, but the customers favored wines and liquors, Robert E. Graham, "The Taverns of Colonial Philadelphia," *Historic Philadelphia*, 318-323.

27. Graydon tells an amusing story of the confrontation of Benjamin Chew, lawyer for the Penns and then Recorder of the town and an alderman with two drunken British officers, *Memoirs*, 43-44; an excellent review of travellers and visitor's accounts mentions the importance to the social structure of the town of immigrant societies like St. David's and St. Tammany, Whitfield J. Bell, Jr., "Some Aspects of the Social History of Pennsylvania, 1760-1790," *Pennsylvania Magazine*, LXII (July, 1938), 301.

2

War and the Limits
of the Tradition

When remonstrance turned to rebellion and political disagreement turned to war the exigencies of the conflict broke Philadelphia society apart. Thanks to the town's commonplace ideology of privatism and its inclusive patterns of social and economic intercourse, Philadelphia did not fracture along the lines of class or occupation. As befitted a seaport, merchants predominated in all the political groups of the town: among the moderate Whigs, among the radical Whigs, among the Tories, and among the Quakers. Fighting Quakers and revolutionary Episcopalians crossed boundaries of religious loyalties. With the exception of pacifist Quakers, the groupings of Philadelphia during the Revolution were first and foremost political. The divisions among Philadelphia's citizens reflected personal attitudes toward the revolutionary governments established in Pennsylvania and toward the Continental Congress. The Congress strongly influenced local politics since it then sat in Philadelphia, capital city of the thirteen colonies.

To a modern observer, half-blinded by the scenes of uncontrolled butchery in his own era, the moderation of the conflict among the political and military groups of the American Revolution appears almost incomprehensible.[1] Within Philadelphia, at

1. A good account of the climate of the war as it was experienced by a Tory, "Diary of James Allen, Esq., of Philadelphia, 1770-1778," *Pennsylvania Magazine*, IX (1885), 176-196, 278-296, 424-441.

least, that moderation was sustained against all the temptations and passions of war and revolution by the lines of control which remained intact throughout the war years. The town may have split into four political groups, but each group, being a rough cross section of the community, shared much in common with the others, in experience, in expectations of human behavior, even in ideology. Through the five years of conflict in Pennsylvania (1774-1779), except for the few banished Quakers and colonial officials and the Tories who left when the British troops abandoned the city, Philadelphians of all persuasions continued to do business together and to share the everyday activities of town life. The town's network of personal communications was never severed by the Revolution to the degree that the network of personal communications was later fragmented by the changed structure and scale of the American big city. In the twentieth century we start our riots and wars with less community than the Revolutionary town had even in its most strained moments.

The inflation, food shortage, and political crisis of 1778-1779 demonstrated the interaction of conflict and control in eighteenth-century Philadelphia. During these crises the Pennsylvania and Continental governments which ruled the town struggled against chaos and bankruptcy. The temper of the leaders had been heated by accumulated frustrations. High prices and food shortages at the market set poor against rich. Yet when the crises of a year reached a violent culmination the leaders of the opposed camps turned to pacify the town rather than to seek political victory in an armed witch hunt.

This same series of crises during 1778 to 1779 also demonstrated the limits of the American tradition of privatism in the face of important urban problems. The crises foretold those conditions under which future American cities would repeatedly fail. As in the case of the modern city where the most pressing problems are those of allocating scarce land, tax, and human resources among conflicting public and private purposes, so too, eighteenth-century Philadelphia confronted the problems of allocating scarce resources among the competing demands of the army, of the city, and of trade. The ideology of privatism offered no guide to such allocation problems. It had no rule for parceling out flour to the citizens of the town save letting the buyers compete. Modern, too, was the scale of the inflation and shortages of 1778-1779. As in today's urban employment, housing, segregation, and financial disorders, the area of suffering was the city, while the area of the remedy for that suffering far exceeded the municipal boundaries. It reached beyond Philadelphia into the hinterland of the three middle colonies and beyond to national and international trade and finance.

The course of the Revolution in Philadelphia had been such that by the summer of 1778, when the town began to face its severe inflation and supply crisis, only two groups remained politically active, the radical Whigs and the moderate Whigs. Pacifist Quakers had been discredited by their inaction and had been excluded from government by test oaths. The Tory cause collapsed as an effective movement in Pennsylvania with the withdrawal of royal troops from Philadelphia on June 18, 1778. Some 3,000 Tories fled with the retreating army.[2]

Although their domestic opponents had ceased to be effective in Pennsylvania, the Quakers, Tories, apathetic, and neutral citizens outnumbered the Whigs in Pennsylvania and probably also outnumbered them in Philadelphia. Thus, though common goals and a common enemy held the Whigs together, even in their most harmonious moments they constituted a minority and their government suffered all the weaknesses and dangers of minority rule. Unable to mobilize more than a fraction of the wealth and power of the commonwealth, the Revolution in Pennsylvania had created many scenes like Valley Forge with the army starving in a region of full barns. Taxes went uncollected for lack of minor officials and petty courts. Late-arriving and unfilled quotas for troops and supplies and a hodgepodge of expedient programs characterized all levels of government.

Under such conditions the great danger to the society lay in the political temptation to bolster public enthusiasm by witch hunts in which all opponents would be branded as Tories and traitors to the cause. A farmer or merchant who did not come forward with grain in response to an offering of depreciated Continental currency could be branded "Tory." The search and removal of property from Quaker homes, justified by their refusal to pay taxes for the war, could become the occasion for looting "Tory" goods. Most danger-

2. Sylvester K. Stevens, *Pennsylvania, Birthplace of A Nation* (New York, 1964), 114.

TABLE V – PART ONE

TAXABLE WEALTH OF LEADERS OF THE MODERATE WHIGS IN PHILADELPHIA, 1774

Ward	Name	Occupation	Assessment	Gross Income from real property	Rent Paid	Tax Paid
Dock	Gen. John Cadwalader	merchant	£143	£170	£170*	£10.14.6
South	Lambert Cadwalader	merchant	3	0	inmate	1.10.0
Lower Dela.	Andrew Caldwell	merchant	12	0	160	0.18.0
Dock	Thomas Fitzsimmons	merchant	8	0	300†	0.12.0
High St.	Francis Hopkins	lawyer	0	0	60	0.0
North	Whitehead Humphreys	shopkeeper	3	0	12†	0.15.0
Lower Dela.	Samuel Meredith	merchant	15	0	not found	1.02.6
Walnut	Thomas Mifflin	merchant	83	130	100*	6.04.6
Mulberry	Samuel Miles	merchant	105	90	90*	7.17.6
Dock	Robert Morris	merchant	116	94	50	8.14.0
Dock	John M. Nesbitt	merchant	15	0	60	1.17.6
Dock	John Nixon	merchant	108	160	45	8.02.0
High St.	Richard Peters	lawyer	20	4	36	2.05.0
Lower Dela.	John Shee	merchant	12	0	130	0.18.0
Chestnut	Thomas Smith	not given	3	0	inmate	0.15.0
	Charles Thompson	distiller, not on list				
Middle	Rev. William White	minister	10	0	45	0.15.0
	James Wilson	lawyer, not on list				

*These figures are imputed rents, that is, the rental value of property which the taxpayer owned and used himself. The imputed rent was set by the tax assessor.

†These rents were paid by partnerships. The total sum gives an idea of the size of the premises the partners used.

"inmate" is a term used on the tax lists for boarders who were also taxpayers.

TABLE V – PART TWO

TAXABLE WEALTH OF LEADERS OF THE RADICAL WHIGS
IN PHILADELPHIA, 1774

Ward	Name	Occupation				
North	Owen Biddle	merchant	8	0	82	0.12.0
Southwark	Capt. Joseph Blewer	sea captain	20	20	20*	1.00.0
Chestnut	William Bradford	publisher	10	0	120	0.15.0
Dock	George Bryan	merchant	6	8	33	0.09.0
South	Dr. Thos. Cadwalader	doctor	140	196	90	10.10.0
Dock	James Cannon	school master	25	35	15*	1.17.6
Dock	George Clymer	merchant	230	293	85*	17.05.0
	Dr. James Hutchinson	not on list				
	William Clingan	not on list				
Mulberry	Fredrick Khul	merchant	204	327	60*	15.06.0
Mulberry	Christopher Marshall	ret. pharmacist	70	128	20*	5.05.0
Dock	Timothy Matlack	merchant	7	15	15*	0.10.6
	Thomas Paine	not on list				
	Charles W. Peale	painter, not on list				
North	Joseph Reed	lawyer	10	0	100	0.15.0
North	David Rittenhouse	instrument maker	12	20	30	0.18.0
Upper Dela.	Gen. Daniel Roberdeau	merchant	59	40	100	4.08.6
Lower Dela.	Benjamin Rush	doctor	3	0	70	0.15.0
	James Searle	merchant, not found				
North	William Shippen	doctor	575	671	80*	43.02.6
Upper Dela.	Col. Johnathan B. Smith	not given	8	0	80	0.12.0

Source: This list was compiled from names of persons mentioned in four books as leaders in the Whig conflicts of 1776-1779:
Robert L. Brunhouse, *The Counter-Revolution in Pennsylvania* (Harrisburg, 1942), Kenneth R. Rossman, *Thomas Mifflin and the Politics of the American Revolution* (Chapel Hill, 1952), David Hawke, *In the Midst of a Revolution* (Philadelphia, 1961), and Brooke Hindle, *David Rittenhouse* (Princeton, 1964). The names were then checked against the Seventeenth Eighteen Penny Provincial Tax List for Philadelphia, 1774.

ous of all, the social fabric of the town and colony could be so rent by a few years of such political deception, fear, and terror that nothing would prevent the two wings of the Whig party from turning on each other, and thereby destroy with internecine conflict the chance for the expanded democracy which most of the society wanted.[3] Not until one group of the Whigs had peacefully replaced another in orderly democratic succession would this danger of revolutionary tyranny be passed.

The Whigs had divided into radical and moderate camps back in 1776 when the colonial Assembly's wavering opposition to independence forced the radical remedy of a declaration of independence and seizure of the government. Evidence from old tax lists suggests that the split among the Whigs was political and social, not economic. It was a division of a single class, not a war between classes. With few exceptions the leaders of the moderates were merchants. Among the radicals, too, the merchants were the largest group and the radicals could boast of several followers with heavier assessments than their rivals. However, the larger proportion of "new" money as opposed to "old" money, of professionals, of intellectuals, and of persons marginal to the established merchant group of Philadelphia seems to have distinguished the radicals from the moderates (Table V).

The moderates had been leading the opposition to England up until the spring of 1776. Then they hesitated. They hoped for compromise with London. They feared violence and destruction. They wanted to move slowly. The old Pennsylvania colonial Assembly did not have enough radical members for it to establish a new government free from any allegiance to the Crown. The radicals called a town meeting for May 20, the day of the Assembly's opening. Four thousand persons stood in the rain in the State House yard listening to militia officers and cheering for independence. The officers called for a constitutional convention to frame a new government. The Assembly, divided, harassed, and confused, succumbed and the radicals seized power, first in Philadelphia, then in all Pennsylvania.[4]

3. The radical pamphleteer Thomas Paine was later imprisoned by Robespierre for his vote to spare the life of the King and for his espousal of moderate causes in the French Revolution, Alfred O. Aldridge, *Man of Reason, The Life of Thomas Paine* (Philadelphia, 1959), 188-221.

4. For an excellent account of the steps leading up to independence in Pennsylvania, David Hawke, *In the Midst of a Revolution* (Philadelphia, 1961).

Test oaths and armed militia guaranteed the outcome of the subsequent election of delegates to the constitutional convention.

The convention first established a temporary government and then wrote a constitution for the state. The radicals, however, were too uncertain of their support in the fall of 1776 to risk submitting their constitution to the voters. Instead, pleading wartime emergency they proclaimed it.[5] This irregularly established constitution became, and remained for the next fourteen years, the major issue of contention between radicals and moderates in Pennsylvania. Within two years the radicals had adopted the name of the Constitutional Society, the moderates the Republican Society.

While the struggle between radicals and moderates for control of the government of Pennsylvania tended to drive the two wings of the Whigs apart, the events of the early years of the war forced them to work together for their mutual defense. Pennsylvania Whigs of every opinion served in the New York, New Jersey, and Pennsylvania campaigns of 1776-1778. In the summer of 1776, after his retreat from Boston, General Howe moved his troops to New York where he won a series of victories and almost destroyed Washington's army that first fall. The following summer, in August 1777, Howe moved into Pennsylvania. He defeated Washington again at the Brandywine River and occupied Philadelphia at the close of September. The victory of the Continentals that same fall in Saratoga, New York, however, encouraged the French, who signed an alliance with the Americans in February 1778.

In the expectation that the French fleet would attack New York the British evacuated Philadelphia in June 1778. This retreat removed the restraining hand of fear of the enemy from the Whig political conflict in Pennsylvania. By the same event, politics in Philadelphia—capital of the state and the nation, and center of the middle states supply region—became suffused with the issues of wartime supply, finance, and trade.

No sooner had the British evacuated the region than provisions ran short. The wheat crop was poor. Such as it was, the Maryland and Pennsylvania harvest faced the demand of Continental and British forces as well as the needs of Philadelphia and the export trade. Prices of wheat, flour, and bread began to rise, and they rose

5. Theodore Thayer, *Pennsylvania Politics and the Growth of Democracy* (Harrisburg, 1953), 186-197.

ever higher under the spur of repeated issues of Pennsylvania and Continental loans, paper money, and quartermaster's receipts.[6]

As always, inflation laid its heaviest tax upon those least able to pay, the poor and the common citizen. Its political direction was to array poor against rich. Moreover, since this 1778-1779 economic dislocation affected the prices and availability of staple items, it created daily grievances.

No state or local government could ignore the clamor. In August 1778 the radical-controlled Pennsylvania Council of Safety, foreseeing shortages, forbade the export of all provisions from the state. There is no way to tell whether farmers and merchants respected this order, but to the extent that it was followed it bottled up Pennsylvania supplies and thereby further deranged the northeast-middle states grain trade. In November, by a similar ruling, the Council forbade the export of flour.[7]

Prices did not figure directly in the October state elections, although they had been rising steadily since July. The moderates charged extravagance and inefficiency and repeated their demand for a new constitutional convention. The radicals pointed with pride to their role as leaders at the moment of independence, and tried to label their opponents "Tory." The moderates gained a few seats, but their delegation to the Assembly amounted to less than one-third of the total seats. After the election, in the maneuvering over the choice of President of the Supreme Executive Council of Pennsylvania, the moderates did score a temporary victory. Joseph Reed (1741-1785), a radical lawyer, and former military secretary to General Washington, wishing to strengthen his administration, struck a bargain with the moderates. If they would support his election he agreed to call the constitutional convention which they had repeatedly demanded. On December 1, 1778, the Assembly voted him President, the highest office in the state.[8] The manner of his election, of course, rekindled the debate on the merits of the Pennsylvania constitution of 1776.

6. Anne Bezanson, *Prices and Inflation during the American Revolution, Pennsylvania 1770-1790* (1951), 84-88; Robert A. East, *Business Enterprise in the American Revolutionary Era* (1938, Gloucester, Massachusetts reprint, 1964), 149-154.

7. Anne Bezanson, "Inflation and Controls, Pennsylvania 1774-1779," *Journal of Economic History, Supplement III* (1948), 14-19.

8. Robert L. Brunhouse, *The Counter-Revolution in Pennsylvania 1776-1790* (Harrisburg, 1942), 53-57.

Philadelphia radicals asked Thomas Paine (1737-1809), a member of their Philadelphia Whig Committee of Correspondence, and the author of the immensely successful *Common Sense* and *The American Crisis* pamphlets, to write a newspaper series in defense of the Constitution. Paine's essay appeared serially in the *Pennsylvania Packet* from December 1 to 12, 1778.[9]

Paine's essay provided two important pieces of evidence about eighteenth-century Philadelphia. First, it showed that the assumption of privatism ran as strongly among radicals as it did among moderates. Second, it revealed the radicals' extremely small-scale, local vision of the city, its business and its government. Both sets of attitudes would prove in 1779, as in all later years, costly blinders upon the vision of city dwellers.

Paine first reviewed the standard assumptions of the radical view of government and society. These were the views of America he had previously set forth in his *Common Sense:* America was a land of unlimited natural resources and hence a place where every man had a chance to get rich; democratic government was necessary to ensure the free private development of these resources; taxpayer suffrage and majority rule were the essence of democracy.[10]

The localism and little government favored by the radicals appeared in Paine's repetition of the familiar radical demand that government must be severely limited lest in peacetime, when public watchfulness diminishes, officials will govern too much. Finally, in discussing the merit of elected, as opposed to appointed, magistrates Paine disclosed his conception of a volunteer, citizens' government. Logically enough, for a Philadelphian who had been watching the town's revolutionary committees function, Paine assumed that ordinary middle-class citizens would constitute the general run of government officials. They would be the successful and respected men of their neighborhood, or county. Such men's practical knowledge, gained as artisans, farmers, or ordinary merchants, would be adequate to the tasks of ruling.[11]

Such a view of politics, presented in this essay as a contrast

9. Aldridge, *Man of Reason*, 62-3.

10. The radical view of democracy including the necessary assumption of unlimited resources appeared in "Common Sense," *The Complete Writings of Thomas Paine* (Philip S. Foner, ed., New York, 1945), I, 5-6, 31, 34, 36-7.

11. Paine, "Serious Address to the People of Pennsylvania on the Present Situation of Their Affairs," *Complete Writings*, II, 282-287, 290-291, 293, 300.

between an over-governed Europe and a free America, left no room for international affairs, or big projects. Indeed, it even misled its contemporary readers about the way the war was being won— through foreign credit, foreign supplies, and since April 1778, an open alliance with the French royal bureaucracy, army, and navy. For the future of Philadelphia and Pennsylvania the popular radical view not only caused the disorders of parochialism, but it also proved unable to accommodate changes in the structure of the society. In time, as industrialization and urbanization progressed, the average, middle-class citizen would no longer present himself for election, nor would voters choose him. Indeed even common-sense knowledge would fail as in modern times few men would comprehend the city as a whole, or even know several of its wards.

Even as Paine wrote his defense of the Pennsylvania Constitution, the war and the economic dislocations of the war, mocked his picture of the world. The very subjects on the colonial landscape which he had neglected now controlled daily life in Philadelphia— the movement of large armies, the inadequacies of the merchant supply network, the provisioning of the French fleet, the financing of the Continental cause.

On December 5, 1778, while Paine's essay was appearing in the *Packet,* angry Congressional conflicts intruded upon the political life of the capital town. That day Silas Deane (1737-1789) published in the same newspaper his attack on Congress and some of its radical leaders. He charged them with delaying the review of his supply dealings with France in order to foster their own political ends. This charge exposed a new side of the war to public view. Since 1776 the Philadelphia scene had been dominated by militia officers and their volunteer companies, by conventions, by town meetings and by *ad hoc* committees of every kind. Citizen volunteer government manifested itself everywhere. Now the other side of the Revolution, secret diplomacy, dealings with a foreign bureaucracy, and the methods of international merchants, came to the foreground. All were subjects beyond the experience of most Philadelphians; all lent themselves to rumor of intrigue and corruption.

The radicals in Congress and in Philadelphia saw the Deane affair as a chance to discomfort their opponents by showing their leaders to be greedy profiteers. Paine, out of personal friendship for

some of the Congressional radicals, began on December 15, 1778, a
series of attacks on Silas Deane and his Philadelphia associate, the
moderate leader, and merchant Robert Morris (1734-1806). The
ensuing exchanges, which lasted in the newspapers for about a
month, raised tempers but did not settle anything. Paine disgraced
himself by revealing secret information he possessed as Secretary to
the Congressional Committee for Foreign Affairs. Robert Morris
justified his actions by saying that his service on Congressional committees did not prevent him from engaging in private business,[12]
but such a defense could not dispel the popular impression that
somehow he and Silas Deane had been profiteering.

Historians have subsequently untangled a good deal of the ob-
scure diplomatic and trade arrangements of the first years of the
American Revolution. The essence of the situation lay in the
French need to proceed secretly in order to preserve the appearance
of neutrality, and the American need to depend upon informal private arrangements of merchants. The resulting attenuation of control added to the sources of trans-Atlantic confusion.

The Second Continental Congress, as early as 1775 when fighting broke out in Massachusetts, had set up a Secret Committee of
Commerce to procure arms from abroad. The chairman of this committee was Thomas Willing (1731-1821), a young but well-established
Philadelphia merchant who had been a leader in the opposition to
England for the past decade. Willing appointed his partner, Robert
Morris, a newcomer to Philadelphia and a self-made man, to the
committee. In December 1775 Willing retired from the committee
and Morris assumed the chairmanship, which he held along with
other Congressional positions until January 1778 when he resigned
in order to devote himself full-time to private business.

In the spring of 1776 the Secret Committee of Commerce had
ordered Silas Deane, then a delegate from Connecticut, and also a
self-made man like Morris, to go to France to seek military supplies.
On the way Deane stopped in the West Indies to make complimen-
tary trading arrangements with William Bingham, (1752-1804) a
Philadelphia merchant now also serving as Congress's agent there.
Thus, in the summer of 1776, there began the Morris-Deane-

12. *Pennsylvania Packet*, January 9, 1779; Brunhouse, *Counter-Revolution*, 61; Aldridge, *Man of Reason*, 71.

Bingham association out of which Morris made his huge fortune. Over the next five years working from this basic Congress-West Indies-French combination Morris built up nine separate partnerships with Philadelphia, New York, French, and English merchants. As a group the partners were aggressive speculators and traders in West Indian goods, flour, tobacco, drygoods, and military supplies. Late in 1777 Morris amicably dissolved his partnership with Willing when Willing stayed in Philadelphia during the British occupation. By 1781 Morris was the most influential and wealthiest merchant in America.

As early as the fall of 1776 complaints began in Congress that Willing and Morris were making exorbitant profits on Continental orders. Later examination of Morris' transactions by the Continental Congress and a careful review of Morris' papers by a modern scholar has failed to show that he profiteered at public expense. Morris was as much a patriot as any of his contemporaries, and he worked long and hard for the cause. He grew very rich, as politically connected businessmen have always grown rich in wartime. Government contracts gave him the credit, capital, and connections needed to do a large-scale business. His volume of trade exceeded by far anything any merchant had handled in pre-Revolutionary times. Inflation, shortages, and the breaking of established paths of commerce guaranteed huge profits to any who could command large quantities of capital and supplies. Morris entered the Revolution as a well-trained, ambitious, and skillful merchant; he saw his opportunity, he took big risks, and he made an enormous fortune.[13]

In January, 1779, while the Deane, Paine, and Morris controversy boiled on, the Supreme Executive Council of Pennsylvania issued a proclamation against monopolizers and forestallers who cornered provisions to raise the price of "bread and other necessaries of life" . . . until "they became ruinous to the industrious poor. . . ." The Council also appointed a committee of radicals to inquire into rumors of monopolization, but nothing came of the investigation.[14] Flour, sugar, rum, and molasses were all selling that month at 100 percent their prewar prices on a specie basis. Because of the

13. The dealings of Deane and Morris and their relations with the Congressional secret committees are carefully reviewed and placed in the business setting of the time by Clarence L. Ver Steeg, *Robert Morris, Revolutionary Financier* (Philadelphia, 1954), 28, 39-41, 58-60; and East, *Business Enterprise*, 126-139, 149-150.

14. *Pennsylvania Gazette*, January 20, 1779; Brunhouse, *Counter-Revolution*, 68.

enormous issues of paper money, wheat sold then in Continental currency at 465 percent and flour 936 percent of its prewar price.[15]

When addressing the Assembly in February, President Joseph Reed spoke out strongly against "forestallers of flour and other provisions" but noted that despite diligent inquiries few prosecutions had been undertaken or were successful. He said a stronger public opinion against the price-fixers would be necessary to control such evil practices. In a city of merchants, shopkeepers, and artisans perhaps it seemed extraordinary to many to condemn a man for selling goods for the most he could get.[16]

Throughout the winter and spring, prices of food rose month by month; shoes and clothing became dear. The newspapers published long letters complaining that society had become deranged by the inflation of currency since an ordinary man could no longer benefit by honest industry and saving. "Our people have become indolent and depraved. . . ." New men of immense wealth and extravagance were rising on the fraud and waste of wartime spending. During these early months of 1779 Army purchasing agents exacerbated the crisis by overbuying.[17]

On April 5 the Pennsylvania Assembly passed additional laws aimed at attacking some of the current abuses in food marketing. No vendor was to refuse to accept Continental currency, and no dealer, except butchers and innkeepers, was to drive out to meet the farmers coming into the public markets with provisions. Finally, any three Justices of the Peace could sit as a committee to set an assize of bread; that is, the Justices could fix the price and weight of bakers' loaves in their town.[18]

Early in May a mob seized a merchant and accused him of exporting flour just brought into the city for the prison. The accusation was entirely false. He was saved only by an alert city official who put the merchant temporarily in jail, secure from the mob. In the same month the militia petitioned the Council against merchants and others who grew rich instead of serving their country.[19]

15. Bezanson, "Inflation and Controls," 15.
16. *Pennsylvania Gazette*, February 10, 1779.
17. *Pennsylvania Gazette*, March 31, May 19, 1779; Bezanson, "Inflation and Controls," 18.
18. *Pennsylvania Gazette*, April 7, 1779; a Philadelphia assize of bread, April 28, 1779.
19. Brunhouse, *Counter-Revolution*, 69-71.

As the month of May wore on, rumors against merchants grew more insistent. A French ship, the "Victorious," had been lying at anchor for several weeks past, and a public guard had been posted on it. It was said about town that a number of merchants had tried to purchase her cargo, and that the Commerce Committee of Congress, seeking to purchase supplies for the army, had even been refused. For some reason the ship stood full loaded. Robert Morris was the agent for the ship; maybe he was trying to drive prices up.[20]

Radical leaders could no longer ignore the drift of popular thinking and the unrest among their followers in the town. Perhaps a revival of the voluntary committees of inspection, successfully used in the 1774 embargo against England, would answer the public clamor against shortages and increasing inflation. The prices of commodities could be fixed and a few speculating merchants made public examples. Best of all, if Robert Morris could be exposed the moderate opposition would be routed. The politics of price control made a dangerous game for the town. The game meant that one group of merchants (the radical leaders) played upon popular frustration and unrest to defeat the political opposition of another group of merchants (the moderate leaders).

The radicals announced a town meeting for Monday, May 24, 1779. For several days prior to the meeting small bands of men cruised the streets cursing monopolizers and looking for trouble. Some observers feared storehouses would be broken into.[21]

A large crowd assembled in the State House yard on the appointed afternoon. General Daniel Roberdeau (1727-1795), a merchant, radical, and popular militia leader was elected chairman and addressed the meeting.

> The dangers we are now exposed to arise from evils amongst ourselves. I scorn, and I hope every citizen here scorns, the thought of getting rich by sucking the blood of his country; yet alas! this unnatural, this cruel, this destructive practice, is the greatest cause of our present calamities. The way to make our money good is to reduce the prices of goods and provisions.
>
> I have no doubt but combinations have been formed for raising the prices of goods and provisions, and therefore the community, in their

20. The complexities of the charges against Morris during the spring and summer of 1779 have been unravelled by Hubertis Cummings, "Robert Morris and the Episode of the Polcare 'Victorious,' " *Pennsylvania Magazine*, LXX (July, 1946), 239-257.

21. Brunhouse, *Counter-Revolution*, 69-71.

own defense, have a natural right to counteract such combinations, and to set limits to evils which affect themselves.[22]

The General next suggested that prices be lowered in monthly stages, as he observed they had been raised. After concluding his short speech Roberdeau read the radical's program for price control to the crowd a paragraph at a time. Item after item carried by acclamation.

The very first resolution following a preamble deploring the high prices of provisions attacked Robert Morris for creating a new inflation—in dry goods. "Since the late importation of a cargo of goods . . . the prices of all kinds of dry goods have been greatly advanced, to the injury of the public and to the detriment of trade." A committee of leading radicals, including Thomas Paine, was appointed by the meeting to wait on Mr. Morris for his explanation.

The meeting also appointed two committees to control prices. One, the Committee on Prices, was to set the monthly price schedule for all Philadelphia transactions in listed commodities; the other, the Committee of Complaints, was to sit at the courthouse from nine to noon every day to hear complaints of infractions. Offenders were to be punished by publication of their names and by referral of their cases to later town meetings for possible further punishment. The meeting adjourned with a resolution that all Tories should be banished from the town.

On June 2 prices were announced for tea, sugar, and molasses, rum, whiskey, rice, flour, coffee, and salt.[23]

The investigation of Robert Morris became a total fiasco. The cargo of the "Victorious" had been consigned to him by a Baltimore merchant. Thereupon Morris had given the Congressional Committee on Commerce the first choice of goods aboard and "very moderate" prices for their selections. The public guard, the delay, and mystery of the ship grew out of confusion over Morris's contract with the Baltimore merchant and the ensuing necessity to renegotiate the prices of goods he had offered for sale.[24]

On June 17 the Philadelphia Committee of Complaints tried to renew the attack when it learned of a purchase of flour for Morris's

22. *Pennsylvania Gazette,* June 2, 1779.

23. For a complete account of the Town Meeting and a listing of the prices set by the committee a week later see, *Pennsylvania Gazette,* June 2, 1779.

24. Cummings, "Episode of the 'Victorious'," 240-246.

account in Lancaster County. The price had exceeded that set for Philadelphia and the Committee feared that such purchases in the country would inevitably advance prices in Philadelphia. This purchase, Morris replied, had been made for the French Navy.[25]

The French Minister in Philadelphia angrily protested such investigation by a Philadelphia town committee and demanded that Congress put a stop to the proceedings. Congress debated the issue without resolution; it feared offending the French, and it feared offending its radical supporters in Philadelphia. As the month of June wore on inflation did not abate. Throughout the colonies the wholesale prices of all major commodities, except sugar, rose sharply all summer. The Philadelphia Committee on Prices responded by adding to its list. By July iron, leather, candles, soap, cotton, and shoes, joined the first items. Altogether the radicals were attempting to control the Philadelphia wholesale and retail prices of thirty-two different goods and commodities.[26] In normal times the prices of these items would have been set by the interactions of trading at Philadelphia for local, regional, and international buyers and sellers.

In an attempt to strengthen support for price control, the radicals returned once again to the militia tactics of 1776. The First Artillery Company of Philadelphia, using as an excuse its absence on garrison duty during the May town meeting, published its resolutions of support in the July 1 newspaper. The formal excuses for the letter concluded with a statement that the company's men had now returned to the city. "We have arms in our hands and know the use of them." After reviewing with approval the monthly roll-back scheme the letter concluded with an ominous bit of bravado " . . . we will see the virtuous, innocent and suffering part of the community redressed, and endeavor to divest this city of the disaffected, inimical, and preyers on the vitals of the inhabitants, be their rank or station what it may."[27]

On the same day a committee of tanners, curriers and cordwainers announced that they would not be bound by the prices for leather and shoes set by the Committee on Prices because controls

25. Cummings, "Episode of the 'Victorious'," 248-249.

26. Bezanson, *Prices and Inflation*, 13, 87-91, 134, 195-6, 213; *Pennsylvania Packet*, June 29, 1779.

27. *Pennsylvania Packet*, July 1, 1779.

had failed to protect the men's living costs. They would set the prices for their work as they saw fit.[28]

The following Saturday the Committee on Prices renewed its attack on Robert Morris. It had learned from another citizens committee in Wilmington, Delaware, that Morris's agent had purchased 182 barrels of flour in that town and "the price given exceeds the regulated market price."[29] The citizens had again seized flour bound for the French fleet. This time the Philadelphia committee found itself in the untenable position of trying to regulate sales of flour in Wilmington, Delaware, which had been negotiated by an agent for a Philadelphia merchant, and was bound for shipment to an allied fleet then heading toward Savannah, Georgia. The inappropriateness of the Philadelphia committee's action made Morris's defense easy. Nevertheless, neither the rightness or wrongness of Morris or the committee would make inflation go away. Prices continued to rise and the controversy dragged on in the Philadelphia press and in Congress all summer.[30]

The following week the Philadelphia Committee on Prices proposed a fiscal attack on high prices. In July, monetary control seemed a more important problem than the direct physical regulation of goods in short supply. The summer crops were good, but farmers would not sell except when they wished to purchase for themselves. They lacked any confidence in the Continental paper money. Judging the situation correctly, then, the radicals proposed a cessation of all further paper issues by Congress. Next the supply of money was to be reduced and Continental needs met by a massive door-to-door subscription of the citizens. Each citizen would be asked to contribute Continental currency to support the war. In return, he would be allowed to apply the amount of his subscription against the next three years' taxes.[31] Unfortunately for the hopes of the scheme, those Philadelphians and Pennsylvanians who were active politically still favored the radicals over the moderates, but no

28. The cordwainers committee is referred to in Gen. Cadwalader's letter, *Pennsylvania Packet,* July 31, 1779, and in Brunhouse, *Counter-Revolution,* 74.

29. *Pennsylvania Packet,* July 3, 1779.

30. Morris's first public defense of his conduct, *Pennsylvania Packet,* July 8, 1779; the full report of the Town Meeting committee who were investigating him, *Packet,* July 24, 1779; report of Morris's Wilmington Delaware agent, *Packet,* July 31, 1779; Morris reviews all the attacks upon him and makes his full defense, *Packet,* August 5, 1779.

31. *Pennsylvania, Packet,* July 10, 1779.

longer trusted their government with credit. The rest of the public
was tired of appeals to patriotism, calls for sacrifice, voluntary committees, and the war itself.

Prices remained high all summer and the normal expectation of
Philadelphia citizens of cheap and plentiful food could not be satisfied. Merchants became restive under the stagnation of regulated
local trade. There were signs that the radical policy was dividing the
town between merchants on one side and artisans and poor citizens
on the other. The radicals sought to counteract the summer's failures by a further infusion of voluntarism. They called for a Town
Meeting to consider the election of a committee of 120 members
from Philadelphia, Northern Liberties, and Southwark to represent
all opinions and interests. On the Saturday before the town meeting, a mob led by two radicals unsuccessfully attacked a merchant's
house. The merchant had given offense by publishing an unpopular
article in an unpopular newspaper.[32]

A large group of opponents of the radical regime are supposed
to have attended the town meeting on Monday afternoon, July 26.
The radical, General Roberdeau, was again chairman of the meeting. He reported subsequently in the newspapers that the "plan for
stopping emissions and raising a revenue by subscription was unanimously approved" and the "association for regulating prices" was
renewed until the end of the year "with only a few, it is thought not
more than four, dissenting voices." Rain broke off the meeting until
9:00 the next morning.[33]

After re-opening, and settling the business of the method of
electing the committee of 120, the meeting proceeded to the consid-
eration of offenders of price regulations. Robert Morris defended
himself in person by denying that he or the French consul had
violated any rule of the Congress or the Philadelphia committee.
Next, General John Cadwalader (1742-1786) a moderate and leader
of the city's "Silk Stocking Company," began to address the crowd
from the speaker's platform on the subject of price controls. As
often as he began he was hooted down by a "body of about 100 men,
armed with clubs, who had marched in array, under their officers,
with fife and drum, and placed themselves near the stage . . ." General Roberdeau could not quiet the militia, even though a voice
vote of the meeting called for Cadwalader to speak.

32. Brunhouse, *Counter-Revolution*, 71-73.
33. *Pennsylvania Gazette*, July 28, 1779.

The angry moderates then left the meeting and formed again two blocks away in the college yard on Fourth Street, between Market and Mulberry. This rump group chose Robert Morris chairman, and proceeded to pass resolutions protesting the denial of free speech, voting to acquit Morris of all charges made against him, and agreeing to participate in the forthcoming election of the committee of 120. Simultaneously, the radicals remaining in the State House yard resolved unanimously that Thomas Paine, then under attack from the moderates for his part in the Deane-Morris controversy, was "a friend of the American cause."[34]

On Saturday, July 31, just before the election, Cadwalader published his appeal for the abolition of all price controls in the *Packet*. He began in a characteristic eighteenth-century way, identifying himself by his economic interest. "I am not, directly or indirectly, engaged in any kind of trade; I am a private citizen, and live upon the income of my estate." He correctly observed that regulation had so far worked to strangle the Philadelphia market. Price controls "must inevitably produce immediate ruin to the merchants and mechanics; and a scarcity, if not a want of every necessary of life, to the whole city."

He then noted that the tanners and cordwainers had refused to be bound by the committee's prices. A complete breakdown surely threatened as other trades would soon form committees and announce non-compliance just as the leather and shoe workers had. The state-by-state regulations were a further disruption of the market in keeping the natural surpluses of one state from reaching others. If there were to be regulations then they must "be undertaken by the united Councils of the states . . ." , in short, control must be national.

Cadwalader concluded by asking his fellow Philadelphians to disband their price association and to petition Congress for the end of all restrictions on interstate trade. "A plentiful harvest has filled the country with an abundance . . . and a market would bring such quantities to the city, that there would be no want of these necessaries in the future."[35]

Although Cadwalader's letter accurately stated the supply conditions in Pennsylvania and the effects of the regulatory associations,

34. Quotations and full account of the Town Meetings, *Pennsylvania Gazette*, July 28; *Pennsylvania Packet*, July 29, 1779.
35. Cadwalader's Letter, *Pennsylvania Packet*, July 31, 1779.

few Philadelphians were yet ready to abandon controls. The harvest did promise well but farmers were selling very cautiously and prices continued to rise. The merchants, though restive under the stagnation of local trade, could continue their regional and export trade on a barter basis. In August the danger of political disorders which might attend an abolition of price control must have appeared to moderate merchants to outweigh the advantages of unfettered trading. The new committee of 120, which contained some moderates, therefore carried easily 2,115 to 281 votes.[36]

The new giant committee enjoyed no more success than its small predecessor. Philadelphia trade was dead; the merchants sold only very small quantities of goods at the regulated prices; throughout the colonies wholesale prices continued to rise steeply. Major trading in army supplies went on at free market prices beyond the city.

Congress itself pursued a conflicting and disruptive economic policy. In August it rescinded all restrictions on interstate trade. Then, in response to continued radical pressure for price control, especially from Massachusetts and Pennsylvania, it resolved that the individual states set up price control committees of their own—as if thirteen lists of state prices and thirteen different investigating committees could have brought order to Congress's supply and financial confusions. In September a group of Philadelphia merchants proposed as an alternative that taxes be levied monthly so that government finances could keep up with the onward rush of current prices.[37]

Altogether, the summer's price-control attempts served only to heighten tensions in the town and to open a cleavage between rich and poor. The charges and counter charges in the press and the town meetings aroused the public against the merchants; yet the price-control committees created by the public clamor failed to bring the price relief the public wanted and needed. Nor could the committee have been effective, given the absence of a public granary system, of arsenals, and of an effective bureaucracy in the colonies. Repeated radical attacks on Quakers and Tories, perhaps conceived

36. *Pennsylvania Packet*, August 5, 1779. The moderate leaders on the new committee were: John Shee, Thomas Fitzsimons, Francis Hopkinson, and Andrew Caldwell.
37. *Pennsylvania Packet*, September 10, 1779; Brunhouse, *Counter-Revolution*, 74, 84-85.

to distract public attention from the inevitable failures of the radical program, only increased the popular appetite for direct action. Moreover, the use of militia companies for threats of political reprisal strained the town's capacity for common-sense control of violence.

On the eve of the October general election of state, county, and local officials the temptations that had lurked in the conflicts of the summer broke forth. At a militia meeting to consider still another drive to rid the city of Tories and "political Quakers" the group clamored to include some moderate leaders in the sweep. James Wilson (1742-1798), a lawyer, prominent moderate leader, and defender of Robert Morris, was singled out.

Late in the morning of Monday, October 4, just eight days before the election, a band of militiamen began rounding up Quakers. In the early afternoon, after allowing their prisoners to go home for dinner, they paraded their captives through the streets of the town picking up a crowd as they went. James Wilson, meanwhile, somehow learning of the danger to himself called for protection upon the Pennsylvania Assembly, then sitting in Philadelphia. General Cadwalader's "Silk Stocking" brigade patrolled in front of Wilson's house in the morning and then, thinking all was safe, went home to dinner. As additional protection Wilson had also gathered an armed group of fellow moderates at his own home. Soon the militia band, swelled by the curious, drew up before Wilson's door. Shots were fired from the house and three militiamen killed. The angry crowd stormed the door and would have murdered everyone in the house had not Joseph Reed, President of the Pennsylvania Supreme Executive Council, arrived just at this moment with a troop of cavalry and a brigade of foot soldiers. The President's troops dispersed the militia and crowd and succeeded in quieting the city.[38]

The incident frightened both radical and moderate leaders. Both sides attempted to prevent further confrontation of mobs and merchants; both sides rushed to use the town's traditional voluntary social controls. Francis Hopkinson, a moderate, published a "Plan for the Relief and Support of the Poor and Distressed Families of . . . Philadelphia," and began a ward-by-ward canvas for funds. The radicals announced a subscription for the families of three dead

38. Brunhouse, *Counter-Revolution*, 75.

militiamen. A person believed to be Thomas Paine wrote a highly distorted and pacifying account of the incident in which he closed by saying this ". . . was not the quarrel of enemies or of parties, but the unfortunate blunder of friends."[39]

The Wilson riot marked the climax of a year's frustration. In the anger of the moment the radicals swept the October elections, but when tempers cooled the riot proved the terminal event in a year of failure of a town's attempts to regulate its own economy. Even in Paine's and Morris's day the business scale of the town had become so large that it had exceeded the political abilities of its local citizens.

In the terms of the moment, the 1778-1779 Philadelphia inflation and provision crisis had been a serious political failure. The confrontation of the popular radical party with the moderate merchant party did not produce any successful institution which could have eased the scarcity and high prices of food. Paine and the radicals had quite properly seen that the free market was not fairly allocating flour and "necessaries" among the citizens of the town. In times of scarcity, just as in normal times, the rich outbid the poor. Morris and the moderates had as properly responded that in their ill-articulated society free, open-market trading by the merchants would in the long run bring relief from shortages and high prices. Both sides spoke half-truths. The radicals failed to recognize the need for the merchants to manage their own private network of traders, and the merchants failed to recognize the immediate needs of the city for a fair, publicly supervised allocation of food.

The political failure of 1778-1779 lay in the inability of the radicals and moderates to work out some limited supply mechanism, perhaps just for bread and flour, which could have taken advantage of the merchant network. One year later Morris and his group organized a supply bank for the Continental Army which suggested how Philadelphia's needs might have been met by a union of merchants back in 1779. Some measure of relief from the inflation and provision crisis of 1778-1779 was not a task beyond the economic capa-

---

39. Hopkinson's subscription, *Pennsylvania Packet,* October 12; relief for the families of those killed, *Pennsylvania Packet,* October 6, 1779. The letter, believed to be Paines', was signed only C—S—. Aldridge, *Man of Reason,* 80, attributes it to Paine although it was not published by Foner in his complete edition of Paine's writings. The letter appeared in the *Pennsylvania Packet,* October 16, 1779.

bilities of the society, but it was a task beyond the political capabilities of the society.[40]

DEMOCRACY VS. PRIVATE ECONOMIC ASPIRATIONS

Such political failures would be repeated over and over again in Philadelphia's later history. The Revolution left the city a tradition of democratic forms and democratic goals grafted upon a society of private economic aspirations. Later political conflict between popular equalitarian goals and the goals of business profit would give rise to the modern municipal corporation and encourage its active participation in transportation, public safety, education, and health. These municipal functions would be the public dimensions of a city of private aspirations. Urban problems that required direct and substantial reallocation of scarce resources, problems like the 1778-1779 crisis, brought failure after failure to the future city. No urban, economic democracy emerged with time because the popular goal of Philadelphia was the individual race for wealth. This was to be the essence of the American, urban experience.

40. Brunhouse, *Counter-Revolution*, 86-87. In 1781 and 1782 Paine was writing for Robert Morris on the necessity for taxes and a stable currency, Aldridge, *Man of Reason*, 89-94.

Part Two

THE BIG CITY 1830-1860

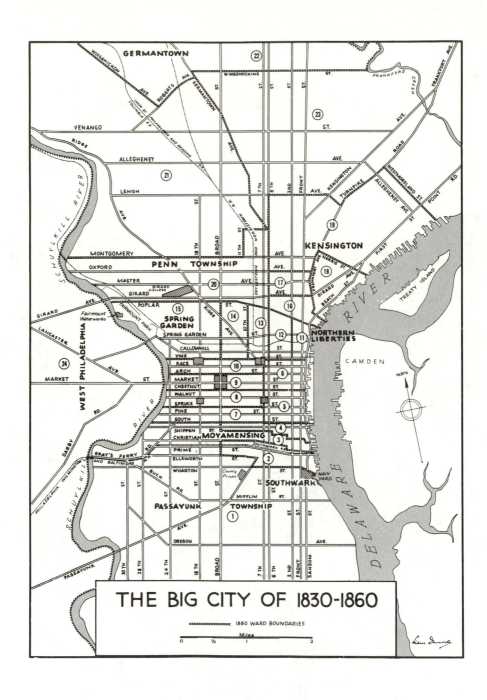

THE BIG CITY OF 1830-1860

············· 1860 WARD BOUNDARIES

Miles

3

Spatial Patterns
of Rapid Growth

A rapid succession of events during the three decades from 1830 to 1860 tested every element in Philadelphia's traditions by relentlessly overturning the commonplace modes of daily life. Methods of business and relationships among men which had sufficed since the first settling of Penn's town were suddenly transformed by an irresistible series of novel events. Speed, bigness, newcomers, and money beat upon settled manners with a rain of harassment and opportunity.

In 1830 Philadelphia had been a booming town, but still a place whose manners followed the familiar paths of English and American provincial towns. By 1860 the flood of change had so far run that Philadelphia had become something new to the world and new to America—a modern big city. Throughout the transition years, in the face of strikes, race riots, plagues, and depressions, Philadelphians clung to their tradition of privatism, failing where privatism doomed them to failure, succeeding where privatism and community could be brought into harmony.

Of all the changes that the shift from old town ways to new big city ways entailed the most important for us to understand today are the changes in community, for disorders in community relationships are now the most serious and intractable problems of our metropolises. In addition to our current needs, concern for the origins of our municipal landscape directs our attention to these years. Many of our urban habits and institutions are survivals from innovations of the nation's first big city era—hospitals, charities, parks, water works, police departments, and public schools. These municipal amenities and institutions are the living reminders of Americans' positive response to the destruction of their old town community.

Despite recurring financial panics and depressions, Philadelphia boomed during the years from 1830 to 1860. Never again would it recapture this pace of its first urbanization and industrialization. In 1830 urban Philadelphia, the old municipality and the densely settled adjacent districts and boroughs, held 161,410 inhabitants; in 1860 the consolidated city of Philadelphia held 565,529 inhabitants (Table VI).

Social and economic heterogeneity was the hallmark of the age. Most areas of the new big city were a jumble of occupations, classes, shops, homes, immigrants, and native Americans. Although by 1860 there were the beginnings of concentrations which reflected the future economic and social articulation of the city—a downtown, three manufacturing clusters, a small slum, a few black blocks, and occasional class and ethnic enclaves—these concentrations did not dominate the spatial patterns of the city. The full development of the segregated metropolis was yet to come.

Although mid-century Philadelphia was a brand-new sprawling port and mill city, as much a novelty as Cincinnati, or St. Louis, or Liverpool then were, no important innovations went into the building of its physical structure. Rather seventeenth and eighteenth-century methods of land division and eighteenth-century methods of housing sheltered most of the big city's families, businesses, and manufactories. The grid street, the narrow house lot, the row house, the interior alley, and the rear yard house or shack were endlessly repeated. When so repeated, however, they lost entirely their eighteenth-century character and took on instead that mixture of dreariness and confusion which so characterized nineteenth-century mass building.

Philadelphia's grid descended directly from the 1682 plan of Penn and his surveyor.[1] During the eighteenth century, despite the

---

1. Anthony N. B. Garvan, "Proprietary Philadelphia as Artifact," *The Historian and the City*, (Oscar Handlin and John Burchard, editors, Cambridge, 1963), 190; an excellent map describing conditions in 1684, "Philadelphia as William Penn Knew It," *Pennsylvania Magazine*, LIX (July, 1935), opposite 209.

TABLE VI

POPULATION OF URBAN PHILADELPHIA 1800-1860

	Approx. wards 1860	1800	1830	1840	1850	1860
Philadelphia, Old City	5-10	41,220	80,458	93,665	121,376	137,756
Blockley-West Phila.	24	—	—	—	11,487	23,738
Frankford, borough	23	—	—	—	5,346	23,985
Germantown, tp. and bor.	22	—	—	5,482	8,336	17,173
Moyamensing	1	—	6,822	14,573	26,979	30,886
Northern Liberties:	11-20	16,970	—	—	—	242,319
Subdiv. 1803-1848 into:						
N. Liberties Dist. (1803)		—	28,923	34,474	47,223	
Kensington Dist. (1820)		—	13,326	22,314	46,774	
Richmond Dist. (1847)		—	—	—	5,750	
Bridesburg Bor. (1848)		—	—	—	—	
Penn Township (1808)		—	—	—	—	
Penn District (1844)		—	—	—	8,939	
Spring Garden District (1813)		—	11,141	27,849	58,894	
Roxborough-Manayunk	21	—	—	5,797	5,346	17,159
Southwark District	2-4	9,621	20,740	27,548	38,799	72,513
Urban Phila. Total		67,811	161,410	231,702	388,721	—
Philadelphia County		81,009	188,961	258,037	408,762	565,529

unfortunate introduction of alleys, Philadelphia's regular streets stood as America's leading example of a handsome and commodious town order. With the increase of the pace of city growth in the nineteenth century, however, other qualities of the street grid than its architectural effect came into prominence.

The rectangular survey of open farm land, the laying out of streets and blocks into even rectangles, the subdivision of blocks into narrow house lots, this was the simplest, cheapest, and clearest way of dividing land for rapid development. It was an ideal method, since it treated all land similarly, for a real estate market composed of hundreds of land speculators and home builders and thousands of petty landlords and small home buyers. Such considerations had led to the introduction of a uniform grid for Manhattan Island in 1811[2] and its almost universal adoption for new towns in the West. Thus, falling in with the rest of the nation, Philadelphians extended their street grid indefinitely along their urban frontier.

Grid subdivision also suited the city's architectural needs. Narrow lots and small row houses could still, as late as 1860, shelter most of the city's families and a good proportion of its workplaces. New construction for Philadelphia's ordinary citizens followed a very simple set of alternatives: shacks, shanties, and back-alley two-room houses for the poor, three-room row houses, or three rooms in multiple-family row houses for the skilled workingman; and six to eight room row houses and flats for middle class managers, prosperous shopkeepers, professionals, and downtown businessmen.[3] Such structures, or stores, barns, and sheds erected on lots subdivided for such structures, contained most of the city's economic activity. The carter kept his team in a stable behind his house, the shoemaker and his journeyman made shoes in his front room, as his predecessors had done in the eighteenth century; men rolled cigars in the local tobacco store while the proprietor's family lived upstairs or in the rear; a small factory of carpet weavers, a foundry or machine shop often took no more than a double lot. Such traditional spatial arrangements of work and housing created the miles and miles of new

2. John W. Reps, *The Making of Urban America* (Princeton, 1965), 296-299.
3. Louis H. Arky, "The Mechanics' Union of Trade Associations and the Formation of the Philadelphia Workingmen's Movement," *Pennsylvania Magazine*, LXXVI (April, 1952), 165-166. See also the house sizes shown in Ernest Hexamer and William Locher, *Maps of the City of Philadelphia* (Philadelphia, 1858), 7 v.

streets and alleys of resident workingmen and shopkeepers.[4] Living among these neighborhood workers, sharing the same streets and housing, were the new commuting workers: the downtown clerks, businessmen and factory workers, and some of the outer-city mill workers.

By 1860 the area of unbroken urban settlement covered about six square miles. The mass of houses spread out over the Delaware and Schuylkill river plain like a man-made savannah of brick and slate, its surface pierced here and there by steeples, gas holders, and the masts of ships. Charles Dickens had sensed the dreary effect when he visited Philadelphia in 1842.[5] The unbroken continuation of the grid burdened the city with more than aesthetic problems; it saddled the city with an increasingly inefficient traffic system. Long before the automobile Penn's streets proved too narrow. First the pedestrians, carriages and wagons, later the added flow of streetcars, overburdened the inner city streets. Yet no municipal board of survey forced subdividers to lay out wider streets in new parts of the city, or forced downtown investors to build farther back from the old street lines. For this generation, and many to come, all urban growth was good and therefore needed no special attention.

The very nature of the grid itself, a system of even-sized, right-angle streets, prevented it from adapting to the strongly concentrated flows of traffic which came from the intensified linkages of modern urban life. The commuters and shoppers moving from the north and west sides of town to the downtown, the business traffic moving from the downtown and the wharves to the industrial clusters to the northeast and the south, and above all the sheer volume of pedestrians, horses, carts and carriages in the downtown itself demanded a few wide streets which would break through the grid to allow traffic to move easily in a few major directions. The inherited

4. A check of the addresses of places of work given in William H. Boyd, *Boyd's Philadelphia City Directory, 1859-1860* (Philadelphia, 1860) shows that cigar makers kept shops in 13 of the city's 24 wards, coopers in 13, carriage and coachmakers in 16, wheelwrights in 20, machinists in 16, iron founders in 14, leather and findings in 14, carpet weavers in 17, dressmakers in 23, tailors in 24, cotton and woolen manufacutre in 13; of course, grocery stores appeared in every ward, while wine and liquor dealers in 22, lager beer saloons in 21, porter houses in 20.

5. "It is a handsome city, but distractingly regular. After walking about for an hour or two, I felt that I would have given the world for a crooked street." Charles Dickens, *American Notes* (Andrew Lang, ed., *Works*, XXVIII, New York, 1897-1899), 116.

diagonal highways of Germantown Avenue and Ridge Avenue on the north, and Passyunk Avenue on the south were themselves too narrow and too few for a city of half a million inhabitants.

Stephen Girard (1750-1831), the wealthy China merchant had early recognized Philadelphia's traffic problems. To remedy the jams next to the wharves and warehouses of the Delaware River he left the city a large sum to tear down houses and build a wide new street parallel to the river. His was the only reform of the Philadelphia street grid in the nineteenth century.[6]

Thoughtless and uncoordinated building on top of the grid lots damaged the city as severely as its inappropriate land division. No attempt was made by this generation to use its large public and commercial structures as a device for creating unified subcenters within the city. The municipal corporation dotted the grid with schools and police stations as if it were salting an egg. Churches sought large cheap lots anywhere within the bounds of their congregations. The stations built for the new steam railroads in the 1830's and 1840's were scattered at the fringes of the city where land was cheap and abundant. None of the new stations reinforced such public market or crossroads concentrations as already existed at the edges of Philadelphia.[7] Stores, as always, made shopping strips out of the most traveled streets, and beyond the downtown, formed neighborhood crossroads by occupying the four corners of an intersection.

The effect of three decades of a building boom carried forward by such methods was a city without squares of shops and public buildings, a city without gathering places which might have assisted in focusing the daily activities of neighborhoods. Instead of subcenters the process of building created acres and acres of amorphous

6. Delaware Avenue completion, *Public Ledger*, November 22, 1850.

7. In 1834 the Philadelphia and Trenton railroad built its terminal between Front street and Frankford road, north of Harrison street in Kensington, four and nine blocks from the public market stalls of the growing Kensington-Northern Liberties industrial quarter. J. Thomas Scharf and Thompson Westcott, *History of Philadelphia* (Philadelphia, 1884), III, 2183. Other railroad stations were also awkwardly placed. The Germantown and Norristown stopped at Ninth and Willow streets, the Columbia Railroad, the Reading Railroad, and the West Chester Railroad located along Broad street between Vine and Arch streets; the Southwark railroad, and the Philadelphia, Wilmington, and Baltimore Railroad skirted the southside settlement, making a dash from Gray's Ferry road across Prime street to the old Navy Yard at the Delaware River. H.S. Tanner, *Map of Philadelphia*, 1836; *Barnes' Map of Philadelphia Revised for McElroy's City Directory of 1860.*

TABLE VII

LOCATION OF FOREIGN BORN, NEGROES, AND SELECTED OCCUPATIONS TENURES AND RENTS, BY PERCENT IN CORE OR RING 1860, 1930

- 1860 -

	Negro	Foreign Born	Britain	Germany	Ireland	Total Population
Ring	34.9	62.1	73.7	60.4	60.8	61.9
Core[1]	65.1	37.9	26.3	39.6	39.2	38.1
Total Number	22,185	168,556	22,398	43,833	94,989	565,529

	Laborer	Clerk	Carpenter	Machinist	Shoemaker	Tailor	Sample
Ring	75.5	40.6	61.7	69.5	66.9	68.9	58.9
Core	24.5	59.4	38.3	30.5	33.1	31.1	41.1
Number in Sample	442	283	149	82	181	122	4,740

- 1930 -

	Negro	Britain	Germany	Ireland	Italy	Poland	Russia	Total Population
Ring[2]	19.7	52.6	43.8	52.0	29.5	27.4	30.0	70.0
Core	80.3	47.4	56.2	48.0	70.5	72.6	70.0	29.6
Total Number	222,504	36,593	38,066	31,359	68,156	30,582	80,959	1,950,961

	Own Their Home	Rent at Under $15	Rent $15-29	Rent $30-49	Rent $50-99	Rent $100 and up	Total Families
Ring	52.4	10.9	16.8	40.3	60.5	44.2	44.2
Core	47.6	89.1	83.2	59.7	29.5	55.8	55.8
Number of Families	232,591	10,142	63,432	96,026	36,427	6,538	448,653[3]

tracts—the architectural hallmark of the nineteenth and twentieth-century American big city. For a city, like Philadelphia, simultaneously undergoing the transition to bigness and the social revolution of industrialization this weakly structured physical form proved a serious handicap. Whatever community life that was to flourish from now on would have to flourish despite the physical form of the city, not because of it.

The social geography of the big city of 1860 was almost the reverse of the late nineteenth and early twentieth-century metropolis. Today's core of poverty and ring of affluence dates from the late nineteenth century[8] and was not characteristic of the first wave of urban growth (Table VII). Because Philadelphia grew so rapidly in the first half of the nineteenth century, and because it grew from such small beginnings, no large stock of old housing existed to absorb and to ghettoize the waves of poor immigrants.[9] There were some run-down alleys adjacent to the wharves and south of Walnut Street, odd-lots not yet claimed for industry and commerce, but these pockets could not begin to hold the rush of newcomers. Philadelphians of all income levels had to locate in new construction. The shanties, shacks, backyard houses, and alley tenements reported by early investigators like Mathew Carey and Isaac Parrish testify to the unpleasant meeting of low incomes with the costs of new construction.[10] Segregated slums, however, did not result. Instead of large tracts of run-down houses occupied by Negroes or Italians or Jews, as in the twentieth century, Irish peasant immigrants flooded into every ward. The German immigrants, though continuing and enlarging their concentration on the northside of town, also lived in large numbers in most of the wards of the city (Table II). By 1860

8. Sam Bass Warner, Jr., *Streetcar Suburbs* (Cambridge, 1962), 15-34.

9. In 1860 the Negroes were the only group of poor people strongly concentrated in the core wards. If laborers be used as a proxy for low incomes, then low incomes were more heavily concentrated in the ring than in the core. If personal property taxes on furniture, watches, and carriages be used as a measure then the core city was indeed richer than the outside districts, *Public Ledger*, January 23, 1843. This analysis is confirmed by a study of church location and membership, Norman J. Johnston, "The Caste and Class of the Urban Form of Historic Philadelphia," *Journal of the American Institute of Planners*, XXXII (November, 1966), 334-349.

10. High cost of housing and Front street tenements, Mathew Carey, *A Plea for the Poor* (Philadelphia, 1837); alley housing of the poor, Isaac Parrish, "Report on the Sanitary Condition of Philadelphia," *Transactions of the American Medical Association*, II (Philadelphia, 1849), 463-470.

Philadelphia's population was 30 percent foreign-born; it included 95,000 immigrants from Ireland and 44,000 immigrants from Germany. Whatever accommodations had to be made within the city to incorporate this flood of newcomers into a new pattern of city life, and there were in these years many tensions and much violence, that integration took place in heterogeneous neighborhoods where almost every trade, nationality, and religion lived near every other. This was the pattern of the early big city, the way of the first era of the urban melting pot.

The scattering of immigrants through the wards of Philadelphia had been fostered by the rapid multiplication of traditional occupations during the years 1774-1860. Although industrialization was transforming the conditions of employment and market relationships of most occupations, these changes had only begun to be reflected in neighborhood settlement patterns. Of the fifteen major occupations which together employed 30 to 40 percent of all Philadelphia's adults, only two were new since the eighteenth century—machinist and factory operative.[11] The big office and factory style of doing business would in time produce both neighborhoods of workers clustering near their mills, and, more commonly, all-residential neighborhoods of workers who commuted to their jobs. In 1860, however, the big office had yet to come and the big factories only dominated manufacturing of locomotives, cottons, gas fixtures, umbrellas and parasols, clothing, trimmings, bricks, hosiery and iron machinery (Table IX).[12] Thus, the occupations of Philadelphia in 1860 remained much as they had in 1774. The city was still an agglomeration of old trades—laborers, clerks, carpenters, tailors,

11. The sample drawn from the original schedules of the Eighth Census is in effect a sample of all occupations since the Census taker recorded the name of every member of a household and put beside each name an occupation, if the member styled himself as having one. The street Directory was much less inclusive, more in the nature of a head-of-household census, although minors and women who wanted to be listed by occupation could be so listed if they took the trouble to inform the Directory canvasser. See notes to Table II for a comparison of the two samples of Philadelphia occupations in 1860.

12. The origin, growth, and location of these large factories are sketched briefly in John Leander Bishop, *A History of American Manufactures from 1608 to 1860* (Third edition, Philadelphia, 1868), III, 18-95. His only additions to the high average size firms shown by the 1860 Census are brewing, a marble works, paper, and chemicals. Significantly he doesn't mention shoes, clothing, rugs, hats, woodworking, furniture— all major industries still organized in small shops.

weavers, shoemakers, grocers, liquor dealers, butchers, tobacco dealers, cordwainers, blacksmiths, and cabinetmakers.[13] The small size of
the shops in which most of these trades were practiced had made the
mixed wards of homes, workplaces, foreign-born and native Americans possible.

On top of this remarkably even grain of settlement the new
industrial ways of the mid-century had begun to lay some of the
patterns of the coming metropolis—especially the beginnings of a
downtown, and some manufacturing sectors. The downtown[14] had
grown out of the expansion and differentiation of the old eighteenth
century Delaware river importing merchant's district. Undifferenti-
ated importing began to split up during the Revolution and in time
the activities of the old general merchant multiplied into hundreds
of wholesale and retail specialties. Manufacturers moved in next to
these new dealers to supply some of their needs, and it was this
manufacturing that gave the early nineteenth-century downtown its
size and bulk. The downtown in 1860 was not, as it is today, a mere
creature of offices and stores.

A quarter of all the city's manufacturing workers, 30,000 and
more men, women, and children, worked in the principal downtown ward of Philadelphia.[15] The garment industry in all its
branches, boot and shoe makers, bookbinders, printers, and paper
box fabricators, glass manufacturers, machinists, coopers, sugar re-
finers, brewers, and cigar makers especially concentrated here.[16] The
city's newspapers, banks, theatres, and restaurants, and many of its
retail stores concentrated here too. Thousands of workers walked to
the downtown every day, while omnibuses, and just before the Civil
War, horse-drawn streetcars brought shopkeepers and customers.[17]
No tall office buildings yet outlined the downtown, no manufactur-

13. Occupations listed in rank order with operative and machinist omitted, see notes
to Table II.

14. For purposes of simplicity the downtown is here defined as 1860 Ward Six. The
dense manufacturing, wholesaling, and retail district included parts of Ward Five as
well.

15. The location of manufacturing establishments and the number of manufacturing
employees is given by ward in *U.S. Eighth Census: 1860*, III, *Manufactures*, 536.

16. The concentration of specialties in the downtown was estimated from addresses
of business establishments listed in *Boyd's Philadelphia City Directory, 1859-1860*.

17. George Rogers Taylor, "The Beginnings of Mass Transportation in Urban
America" Parts One and Two, *The Smithsonian Journal of History*, I (Summer and
Autumn, 1966), 35-50; 31-54.

ing lofts filled entire blocks, but the basic manufacturing-wholesale-retail-financial elements had already been assembled by 1860 for the future metropolis.

Beyond the downtown convenient transportation had encouraged additional manufacturing clusters. They took the common American pattern of radiating out from the original urban core like a crude spiderweb spun through the blocks of little houses. As the city grew along the Delaware shore, manufacturing sprang up behind its wharves and shipyards. To the north stood the leather and wool district (1860 ward 11), and the machinery and the textile mills (1860 ward 18). On the southside garment sweatshops scattered through the city's first slums (1860 wards 4 and 5). To the west, Market street, for many years the only road with a permanent bridge across the Schuylkill River, had become a manufacturing axis, especially for furniture, woodworking, and packing houses (1860 ward 9). On the northwest the new railroad yards there made that section the home of locomotive building and metalworking.[18] Beyond the stretch of continuous settlement there were, as well, mill towns like Manayunk on the Schuylkill, or Kellyville in West Philadelphia, but these were not as yet part of urban Philadelphia.

These manufacturing concentrations introduced Philadelphia to some of the diurnal rhythms of an industrial metropolis. Work began to be separated from home neighborhood. It is difficult today to estimate the number of commuting workers, as opposed to those employed within their own neighborhoods. Some estimate can be made, however, by comparing the residential information of the Street Directory of 1860 with the workplace information of the U.S. Census of the same year. In those wards where the jobs for men in manufacturing establishments exceeded the number of adult males in manufacturing occupations living in the ward there must have been strong daily inflows of workers. Wards where adult males engaged in manufacture exceeded the needs of resident establishments supplied workers to the deficit wards (Table VIII).

By this very crude measure, the downtown and Market Street manufacturing clusters must have been the destination of thousands of workers. At least 20,000 persons, men, women, and children, must have come each day to staff the garment and shoe factories,

18. Concentrations estimated from listings in *Boyd's Directory, 1859-1860*, and addresses in Bishop, *History of American Manufactures*, III, 18-95.

printing plants, and furniture mills of the downtown. Market Street must have needed several thousand more workers.[19] It seems most likely that the bulk of these early commuting workers came from the poor districts on the south side (1860 wards 2, 3, 4), while the skilled workers came from the northside residential concentrations

TABLE VIII

ESTIMATE OF THE FLOW OF MALE MANUFACTURING EMPLOYEES
TO OR FROM THE WARDS OF THEIR RESIDENCE, 1860

Ward	Percent of a Ward's Male Residents Engaged in Manufacture	Male Employment in a Ward's Mfg. Establishments as Percent of Ward's Males 15 yrs. and older	Approx. Flow of Male Employees	
			Volume	Direction
1	34.3	25.8	+ 8.5%	
2	30.2	10.1	+ 20.1	Out
3	32.1	8.9	+ 20.1	Out
4	26.8	7.3	+ 19.5	Out
5	17.4	75.5	− 58.1	In
6	15.9	324.4	−308.5	In
7	14.1	12.9	+ 1.2	
8	13.5	33.6	− 20.1	In
9	15.3	91.5	− 76.2	In
10	20.5	28.9	− 8.4	
11	33.1	56.5	− 23.4	In
12	30.9	28.7	+ 2.2	
13	26.5	16.1	+ 10.4	Out
14	24.1	34.3	− 10.2	In
15	24.8	43.6	− 18.8	In
16	42.0	46.6	− 4.6	
17	44.4	26.7	+ 17.7	Out
18	37.9	35.5	+ 2.4	
19	36.4	29.3	+ 7.1	
20	28.4	14.0	+ 14.4	Out
21	34.3	39.8	− 5.5	
22	26.6	26.7	− 0.1	
23	24.9	34.8	− 9.9	
24	26.7	35.6	− 8.9	

19. These location estimates are confirmed by the presence of industrial structures shown in Hexamer and Locher, *Maps of the City of Philadelphia*, I-III. According to the *U.S. Eighth Census: 1860*, III, *Manufacturers* 536, the downtown wards (5 and 6), employed 37,268 men and women, Market street (ward 9) 6,435, or together these two manufacturing districts employed 43,703. This total for the two districts was 44.2% of the 98,983 workers given by the census for the entire city.

(1860 wards 13 and 20). The northwest locomotive and metalworking center, the Kensington textile center, and the new Southwark mills must have been manned by workers living nearby (Table VIII). Altogether perhaps a third of Philadelphia's manufacturing workers were commuting to jobs in the manner of the majority of their successors in the twentieth-century industrial metropolis.

By 1860 the combined effects of Philadelphia's rapid growth—the endless grid streets, the scattering of churches, stations, and factories, the flood of immigrants, the novelty, the sheer size, and pace of the big city—all its elements of change contributed to the thorough destruction of the informal neighborhood street life which had characterized the small-scale community of the eighteenth-century town. In response to these new conditions all Philadelphians, of every class and background, reacted in the same way to the loss of the old patterns of sociability and informal community. They rushed into clubs and associations.

The mid-nineteenth century was *par excellence* the era of the urban parish church, the lodge, the benefit association, the social and athletic club, the political club, the fire company, and the gang. Over the whole range of sociability from the parties of the wealthy to the meanest boy's gang all Philadelphians sought a sense of social place and community in club life. It has been estimated that in 1861 there were four hundred parish churches in Philadelphia, or about one for every 750 adults.[20] There must have been twice that number of organized lodges, clubs, and benefit associations.[21]

Most enduring and best known were the British and Irish organizations and their American copies: the imported Masons, Odd Fellows, Druids, Foresters, and the native Sons of St. Tammany, and Society of Red Men.[22] A typical daily newspaper of 1850 would

20. Timothy L. Smith, *Revivalism and Social Reform* (New York, 1957), 20.

21. Some idea of the sheer volume of clubs and associations can be formed by looking at the listing of participating organizations in President Harrison's funeral parade, *Public Ledger,* April 21, 1840; also Scharf and Westcott, *History of Philadelphia,* II, 1092-1098, 1449-1941; III, 2062-2084; outlines of workingclass mutual benefit associations from Philadelphia Society of Friends, *A Statistical Inquiry into the Condition of the People of Color of the City and Districts of Philadelphia* (Philadelphia, 1849), 22-23.

22. Noel P. Gist, "Secret Societies: A Cultural Study of Fraternalism in the U.S.," *University of Missouri Studies,* XV (October, 1940), 32-39; Charles W. Ferguson, *Fifty Million Brothers, A Panorama of American Lodges and Clubs* (New York, 1937), 22-30, 218.

carry a column or more of advertisements announcing meetings, lectures, and balls of these lodges and their many imitators. The programs ranged from the improving topics of the lyceums, mechanics institutes, temperance and anti-slavery societies to the mere sociability of the ethnic club or the firehouse ball. So severe was the mid-century Philadelphian's sense of loss of community that radical associations proposing cooperative living in the city or communist communities in the country enjoyed large audiences at their meetings and considerable support for their experiments.[23]

The flood of Irish immigration gave rise to two opposing groups, the Loyal Orange Institution and the Ancient Order of Hibernians. These lodges, as well as the firehouses and gangs of similar loyalty continued Irish warfare on the streets of Philadelphia. Then, in the mid-1840's when all the stresses of the city began to focus on the issue of Catholic immigration Nativist clubs sprouted up in most of the wards of the city: Order of United American Mechanics, Wide-Awakes, Native Sons of America, Know-Nothings.[24]

On balance, despite the public conflict some of these groups caused, the club and association response of this first generation of big-city dwellers was probably a necessary and wholesome one. It helped to preserve the mental health of the joiners by offering a replacement for the old street, shop, and neighborhood life of eighteenth-century town conditions. Yet, as so often happens with cities, an adaptation which served the interests of individual citizens, did not when repeated a thousandfold create a good public result.

Clubs, lodges, parishes, and gangs were not media which could nourish effective and inclusive community growth. A city of such private associations was a city of closed social cells; such a city could not imitate the open, easy neighborhood life of the town, nor could it establish a sufficiently inclusive system to maintain order against the stresses of industrialization. Only after decades of disorder would some of the functions of the former town pattern be redistributed in their modern form.

23. John R. Commons, ed., *History of Labor,* I, 519-521.
24. Ferguson, *Fifty Million Brothers,* 296-351.

4

Industrialization

Though the spatial patterns of rapid growth greatly disrupted Philadelphians' traditional ways of living, still more unsettling were the events of industrialization. The rapid transition from the preindustrial town economy to the industrial, big-city, regional economy created both great opportunities for personal wealth and widespread dislocation and personal defeat.

Industrialization manifested itself as an increase in the reach of the city and its businesses. This gain in reach brought with it a speeding of the pace of all its work. First came the succession of changes in transportation, the new turnpikes, canals, railroads, and telegraph lines, and the improvements in sailing ships, navigational aids, express and postal service. This series of changes which began in the late eighteenth century and reached full expression on the eve of the Civil War, speeded men's reckoning of time and accelerated their business aspirations. By 1840 freight moved from Philadelphia to New York in hours instead of days, to Pittsburgh in days instead of weeks.[1] Trading areas grew, accounts were settled faster, and the volume of all kinds of transactions doubled and doubled again.

Next, the opportunity to do a big business created the opportunity to make a big profit by arranging large-scale production. Although the introduction of some new machine was often the

1. George R. Taylor, *The Transportation Revolution 1815-1860* (New York, 1951), 138-152.

occasion for change, specialization and rationalization of traditional tasks were the key elements in the first stages of industrialization. The old general merchant who assembled goods from abroad and from local artisans for shipment to country shopkeepers, or for retail at his own store, gave way to wholesale and manufacturing specialists. These new men restricted themselves to one line of goods, like jeans, women's shoes, or woodenware. They reorganized the artisans of that specialty, or rearranged production to use machines, unskilled immigrants, or women and children, so that their line could supply a city-wide or regional market.[2]

Improved long-distance transportation and large-scale production, in turn, tied the city ever more closely to national and international business conditions. Peaks of prosperity, and deep depressions, for the first time became characteristic of the city's economic life. Depressions struck in 1819 and again in 1837; in the 1840's business was often slack, and there was another sharp panic in 1857. These bad years gave harsh evidence of the city's loss of control over its own fate. The collapse of the Bank of the United States, Philadelphia's and the nation's largest, and the failure of important merchants in every panic made dramatic displays of the instability of the new business.[3]

The story of Philadelphia's first experience with industrialization can best be told by distinguishing two different groups: one, the artisans and unskilled workers of the city;[4] the other, its business and political leaders. For the former, the crucial event of the first

2. The effects upon sales areas brought about by successive improvements in transportation are carefully documented in Elva Tooker, *Nathan Trotter, Philadelphia Merchant 1787-1853* (Cambridge, 1955), 118-131. Trotter was a conservative Philadelphia merchant trading in imported metals. New transportation brought him far-flung customers, but also new competition—Phelps Dodge of New York came to dominate Trotter's line of goods.

3. The failure of large, well-established firms in depressions was one of the novel, but characteristic and unsettling, aspects of the new scale of nineteenth century business. Philadelphia's experience began with the shocking failure of Robert Morris in 1797. Most dramatic, since it signalled the end of the financial hegemony of the city was the closing of the Bank of the United States in the long 1837-1843 depression. Even a short panic, like the break of 1857, however, would bring down some reputable firm. For instance, the successful banker, Caleb Cope (1797-1888) lost his silk business in 1857.

4. It would take a special research project to classify the population of Philadelphia during the years 1830-1860 according to modern usage of upper middle class, middle class, working class, and lower class. For purposes of analysis of the events of this

half of the nineteenth century was the reorganization of the conditions of their work; for the latter, the crucial event was the change in their relations to the city and to the world beyond the city's boundaries.

The history of Philadelphia's artisans and unskilled workers comes down to us from several sources. The unions, strikes, and workingmen's parties of the 1827-1837 decade tell of the aspirations of these ordinary citizens and their complaints against industrialization. The demands of the revived unions of the 1850's and the contemporary descriptions of manufacturing in the city tell something of the direction that industrialization took, and what the rate of change had been, over the years 1830-1860.

During this first era of industrialization, from the revival of prosperity in 1827 to the eve of the Civil War, Philadelphia's artisans suffered from two disturbances: a loss of relative standing in their city, and a revolution in the terms and conditions of their work. The first disturbance amongst the artisans took the form of frustrating their rising expectations; the second disturbance took the form of unhinging the craft traditions of a century and setting men to work at longer hours, at a faster pace, and in a more socially isolated and economically insecure environment than they had ever labored in before or ever would again.[5]

Many of the tensions of early nineteenth-century Philadelphia came from the frustration of rising expectations of the city's large artisan class. The process of industrialization by breaking down old crafts into new specialties raised some artisans into the rank of the new middle class—it made businessmen, downtown retailers, factory

period a three-part division has been employed; the *new middle class,* downtown businessmen, downtown retailers, owners and superintendents of manufacturing establishments; *artisans,* skilled workers in factories, skilled workers laboring in their own homes and own shops, or outside on contract for others, and artisans who both manufactured and sold wholesale and retail on their own account; *unskilled,* laborers, sales clerks, unskilled and semi-skilled factory operatives, apprentices, women, children, sailors, and Negroes. The justification for this three-part division is that it calls attention to the split-up of the old artisan-shopkeeping unity of the eighteenth century mode into a new middle class and two skill levels of workers.

5. Leonard Bernstein, "The Working People of Philadelphia from Colonial Times to the General Strike of 1835," *Pennsylvania Magazine,* LXXIV (July, 1950), 333-339; William A. Sullivan, *The Industrial Worker in Pennsylvania 1800-1840* (Harrisburg, 1955), 29-83; Norman Ware, *The Industrial Worker 1840-1860* (New York, 1924), 18-70; John R. Commons, ed., *History of Labour in the United States* (New York, 1918), I, 351-365, 381-423, 487-492, 536-546, 575-607.

owners, and mill supervisors out of them. Others it lowered to the level of permanent employees. This splitting up of the city's traditional artisan-shopkeeper group would have been a troublesome process in its own right since it frustrated so many men's expectations for a shopkeeping, master artisan role for themselves and their families. In addition to this frustration, the rising productivity of industrialization exacerbated artisan grievances by raising the level of the new middle class's consumption while skilled workers gained little.

One need not recall the extreme symbol of the lavish furnishing of the Victorian *haut bourgeois* house to appreciate the tensions set up by the unequal distribution of the first fruits of industrialization. In the years between 1827 and 1860 the new middle class enjoyed a number of important advances in everyday consumption. The bare floors, whitewashed walls, and scant furniture of middle-income eighteenth-century homes gave way to wool carpeting, wallpaper, and all manner of furnishings. The houses themselves became relatively cheaper and grew in size from three rooms to four-to-six rooms in row houses or flats in row houses. The children slept one to a bed, and indoor toilets became common in their homes. In contrast to the eighteenth century when the middle-income house generally included the shop, the husband now commonly worked in an office, store or shop outside his home, and the first-floor, front room became a parlor instead of a work room. Mid-nineteenth-century families of the new middle class did not need to put their children to work in the family trade or shop; they could take full advantage of the new public grammar school education. Finally, they had grown prosperous enough to attend the increasing variety of offerings of commercial downtown entertainment.[6]

Almost every item on this list of middle-class consumption gains lay beyond the reach of Philadelphia's artisan population.

6. This description of the rising standards of living among Philadelphia's new middle class during the years 1825-1860 is an impressionistic summary which attempts to reconcile the pessimistic accounts of labor histories with the more optimistic indices of economic historians. Most useful for specifics are, Edgar W. Martin, *The Standard of Living in 1860* (Chicago, 1942), 95-105, 110-115, 121-123, 168-180, 343-345, 359-380, 393-404; and Richard O. Cummings, *The American and His Food* (Chicago, 1940), 27-28, 54-55, 242-244; suggestion of improvement in housing, Robert E. Gallman, "Commodity Output, 1839-1899," *Trends in the American Economy in the Nineteenth Century* (National Bureau of Economic Research, Princeton, 1960), 29-42.

Though the subject is a vexed one, it seems likely that artisans' and unskilled workers' real income rose only slightly during the years 1827-1860.[7] Presumably whatever the artisan lost in money wages he regained in the cheapening of the prices of clothing, shoes, fuel, furnishing and household wares, and in the slight enlargement in the size of cheap houses. Some of these modest changes in artisan consumption had been won by the new technology of industrialization: the cheaper coal made possible by canals, the cheaper cloth by textile mills, the cheaper ironware by improved foundries. Other consumption gains had been achieved by driving the artisans themselves; the lowering of prices for clothing, shoes, and housing could be attributed more to a faster pace and new organization of tasks than to new machines.

At the very least, the net result of early nineteenth-century industrialization was to leave the unskilled workers close to eighteenth-century poverty, and to widen the difference in consumption ability between the artisans on the one hand and the new middle class on the other. The city's streets lined with little stores and the scattering of middle-class houses in every neighborhood were daily reminders of the artisan's relative loss of ground. These streets, the growing luxury and number of downtown shops, and the popular newspapers and magazines of the day were all enormously successful in heightening the common man's appetite for consumption.[8]

At the very same moment when artisan expectations for consumption and status rose, the transformation of the work habits of many old skilled crafts attacked the traditional psychological modes and economic stability of many Philadelphia families. The key change going forward was the introduction of wholesalers or capital-

7. The literature of economic history does not deal with trends in one city and therefore I have felt justified in discounting somewhat the strong national 1819-1850 rise in real income estimated by Stanley Lebergott, *Manpower in Economic Growth, The American Record Since 1800* (New York, 1964), 139-154, because of the reports of stagnation and loss of real income stated by the labor historians Commons, Sullivan, and Ware.

8. The theme of foolish wives and husbands consuming beyond their means abounded in the sentimental novels and household guides of the period. Men were especially prone to speculation and gambling, instead of patient accumulation, women were prone to extravagant display, social climbing, and bad management. For instance, examples from two of the most popular contributors to Philadelphia's ladies magazines, Lydia Maria Child, *The American Frugal Housewife, Dedicated to Those Who Are Not Ashamed of Economy* (Boston, 1835), and Timothy Shay Arthur, *What Can Woman Do?* (Philadelphia, 1860).

ists who speculated in advance of orders and who organized their business for quantity production. These men, pricing their goods, putting out their work, setting their wages, and hiring and firing according to the flluctuations in city and regional markets, took control of most of the commonplace crafts in the 1820's and 1830's. With the exception of the bakers and the unskilled workers who joined the artisans in the great Ten-Hour Movement of 1835-1836, all the trades societies of that popular outpouring represented men who were trapped in the painful transition from eighteenth-century small-scale work to nineteenth-century large-scale, speculative production.[9] For some the new scale of production came from the growth of Philadelphia itself to a big city; for others the new scale came from the seasonal output of wholesale goods for southern and western shopkeepers; still others sold in the competitive east coast inter-regional trade.

By the 1850's Philadelphia's artisans had been organized in a curious network of large and small enterprises in which large-scale production emerged from a mixture of old and new ways. Shoemaking, for example, now reflected the interaction of seasonal business, big city growth, mechanization, and inter-regional specialization. Individual shoemakers no longer made shoes on order for customers who came in off the street. Instead, most of Philadelphia's 7,000 shoe workers were organized for production for jobbers and retailers. In Lynn, Massachusetts, shoe factories had captured the dominant share of the cheap shoe trade of the east coast, including Philadelphia. Lynn shoe parts were often used, too, by Philadelphia shoe manufacturers. Philadelphia's specialty had become ladies' shoes and expensive men's shoes and boots. The work was cut by skilled men at the manufacturer's shop and then given out to men who worked in their homes or in little shops about the city. Often the outside workers contracted to do just one operation, like forming on the last, sewing the uppers, or attaching the heels. German immigrants had moved especially into shoemaking. The introduction of a pegging machine and sewing machines had not as yet concentrated the trade in big factories, but only increased the role

9. The bakers were fighting the traditional Saturday and Sunday night work of their trade while the unskilled workers, coal heavers, seamen, wood cutters, seamstresses and tailoresses were fighting for subsistence wages and public recognition, Sullivan, *Worker in Pennsylvania,* 119-144.

of women in making soles and uppers. Finally, there was a special tenement adaptation of the industry which fitted the influx to cheap immigrant labor to the competition with New England. Small shops of "garret bosses" employing one to ten workers turned out low-priced shoes for local retailers and jobbers.[10]

The clothing industry had early been organized to take advantage of cheap female labor. Mathew Carey had published his complaint against the abuses of this trade in 1837, just before the rapid expansion of the ready-made clothing industry.[11] Improvements in transportation and the influx of immigrants perpetuated similar conditions of exploitation until well into the twentieth century. Improved transportation created the western and southern market for Philadelphia's ready-made clothing, but it also opened up an unhappy competition between underpaid Philadelphia seamstresses and rural pieceworkers. As in the case of shoes, much of the garment industry was organized around small shops and sales offices where skilled men did the cutting and parceled out the thread, buttons, and trimmings to the women and children who did the work at home. Sewing machines had just begun to become important in the 1850's, especially in shirtmaking. In some lines, in men's and boy's garments especially, there were large factories where tailoring was done on a highly specialized and rationalized basis.[12]

Philadelphia in the 1850's was, as it had been since the Revolution, the nation's largest textile city. Its 10,000 and more textile workers were organized in a special mix of modern mill and old fashioned cottage work. Carpet weaving took a form similar to that of the garment industry. Manufacturers most commonly were small organizations which took orders, prepared the yarns, and set up the looms of weavers who worked up the carpets in their own homes or in backyard sheds. There were about a hundred such manufacturers, who kept 1,500 hand looms going. Under the pressure of power-

10. This description of conditions in the shoe trades, and the descriptions that follow for other trades are derived from material in Edwin T. Freedley, *Philadelphia and Its Manufactures, A Handbook Exhibiting the Development, Variety, and Statistics of the Manufacturing Industry of Philadelphia in 1857* (Philadelphia, 1858), 185-189. Freedly's information has been altered when in conflict with *U.S. Eighth Census: 1860* data. Also, Sullivan, *Worker in Pennsylvania*, 114-116 has useful material on the plight of the cordwainers.

11. Mathew Carey, *A Plea for the Poor* (Philadelphia, 1837).

12. Freedley, *Manufactures*, 232-234.

driven factory competition from New England prices for weaving were low, and consequently English, Irish, and German immigrants continued in the trade, not native-born Americans. There were in Philadelphia in the 1850's a few large employers who combined power-driven looms with hand weaving and the industry was rapidly moving in the direction of mechanized production in large factories.[13]

Cotton and woolen hosiery, Philadelphia specialties since before the Revolution, stood at every stage of modernization from the cottage use of old wooden hand-powered knitting frames to factory-organized power-driven circular knitters which "will do a day's work before breakfast." About one thousand knitgoods workers lived on the northside, in Germantown and Kensington, following the old style of cottage labor. Prices were high and these skilled workers, mostly immigrants from the English center of the trade in Leicester and Nottingham, still prospered. Large factories had entered the business, however, and one integrated mill employing 500 used power machinery for all aspects of the business from scouring and spinning the wool, to circular and flatbed knitting of hosiery, scarfs, comforters, and fancy goods.[14]

The weaving of silks and narrow goods and the manufacture of sewing thread were new industries to Philadelphia and had been entirely assumed by a few large factories using the latest power-driven machinery.[15] Cotton and woolen cloth emerged from every possible kind of urban manufacturing organization. Big mechanized mills using steam-powered machinery and cheap female and child labor were moving into the city. Earlier organizations, however, persisted. Some mills employed both hand weavers and power-driven looms. Still other firms spun or purchased thread, and gave out orders and set the looms of domestic hand weavers. In 1853 there were still 2,000 hand-loom weavers reported working both in the north and southsides of Philadelphia. Machine and factory competition, however, had driven them out of many lines; prices were low, and even if they managed to find regular work they were paid "a sum seemingly inadequate to support a family."[16]

13. Freedley, *Manufactures*, 239-240; Arthur H. Cole and Harold F. Williamson, *The American Carpet Manufacture* (Cambridge, 1941), 26, 53-58.

14. Freedley, *Manufactures*, 240-244, 255.

15. Freedley, *Manufactures*, 244-249.

16. Freedley, *Manufactures*, quotation, 254, cotton and woolens 234-239, 250-263.

There seems to have been a tradition in textiles for skilled workers to migrate from England, Scotland, Ireland and Germany to Philadelphia, where they practiced their trades in the city until they were forced by modernization into factories or out of the craft altogether. The effect upon the city of this immigration was to maintain strong tension throughout the first half of the nineteenth century as one specialty after another succumbed to industrialization.

The whole city was a mix of old and new. At the Baldwin and Norris locomotive works hitherto unprecedented industrial armies of 600 workers using the latest machinery turned out these novel machines. Philadelphia's foundries and chemical companies, though not all large, had a national reputation for quality and modernity. The new furniture manufactures had been organized in about ten showrooms with the work being done in about one hundred small shops. Carriages, another new Philadelphia specialty, had captured some of the northeast and western trade. Carriage production took the form of concentrating sales and assembly in a few firms. The parts of the carriages, however, were manufactured in shops of all sizes and types located throughout the city. The brass lamp, gas fixture and gas fitting industry developed into a few big factories, as did umbrella manufacture. At the other extreme, about a thousand cigar manufacturers, employing only one to five workers, rolled cigars by hand in tiny neighborhood shops.[17]

Perhaps the only uniformities common to all these many different arrangements of urban manufactures were that all were responses to the new opportunities of the city. The pace had quickened, competition from others was often keen, the threat of new machines and new methods was continuous, and the possibility of new modes of organization pervaded every old craft as well as every new skill.

It is against this background of ceaseless industrial change that the union movement and labor politics of Philadelphia can best be understood. Of the sixty-one trades reported by labor historians to have organized or have gone on strike during the three decades 1830-1860, forty-two were reported as being practiced in the city as far

17. Freedley, *Manufactures,* chemicals 206-211, 214-220; locomotives 306-314; foundaries and iron works, 283-342; furniture 271-276; cigars 388; umbrellas and parasols, 389-394.

back as 1774.[18] Well before the introduction of factories using new machinery most of Philadelphia's old trades had organized themselves to fight against the consequences of the capitalists' reordering of production. Loss of control over wages and hours and the loss of status in the society were the first and most decisive blows against the city's old artisan-shopkeeper class. Given the speed of the growth of the city and the nation, there was no way these early artisans' unions could control the fate of their members. They could often negotiate for prices and hours with one manufacturer for one job; and in boom times they could negotiate successfully for a whole season; but no amount of organization could protect the crafts from new machines, competition from other cities and regions, cheap rural and immigrant labor, and periodic world and national depressions.

In the late 1820's Philadelphia artisans, encouraged by radical literature from England and using the city's own long-standing tra-

18. The process of industrialization and specialization created the following nineteen trades, none of which appeared on the 1774 Philadelphia tax lists, and all of which were reported by Sullivan and Commons to have organized during the years 1830-1860. Basket makers, carpet weavers (ingrain), chair makers (formerly part of the general trades of joiner and turner), coal heavers, cotton spinners (one spinner and one threadmaker was listed in 1774), factory operatives, gilders, glass cutters (one glassmaker was listed in 1774), hod carriers, hotel waiters, lithographers, moulders (iron), silver platers, slaters, tailoresses and seamstresses, tinplate and sheet iron workers, trunk makers, upholsterers, woodworkers and furniture painters and trimmers (specialties that came out of eighteenth century trades of joiner and turner).

The following forty-two trades were reported as having unions sometime during 1830-1860 and were also found on the 1774 tax list. The trades are given with the number of men practicing that trade reported by the 1774 tax list so the reader can get some idea of the change of occupational scale of the city from 1774 to 1860. These quantities may be compared to the industry size figures of Table IX and the percentages of major occupations in 1860, notes to Table II. Bakers 123, biscuit makers 1, barbers 38, blacksmiths 123, block and pump makers 7, bookbinders and folders 9, brass moulders (1774 brass founders) 4, brewery laborers 19, brick layers 48, brick makers 5, cabinet makers (equivalent to the 1774 trades of carvers 11, joiners 94, and turners 17) 122, carpenters 178, carters 40, coach makers 6, cordwainers 198, glass blowers (1774 glassmaker) 2, hatters 72, horn comb makers (1774 combmaker) 4, laborers 614, leather pressers and finishers (1774 skinners 30, tanners 37) 67, marble workers (1774 marble quarry) 1, masons 22, nailors (1774 nailmaker) 7, oak coopers 132, painters 27, papermakers 4, plasterers 19, plumbers 2, riggers 4, rope makers 13, saddlers, (1774 saddlemaker 32, harnessmaker 8) 40, sailmakers 17, seamen (1774 seaman 1, mariner 163) 164, segars (1774 tobacconist) 19, ship carpenters 112, stockingmakers 58, stone cutters 12, tailors 90, weavers (handloom) 32, wheelwrights 20, wood sawyers 16. This list of 1830-1860 unions was compiled from Sullivan, *Worker in Pennsylvania*, Appendix B, and Commons, *History of Labor*, I, 607.

dition of political organization, established a newspaper and a political party, the Working Men's Party.[19] During the active years of the party, from 1828 to 1831, these artisan groups demanded a number of reforms: a free universal public school system, abolition of the compulsory summer militia training and its related system of fines, abolition of imprisonment for debt, institution of a mechanic's lien law to give workmen first position for debt collection against bankrupts, abolition of lotteries, and tighter regulation of the sale of alcoholic beverages.[20] During the next twenty years the Pennsylvania legislature enacted into law all these useful proposals for easing the workingman's lot; it even passed an irregularly enforced ten-hour day in 1847, but such reforms could not counter the basic anxiety of the Working Men's Party—artisans were working harder but steadily losing ground to the new middle class.

As in Tom Paine's day, these artisans viewed the state and city government as an engine of the wealthy and successful. More specifically, they saw the granting of corporate charters as a device by which the wealthy seized monopoly privileges and thereby gained an unfair competitive advantage over the hard-working mechanic. Like Paine, the followers of the Working Men's Party had no understanding of the society's need for large and settled institutions to accomplish large tasks like building and operating turnpikes, canals, water works, factories, wholesale houses and banks. Such institutions and projects, pointed to by many as the great improvements of the age, were not progress to these artisans; they were seen as taxes laid unfairly upon the artisan who was struggling to feed and clothe his family and to meet the taxes on his small "cabin."[21]

The federalist and the democrat, the administration and the opposition man when in legislative council, urged by one interest, ARE ALL COM-

19. Louis H. Arky, "The Mechanics' Union of Trade Associations," *Pennsylvania Magazine*, LXXVI (April, 1952), 142-176.

20. Commons, History of Labor, I, 216-230; ban on sale of lottery tickets 1833, John S. Ezell, *Fortune's Merry Wheel, the Lottery in America* (Cambridge, 1960), 207-210; enabling act for free public schools 1834, Lawrence A. Cremin, *The American Common School* (New York, 1951), 34-37; mechanic's lien law passed 1836; imprisonment for debt abolished 1844; strict regulation of taverns 1855.

21. *The Principles of Aristocratic Legislation Developed in an Address Delivered to the Working People of the District of Southwark, and the Townships of Moyamensing and Passyunk* (Philadelphia, 1828) Arky attributes this pamphlet to the labor journalist William Heighton (1800-1873), "The Mechanics' Union of Trade Associations," *Pennsylvania Magazine*, LXXVI, 165-166.

BINED IN ONE PARTY, to elevate the lofty and humble the low, to enrich and aggrandize the few wealthy and powerful, and to depress and impoverish the multitude. Thus while our interests and welfare are passed by unnoticed, we see charters, statutes, and enactments, passed from session to session, for the exclusive advancement and benefit of Banking, Inurance, and Mercantile, *master* Manufacturing, Landed, and other monied, monopolizing and speculating institutions and interests: all of which, under the fostering wing of legislative protection, are accumulating their annual millions from the toils and labours of the Operative classes.[22]

For a few years, from 1828 to 1831, the Working Men's Party nominated its own candidates and endorsed sympathetic Democrats and Federalist-Republicans. The Working Men mustered three to six hundred votes in the city and similar amounts in the adjacent county districts. Its leaders, however, were too inexperienced to maintain the difficult third-party position in the face of alternate harassment and blandishment by such professional politicians as Southwark's Joel Barlow Sutherland. Perhaps most important, when President Jackson made the anti-Bank, anti-monopoly, hard-money cause of the workingmen his own, the Working Men's Party evaporated in the general Jacksonian enthusiasm.[23]

In the prosperity and boom of the mid-1830's Philadelphia's union movement, which had been growing since the late twenties, burst forth. In the fifteen months from the spring of 1835 until the fall of 1836 six thousand artisans and unskilled workers of Philadelphia won a series of strikes for a ten-hour day and higher wages. Not until World War I would the unions of Philadelphia recapture such an effective position in the city. The old unity of the artisan-tradesman group expressed itself for the last time when tradesmen supported the artisans in their parades and petitions for ten hours as a decent day's work for a decent man.[24]

Unique to the enthusiasm of 1835-1836 was the first appearance of the unskilled. Such groups had never organized themselves before, nor would most of them be heard from again until the twentieth century. Sailors, coal heavers, seamstresses, and firewood sawyers, all members of traditionally exploited occupations, broke

22. *The Principles of Aristocratic Legislation*, 7.
23. Arky, "The Mechanics' Union of Trade Associations," 171; Philip S. Klein, *Pennsylvania Politics 1817-1832, A Game Without Rules* (Philadelphia, 1940), 365-367.
24. Commons, *History of Labor*, I, 373-401.

through the shell of the city's indifference and hostility for a moment to demand recognition by the general society. Their strikes and parades were the last echoes of the radical demands of the Revolution.[25]

In the nineteenth century, as in the eighteenth, sailors were recruited from the rural and urban lower class. The men were kept in order by the military discipline of the ship. It is testimony to the spirit of the 1835-1836 labor movement in Philadelphia that such a traditionally down-trodden, transient, and ill-trained group was able to come together to sustain a strike for wages.

The Schuylkill coal heavers, too, were lower-class workers, mostly Irish. They labored in gangs, like the canal and railroad construction strikers of the rural areas. This task organization at the piers undoubtedly encouraged their organization into a union. Indeed, it was the month-long strike of several hundred coal heavers that sparked the whole labor agitation of 1835-1836. In the beginning the employers replaced the striking workers by scabs, and fights between strikers and scabs led to arrests of the strike leaders by Mayor John Swift (1790-1873). In assessing the unprecedented fines of $2,500 upon each defendant, the mayor said he hoped these fines would stamp out the union. Frightened by this attack on unionism, the trades societies of skilled men came to the support of the coal heavers. The unions financed a successful appeal of the Mayor's Court fines and the men were ultimately acquitted.[26]

The seamstresses and women tailors of Philadelphia, like the sailors and dock laborers, were a long-exploited group of low skills. Their traditional poverty followed directly from the low status of women in eighteenth and early nineteenth-century America. Because of popular prejudice women could not demand equal pay for equal work, while the lack of employment opportunities for women maintained an abundant supply of female laborers who would work at below the level of decent self-support. The contemporary rationalization of low wages for women rested on the assumption that working women were girls living within their families helping to

25. The appearance of the unskilled in the 1835-1836 labor movement, Sullivan, *Worker in Pennsylvania*, 134-143, 152-157.

26. The workers were, however, not strong enough to defeat Mayor Swift when he ran for re-election in the fall of 1835. Leonard Bernstein, "The Working People of Philadelphia from Colonial Times to the General Strike of 1835," *Pennsylvania Magazine*, LXXIV (July, 1950), 333-339.

supplement family incomes. In fact, however, many were poor women and girls trying to eke out an existence by sewing. Some worked in the downtown factories, many others in tiny rooms in the south-side slums.[27]

Since Anne Parish's work shop of 1795, Philadelphia philanthropists had often set up charity work rooms in hard times. And many winters the girls themselves placed advertisements in the newspapers asking for jobs to tide them over the winter; but most of the time they just fared badly. The successful seamstresses and tailoresses union of 1835 represents the first event in a hundred-year series of needle trades organizations. None of these proved permanently successful until immigration dried up some of the sources of cheap labor, until unionized male workers came to their aid, and until the status of women rose sufficiently in the society to support government regulation of the industry. The one enduring gain of the 1835 strike was publicity. The problems of women in the garment trades became, thereafter, a journalistic formula for pricking the sentimental social conscience of middle-class readers.[28]

Philadelphia sensibilities, however, could not yet reach all citizens. When the lowest class of laborers, the street wood sawyers, spurred by the successes of others, demanded ten to twenty-five cents more for sawing a cord of wood, their strike was met with sneers at their interracial organization and with disbelief that such lowly persons could expect to be taken seriously. "Yesterday there was a turnout among the wood sawyers—some ten or a dozen who claimed affinities with whites and the rest the cullings of a lot of blacks."[29]

The sharp and deep depression of 1837 cut short all the hopes of the unskilled and obliterated both the artisans' unions of 1835-1836 and their gains. The massive immigration of Irish and Germans in the 1840's then turned the city into a surplus labor pool and thereby prevented for fifteen years the revival of effective unions.

27. Mathew Carey, *A Plea for the Poor* (Philadelphia, 1837).

28. Typical shocked editorial on conditions in the needle trades during wintertime, *Public Ledger*, October 17, 1840. The popular novelist Timothy Shay Arthur had been a tailor and he wrote many stories on the plight of the seamstress, *Women's Trials: or, Tales and Sketches from the Life Around Us* (Philadelphia, 1853), "I Didn't Think of That" and "Plain Sewing."

29. *U.S. Gazette*, June 12, 1835, quoted in William A. Sullivan, "A Decade of Labor Strife," *Pennsylvania History, XVII* (January, 1950), 35.

Today one can look back upon the interval between the depression of 1837 and the revival of unions among some skilled workers in the 1850's and see the formation of significant new groupings. These new groupings of the 1837-1853 interval foretold a new accommodation for many skilled workers to urban industrial life. Informal organizations and industry itself began to form a complementary chain. The churches, clubs, lodges, temperance, and reading societies of natives and immigrants encouraged social ties that made the formation of death benefit, accident, and unemployment pools possible. The group organization of work which by the 1850's obtained in many industries (Table IX) taught cooperative life and action to many artisans who had formerly worked alone in

TABLE IX

GROUP ORGANIZATION OF WORK IN MAJOR LINES OF MANUFACTURE
PHILADELPHIA 1860

Total Persons Employed	1860	Average No. Persons Per Establishment
98,397	All lines of manufacture	15.6
1,255	Locomotives	627.5
4,793	Cotton goods	94.0
1,131	Gas fixtures	75.4
3,258	Cotton and woolen goods	63.9
1,021	Umbrellas and parasols	48.6
3,290	Shirts, collars, etc.	45.7
14,387	Clothing, men and boys	40.9
1,219	Silk fringes and trimmings	39.3
1,876	Bricks	38.3
2,285	Hosiery, woolen	32.2
1,613	Machinery, general, of iron	26.4
2,680	Carpets	21.6
1,190	Bookbinders	20.0
1,038	Carriages and coaches	20.0
1,326	Leather	15.8
8,434	Boots and shoes	12.0
1,627	Furniture and cabinetmaker's wares	10.1
1,290	Cigars	5.6
1,138	Millinery, laces, etc.	4.9

54,851

virtual isolation in their own homes or with one or two other men. The revival of the labor movement among skilled men in the 1850's was thus both the response to and expression of the organization of the city and its industries.[30]

For contemporaries, however, for the artisans who lost their hours, wages, and unions in the depression of 1837, and for the unskilled who lost all representation in the society for a lifetime, the forties and fifties presented a bleak outlook—heavy immigrant and machine competition and sharp market disciplines of seasonal work, periodic lay-offs, fluctuating prices, wages, and hours. In the face of such a future their fear and frustration found immediate expression in racial and anti-Catholic rioting, and nativist politics. Their anger brought the final destruction of the unities of the eighteenth century town and forced the city to seek a new order in the rule of political bosses and professional police.

30. Edgar B. Cale, *The Organization of Labor in Philadelphia* (Philadelphia, 1940), 1-41, 113-114 has lists of every workingman's organization mentioned in any Philadelphia newspaper in the fifties; also useful for the 1837-1860 interval are Philip S. Foner, *History of the Labor Movement in the U.S.* (New York, 1947), I, 210-248; and Commons, *History of Labor*, I, 454-471, 487-492, 575-623.

5

The Specialization
of Leadership

Businessmen and politicians were subject to the same forces as their
fellow citizens. Indeed, these were the men who directed the city's
response to the opportunities for regional sales and large-scale production. Together they lobbied for and financed the new private,
state and federal navigation aids, canals, and railroads which made
the industrialization of Philadelphia possible.[1] The resulting size
and reach of the city meant that specialization would yield large
gains in money and power, just as specialization had made the large-
scale production of everyday goods a reality.

As they reorganized the artisans' crafts Philadelphia's business
and political leaders shifted their own roles from generalists to specialists. The former merchant's role split into many fragments: retailer, domestic wholesaler, foreign importer, jobber, commission
agent, manufacturer's representative, auctioneer, marine insurance

1. The transportation history of Philadelphia appears in a number of modern
studies, Wilbur C. Plummer, *The Road Policy of Pennsylvania* (Philadelphia, 1925), 43-
46; James W. Livingood, *The Philadelphia-Baltimore Trade Rivalry, 1780-1860* (Harrisburg, 1947), 100-104; Louis Hartz, *Economic Policy and Democratic Thought, Pennsylvania 1776-1860* (Cambridge, 1948), 86-180; Carter Goodrich, *Government Promotion
of American Canals and Railroads* (New York, 1960), 61-75; Julius Rubin, *Canal or
Railroad? (Transactions of the American Philosophical Society, n.s. LI, November, 1961),*
15-62.

dealer, broker, banker, and factor. The former leadership roles of merchant politician, artisan clubman, and gentleman office holder all gave way to the new roles of professional boss, ward heeler, fire-house gang leader, full-time philanthropist, and professional gentleman democrat. In the late eighteenth and early nineteenth centuries the capabilities and outlook of merchant politicians had determined the city's government. By 1850 the needs and perspectives of the new specialists determined the course of the city's political history.

Historians of the Jacksonian era have yet to undertake the kind of systematic quantitative studies of urban leadership which is now beginning to characterize analysis of early twentieth-century city politics. Until such work is done any account of transitions in political style must remain impressionistic. Four biographical sketches are offered here as examples of the change in leadership which took place during the first half of the nineteenth century. Full documentation of the timing and frequency of these roles must await special studies by a future political historian.[2]

The change from the old eighteenth century civil order to the modern specialized one can be suggested by a few biographical sketches. Thomas Pym Cope (1768-1854) was a good example of the old-style generalist, both in business and politics. Cope, born in Lancaster, Pennsylvania, was apprenticed as a boy to his uncle in Philadelphia. After six years with his uncle, Thomas set up for himself as an importing merchant. He managed his affairs carefully, prospered, and over the years amassed one of the largest fortunes of his time. He was also a popular member of Philadelphia society and one of the city's most useful citizens. Like the famous merchant Stephen Girard, whose friend and executor he was, Cope saw the city as the foreground of a man's loyalty and public concern. Public life, for him, was participation in the management of the city, and he drew no sharp distinctions among public office, municipal committees, and private philanthropic groups.[3]

Cope founded the Philadelphia Board of Trade and for twenty-two years served as its president. As part of his own business he

2. A first step toward quantitative analysis has been made by Gary B. Nash's study of the changing social origins of lawyers, "The Philadelphia Bench and Bar 1800-1861," *Comparative Studies in Society and History*, VII (January 1965), 203-220.

3. Cope's biography, *Dictionary of American Biography*, J. Thomas Scharf and Thompson Westcott, *History of Philadelphia* (Philadelphia, 1884), II, 1475; Commissioners of Fairmount Park, *First Annual Report* (Philadelphia, 1869), 6-12.

established regular packet service between Philadelphia and Liverpool. Also, like all Philadelphia businessmen, he pressed for internal improvements to expand the city's region of cheap, inland transportation. Cope helped finance the completion of the Chesapeake and Delaware Canal and promoted the building of the Pennsylvania Railroad. This latter project was undertaken to modernize the slow and seasonal mixed canal and railway lines which Philadelphia merchants had persuaded the state to build in the late 1820's. Businessmen in both Philadelphia and Pittsburgh promoted the scheme, and the city of Philadelphia alone pledged $5 million of its municipal funds. The project, managed as it was by private directors and non-voting public ones, yet financed by both municipalities and individual investors, was the last of the large, mixed enterprises of the era of the general merchant management of city government.

Cope's view of the city extended beyond the narrow purview of the Board of Trade. As a member of the City Council he worked hard for the controversial and very expensive Schuylkill water works. These works, the first of their kind in the nation, were to cleanse the city in the hope that the city's recurrent summer fevers could be stopped. In time the Philadelphia works became the model for the nation. Later Cope gave large sums to the city to help it purchase private estates around the reservoir and to construct what is now Fairmount Park. In Philadelphia in the 1840's, as in other cities, only a few wealthy men saw the future importance of the city's undertaking to provide the amenities of the gentleman's estate for the public by building parks. Cope was one of this small group. In addition he gave $25,000 to the Zoological Society to help set up a zoo on the Fairmount grounds. Also in his capacity as public citizen he was a founder of the Mercantile Library, a state legislator for one term (1807), and a member of the state constitutional convention of 1837. His political ambitions were limited, however, and he refused offers for nomination to Congress.

Finally in the traditional fields of philanthropy Cope also took an active part. He had been stricken with yellow fever during the great epidemic of 1793. When the fever returned to the city in 1797 Cope followed Stephen Girard's example by staying in the city. He was at that time a manager of the Almshouse and one of the Guardians of the Poor who carried food to the houses of the sick. In addition to numerous minor services to charity he gave $40,000 to the Institute for Colored Youth to found a technical school for Negroes.

The late eighteenth- and early nineteenth-century tradition of merchant leadership implied some wealth and success as a prerequisite for public recognition, but all shades of politics were acceptable. Charles J. Ingersoll (1782-1862) turned against his father's party to support the War of 1812, and later turned against all proper Philadelphians to aid President Andrew Jackson in his attack on the United States Bank. Another Jacksonian, Robert Patterson (1792-1881), a self-made textile magnate, served on many boards, public and private, and was a promoter of Philadelphia transportation. Though a strong Jackson Democrat, he opposed the President's free-trade program.[4]

The great strength of the old merchant system of government lay in the variety of talent, experience, and opinion which it could harness to public commissions, private boards, and elective office. Such a man as Henry D. Gilpin (1801-1860), U.S. Attorney General under President Van Buren, author, editor, and lawyer, sat on numerous Philadelphia boards ranging from the Chesapeake and Delaware Canal Company to the University of Pennsylvania and the Academy of Fine Arts. The merchant Stephen Girard (1750-1831) left almost his entire fortune to the city for various public works and a school for poor white boy orphans. The locomotive builder Matthias W. Baldwin (1795-1866) served on numerous public and private boards, and was elected to the state legislature to help carry through the Philadelphia County Consolidation Act of 1854. Like Girard he was a man of great generosity and definiteness of opinion.[5]

This style of leadership died out in Philadelphia about the time of the Civil War. The men of the Revolutionary and first post-Revolutionary generations could not be replaced by younger successors because both the city and the business environment in which they had been raised and trained had been thoroughly transformed during their lifetimes. By 1850 they were as antique as the hand-loom weavers.

4. Ingersoll and Patterson, *Dictionary of American Biography;* Charles M. Snyder, *The Jacksonian Heritage: Pennsylvania Politics, 1833-1848* (Harrisburg, 1958), 90, 104, 114, 149-150.

5. Gilpin, Girard, and Baldwin, *Dictionary of American Biography; Memorial of Matthias W. Baldwin* (Philadelphia, 1867), 212.

Jay Cooke (1821-1905), the great Philadelphia financier of the Civil War, was the outstanding type of the new era. A frontier lawyer-shopkeeper's son from Sandusky, Ohio, he came to Philadelphia in 1838 to work as a clerk for an express company organized by Democratic politicians to do business on the Main Line. The company failed after six months. Then, in 1839, Cooke found his permanent place in a Philadelphia brokerage house. He was a rapid calculator and a hard worker. His combination of diligence and attractive easy manners made him an instant success. In time he rose from clerk to partner to founder of his own firm. Though he was lively, curious, and open-minded, the sheer discipline of work precluded his making any meaningful contribution to his society outside the specialty of his career of private banker and investment broker.[6]

Confident of himself and his ultimate success and fascinated with the business of making money, young Jay Cooke took easily to the fast pace of the new nineteenth-century downtown life.[7] Far from resenting the discipline of unremitting labor, he gloried in it.

> I write so many letters that I almost lose the form and spirit of a private one and should my business way of expressing things, etc., be displayed, as I doubt not they frequently are, you can lay the fault to the right cause. I write some days fifteen or twenty letters to all parts of the United States, and more than both of my bosses do. At this season of the year, I get up at half-past seven, take breakfast at eight, then go into the counting room and there am busy as a bee until three o'clock, when the banks close and I go to dinner. After dinner I am busy until six o'clock when I leave the office, take tea, do what writing I have to do for Mr. Sturdivant [an evening hotel accounting job he took on to pay for his lodgings], then take a walk up Chestnut street or anywhere else my mind leads me to. At seven all the places of amusement are opened and we have our choice of every variety. I am getting indifferent to them and go seldom. Supper is on the table at any time from nine to twelve at

6. Cooke's biography, Ellis P. Oberholtzer, *Jay Cooke* (Philadelphia, 1907), I; Henrietta M. Larson, *Jay Cooke, Private Banker* (Cambridge, 1936); Larson, "Jay Cooke's Early Work in Transportation," *Pennsylvania Magazine*, LIX (October, 1935), 362-375.

7. From 1845 on the ten-hour day, six-day week was common in wholesale houses and presumably also financial and professional offices. In manufacturing the Pennsylvania law of 1847 and the big demonstrations of 1848 helped to establish ten-hour days, but retail hours remained much longer until the twentieth century. Charles R. Barker, "Philadelphia in the Late Forties," *Philadelphia History*, II (#10, 1931), 256. Compare with Arthur H. Cole, "The Tempo of Mercantile Life in Colonial America," *Business History Review*, XXXIII (Autumn, 1959), 277-299.

night. I generally begin to dream of home about ten to twelve o'clock.
. . . in my position I can see and have a broad space for observing the
different nations of men. Among our customers are men of every age
and every position of society, from the hoary miser to the dashing buck
who lives upon his thousands. Through all grades I see the same all-
pervading, all-engrossing anxiety to grow rich, to snatch from the unwilling hand of fortune that which her caprice will never permit her to
grant them. This is the only thing for which men live here. How they
do in the country I know not, but I see enough to convince me of this
fact. . . .

The confident youth finished his letter to his brother with a
repetition of Benjamin Franklin's formula—one should work hard
in one's youth for wealth in order to enjoy the luxury of a virtuous
and philanthropic old age. "I look upon riches as naught more than
the means whereby one can display his social and generous spirit,
and, if I should ere be the one I may be, I'll be a friend, a man."[8]

It was not Cooke's personal morality that was new, but the shift
of the focus of his concern away from the city which typified the
change of his generation. The city of Philadelphia did not serve for
him, as it had served for previous merchant generations, as an important frame through which he saw the world and out of which he
took action upon the world beyond. No deep knowledge of, or concern for, the general welfare of his city informed Cooke's business,
politics, or philanthropy.[9]

The education he received from his work taught him to concentrate on his business specialty, and unfortunately for Philadelphia, that specialty was not urban in scope. In Cooke's lifetime
banking became fully institutionalized on a national scale. Cooke
himself in his role as salesman of Union war loans and later as a
railroad promoter helped contribute to that nationalization. Within
this focus he made very important contributions to society. Such
concern as he had with politics necessarily looked towards Washington. The problems of Philadelphia were irrelevant to all the major
concerns of his daily life. To Jay Cooke, like many of his fellow

8. Both quotations are from the same letter written to his brother February 28, 1840.
The letter has been lost or destroyed since publication in Oberholtzer, *Jay Cooke,* I,
58.

9. Cooke took a minor interest in Philadelphia religious affairs. He was reported as
an usher at a Dwight L. Moody revival in 1875. Lefferts A. Loetscher, "Presbyterian-
ism and Revivals in Philadelphia since 1875," *Pennsylvania Magazine,* LXVIII (January, 1944), 57-58.

businessmen, Philadelphia's downtown was merely the local center of regional and national transactions. Outside the downtown many of the city's new mills, warehouses, and transportation services were also only urban in location. Thus, for a growing number of Philadelphia businessmen the city was but a place of congregation.

In short, by the process of industrialization and growth Philadelphia was becoming in the mid-nineteenth century an agglomeration of institutions and activities which were not local but regional and national. The new generation of business leaders shifted their activities accordingly. For example, the famous locomotive manufacturer Matthias Baldwin (1795-1866) was active in a number of civic projects, but his partner Mathew Baird (1817-1877) did not participate in public affairs; he ran a succession of businesses instead. Or William Sellers (1824-1905), machine tool designer and one of the founders of a whole new Philadelphia industry, served on a few boards, including the boards of the University of Pennsylvania and the Franklin Institute, but this contribution was directly tied to his business specialty. The new habits of business taught the mid-nineteenth century Philadelphia businessman that the city was not important to their daily lives, and in response these business leaders became ignorant of their city and abandoned its politics.[10]

Yet once Philadelphia became an agglomeration of regional and national business organizations the cure for many of the city's basic problems—especially its maldistribution of personal income and bad physical arrangements—depended upon guiding the activities of these big business organizations both nationally and locally so that the destructive environments of the city would not perpetuate themselves. In America, this essential connection between the modern organization of a large city's economic and social life and the necessary activities of its politics has yet to be made.

The failure of Jay Cooke's generation and later generations of Philadelphia businessmen to take responsibility for the consequences of the scale and organization of their business has turned their personal benevolence to ashes. Jay Cooke was an honest, open-

10. This interpretation of the narrowing specialization of Philadelphia business leaders fits with that of E. Digby Baltzell, *Philadelphia Gentlemen, The Making of a National Upper Class* (Glencoe, 1958), 130-141; and also is in harmony with Robert A. Dahl's findings for New Haven, Conn., *Who Governs? Democracy and Power in an American City* (New Haven, 1961), 11-100.

hearted man. He did not abandon his youthful promise to use his wealth to "display his social and generous spirit." His philanthropy, however was at best peripheral to the needs of the city. Previously the informed, self-interested, and politically active merchants had established in the late eighteenth and early nineteenth centuries most of the modern network of Philadelphia's services. By comparison Cooke restricted his connections with local political groups to those organizations whose activities directly aided his business—the Union League and the Home Labor League (a high-tariff group). He gave some of his wealth to Kenyon, Princeton, and Dartmouth colleges, donated large sums to local charities, was an active supporter of the Y.M.C.A. and the American Sunday School Union, and joined the Academy of Natural Sciences and the Historical Society of Pennsylvania. All in their way were worthy causes, of some help to a few people, but considering Jay Cooke's intelligence, the sum of his benevolence exerted a pitifully small leverage upon the problems of his city.

As businessmen abandoned the city's affairs and its politics new specialists assumed their former tasks. Politics became a full-time business and professionals moved in to make careers of public office. Although the first half of the nineteenth century was a transitional period, populated with many men and women who mixed old forms and modern roles,[11] two thoroughly modern types emerged in Philadelphia's pre-Civil War municipal politics—the boss and the gentleman-democrat. Both symbolized enduring experiences of a city which sought simultaneously to maintain an open society and to reward the successful pursuit of private wealth. The boss portrayed the self-made man; the gentleman-democrat portrayed the union of democracy and wealth.

The new city boss, or self-made politician, bore the marks of the steady battle for control of votes. Philadelphia's first boss, Joel Barlow Sutherland (1792-1861) lacked inheritance and outside income; he had to make politics pay. His plural office-holding, his

---

11. The lawyer politicians of the pre-Civil War era showed more local concern and were more closely tied to the city than later corporate lawyers. For example George M. Dallas (1792-1864) and John M. Read (1797-1874). The era of small-scale personal journalism also produced the transitional figures of journalist-politicians. For example, James N. Barker (1784-1858), mayor 1819-1821; Robert T. Conrad (1810-1858), mayor 1854-1856; Joseph R. Chandler (1792-1880), congressman 1849-1855.

unscrupulousness, and his lack of imagination cast a shadow of uncreative, corrupt municipal management over the future of the city.

A Scotch immigrant's son, Sutherland graduated from the University of Pennsylvania Medical School the year of the opening of the War of 1812. He immediately joined a Philadelphia militia company and rose through militia politics to the rank of lieutenant colonel. Aided by such connections, Sutherland was three times elected to the state legislature. Peace, however, deprived him of the source of his popularity and power and he was forced to take the unglamorous job of doctor to the quarantine hospital of the port of Philadelphia.[12]

Reasoning correctly that law promised a better path to politics than medicine, he studied law and entered the bar in 1819. Two years later he was elected to the legislature and became Speaker in 1825. As Speaker he helped to promote the state canal project which was to give Philadelphia an economical transportation line to the west.[13] It was in these years, too, that he put together his southside political machine which grew in the next decade to be the major Democratic Party force in Philadelphia city and county. The southside of Philadelphia, was a mixed area in the twenties and thirties. Sailors, shipyard workers, longshoremen, and the marine trades clustered along the Delaware shore, especially in the District of Southwark. The south edge of Philadelphia (the Cedar, New Market and Pine wards) bordered on the fashionable and also held the Negro ghetto. Few Negroes voted, however. Some Irish weavers settled in Moyamensing and an Irish colony grew in the western part of the area, along the Schuylkill wharves. Throughout the whole district lived large numbers of unskilled laborers, downtown workers, and local artisans.[14]

12. Sutherland's biography must be patched together out of fragments. *Dictionary of American Biography;* Charles Sutherland, *A Memoir of the Life and Services of Joel Barlow Sutherland, First President of the Society of the War of 1812* (n.d., n.p., pamphlet, Pennsylvania Historical Society, published privately by his son), 5-9; Scharf and Westcott, *History of Philadelphia,* I, 588, 592, 604-608; John R. Commons, ed., *History of Labor,* I, 194-205; Snyder, *Jacksonian Heritage,* 48-50, 86; Louis H. Arky, "The Mechanic's Union of Trade Associations," *Pennsylvania Magazine,* LXXVI (April, 1952), 165-174.

13. Richard I. Shelling, "Philadelphia and the Agitation in 1825 for the Pennsylvania Canal," *Pennsylvania Magazine,* LXII (April, 1938), 175-204.

14. Until the boundaries were changed before the 1836 election Sutherland's First Pennsylvania Congressional District consisted of Southwark, Moyamensing, Passyunk,

Political power centered around the two independent, self-governing Districts, Southwark and Moyamensing. During Sutherland's time both were intensely patriotic, white-equalitarian, anti-Negro, anti-foreigner, in short, strong followers of the old radical Revolutionary traditions of the city. Sutherland's strategy, like that of many Pennsylvania politicians, was to try to balance his constituent's enthusiasm for President Jackson and Jacksonian slogans with a steady support of his district's economic needs.

After two failures Sutherland, in 1826, was elected to Congress where he served for the next ten years.[15] This political success made it possible for him to garner the fruits of power, and during these years he held at intervals the additional offices of Prosecuting Attorney for Philadelphia County and Associate Judge of the Court of Common Pleas. In Congress, as a member of the House Commerce Committee, he promoted the Philadelphia Navy Yard, which was then situated on Federal street in Southwark, and helped to secure the federal appropriation for the important Delaware River breakwater.

In 1834 national events threatened Sutherland's ability to balance Jacksonian enthusiasm with support of Philadelphia's economic interests. The year 1834 saw the crisis of the Bank of the United States. President Jackson had consciously revived the old radical campaign against special privilege to the wealthy and championed the attack on the Bank's charter and federal deposits. In the banking capitals of the Atlantic seaboard municipal politics became strongly polarized between those who felt that a demagogue was

---

the west Philadelphia towns of Blockley and Kingsessing, and the three southside Philadelphia wards of Cedar, New Market, and Pine. *Congressional Directory of the Twenty-Third Congress, First Session* (Washington, 1834). The characterization of this district rests upon guesses from extrapolating back from the 1860 U.S. Census ward details to the thirties. In 1860 the Irish were still very much concentrated at the northern edge of the district in wards 4, 7, and 8. They had not penetrated the heart of Sutherland's old area of popularity. A sample of the occupations on the southside of Philadelphia taken from an 1840 street directory (Table XI) confirms the marine trade, artisan and unskilled characterization of most of the district. Similar hints can be found in *Hazard's U.S. Commercial and Statistical Register*, IV (January-July, 1841), 394, and Norman J. Johnston, "The Caste and Class of the Urban Form of Historic Philadelphia," *Journal of the American Institute of Planners*, XXXII (November, 1966), 334-349.

15. In his first attempt Sutherland was defeated by the well-known philanthropist and school reformer, Samuel Breck (1771-1862). Breck, a Federalist, served one term in Congress only.

attacking the sanctity of personal property and those who regarded Jackson as the savior of democracy. The division in Philadelphia, the home of the Bank of the United States, by no means cut neatly along class lines. Many workingmen joined Whig parades and memorials in defense of the Bank. All spring and summer the Whigs had been strong and active. The Bank, partly out of self-defense and partly in the hope of threatening Congress and the President with a depression, rapidly called in its loans and a severe, if brief, depression fell upon the city and the nation. In the face of these hard times men fell back upon their traditional voting patterns and few Philadelphia seats changed hands.

Spurred by the elections in New York, the Whigs of Philadelphia chose to attempt to unseat the southside Democratic boss, Joel Barlow Sutherland even though Sutherland, otherwise an ardent Jacksonian, had announced himself in favor of the Bank. The Whigs devised the strategy of nominating an Irish mechanic, hoping to swing the election with a combination of native Whigs and new Irish voters. Sutherland's supporters countered with a strong anti-Irish campaign which seems to have united his following. The Whigs, in turn, seem to have expected a violent election; perhaps they intended using force at the polls. Nicholas Biddle of the Bank of the United States sent his family to the country because he feared violence on election day.

On Tuesday, October 14, 1834, balloting proceeded in an orderly way at the polls in the Southwark and Moyamensing parts of the congressional district. Moyamensing had just completed its Commissioners Hall and in front of the new polling place the Democrats had set up tents and the Whigs had rented a house for campaign headquarters. Toward evening as the voters queued up to cast their ballots a fight began in one of the lines and soon the Whigs in the crowd drove all the Democrats from the polls, flattened their tents and cut down the Democratic liberty pole. Since the Democrats were then a minority in Moyamensing, they sought help from adjacent Southwark. Men from this section ran into Moyamensing and soon drove the Whigs away from the polls and into their house. The mob then set about to destroy the Whig liberty pole which was partially sheathed in iron and could not be easily chopped down. While the Democrats milled around the pole some Whigs opened fire from the house wounding fifteen or twenty in the crowd and killing one. The infuriated crowd surged on the headquarters, broke in, and beat persons they caught inside and heaped the furniture about the liberty pole to make a pyre. This street fire spread to a block of nearby houses. When the volunteer fire companies arrived, the mob set upon them, beating the firemen, cutting their hoses, and wrecking their carriages. The fire burned throughout the night unattended. Sutherland was re-elected.[16]

Two years later Sutherland fell victim to the continued confusions of Jackson's war on the Bank. He was caught in one of those painful moments in American political history when a politician cannot safely support both the popular enthusiasms and the economic interests of his constituents. Politics in Pennsylvania during the years 1834-1836 fragmented over three issues: support of the law establishing free public schools, divisions over the location and number of state canals, opposition or sympathy for Jackson's attack on the Bank of the United States. All these issues split the Democratic party of Pennsylvania. Sutherland's wing of the party favored schools, canals, and the granting of a Pennsylvania charter to the Bank.

Many of the Whigs supported the same program. Because of the Democratic division in 1835 a Whig coalition swept the state's gubernatorial election. Sutherland, who had been under heavy attack from Jackson enthusiasts in Philadelphia, decided to try to switch party allegiance in the hope that he could ride a new wave. The state legislature assisted him by changing the First Congressional District so that it included new territory on the northwest side of town where native millworkers and shopkeepers should have responded to Sutherland's type of Whiggery. The Democrats responded by running a well-known Southwark District Commissioner, Lemuel Paynter (1788-1863), against him. Sutherland's machine delivered his old district to him. He carried Southwark and Moyamensing once more, but he lost in the newly annexed areas.[17]

16. Election, Snyder, *Jacksonian Heritage,* 46-49; Scharf and Westcott, *History of Philadelphia,* I, 638-639. Two years later, as a result of this election riot, the state legislature passed an act indemnifying the owner of the houses that had been destroyed and making the city liable for all future damage to property caused by rioting, Act, March 11, 1836.

17. Snyder, *Jacksonian Heritage,* 53-60, 75-81, 85-86; district boundaries and votes, *Public Ledger,* October 13, 1836; Paynter, U.S. Congress, Joint Committee on Printing, *Biographical Dictionary of American Congresses 1774-1961* (Washington, 1961).

The district then alternated for sixteen years among Democrats, Whigs, and Native Americans until in 1850 a new boss, Democrat Thomas B. Florence (1812-1875) took control by reviving Sutherland's old style of friendship to the workingman, attention to patronage and favors, and support for the basic economic interests of the city. Florence was succeeded in turn by the famous speaker of the House of Representatives Samuel Jackson Randall (1828-1890), a skillful practitioner of the same style. Altogether, the bosses of Philadelphia's southside democracy, Sutherland, Florence, and Randall held the Congressional district in steady professional control from 1826 to 1890 with but a single break of sixteen years.[18]

Sutherland's career suggests the new tensions of professional politics. To ensure repeated election to public office the professional must depend upon a mix of popular slogans, local patronage, party discipline, and support for local economic interests. Moreover the professional must maintain this mixture in balance, not being caught, as Sutherland was, with popular enthusiasms overrunning his loyalty to local economic interests. Such a precarious political balance promised weak government for the future of Philadelphia and suggested that such leadership would be slow to respond to change. On the other hand, the rising importance of the professional politicians also meant that it would become increasingly difficult for the city's businessmen to run for office for a term or two in order to accomplish some specific reform. Rather the business specialists would have to seek satisfaction from the political specialists.

Professionalism also manifested itself in the role of the gentleman democrat. The role was not a new one, having been followed by Washington and Jefferson and a number of national figures. In the nineteenth-century city, however, the role took on special significance as the compliment to the new professional boss. Richard Vaux (1816-1895), frequent candidate and second mayor of the consoli-

18. Paynter served only two terms and then retired because of ill health. He was succeeded by Charles Brown (1779-1883), Democrat, a cordwood dealer, city councilor and state senator. In 1842 Edward Joy Morris (1815-1881), Whig, a lawyer, and state representative defeated Brown. In the next election, 1844, Lewis Charles Levin (1808-1860), Native American, a lawyer and journalist, seized the seat and held it for three terms until he was defeated by Florence, a journalist, militia officer and professional Democratic politician. In 1862 Randall, who began his career in the legislature as a dealer in streetcar franchises, defeated Florence and held the seat until his death in 1890. It was, after the Civil War, the only Democratic seat in Philadelphia.

dated city of Philadelphia from 1856 to 1858 was such a figure. A Quaker whose parents were Friends, his father had retired early in life from a merchant career to become a philanthropist. The father is remembered today as a school and prison reformer. The son, Richard Vaux, was educated by tutors and at the Friends Select School, but the pacific teachings of Quakerism seemed to have passed him by. He was a vigorous, direct-action American of the kind so common in the early nineteenth century. After his schooling he read law with a well-known Philadelphia politician and lawyer, and at the age of twenty was admitted to the Philadelphia bar. Before beginning practice, however, he took the aristocratic tour of Europe. He served for a year as private secretary to the American minister at London, but diplomacy did not appeal to him.[19]

Upon returning to Philadelphia in 1839 he found that his friends had nominated him as Democratic candidate for state representative in a hopelessly strong Whig ward (Market Street). Though easily defeated in the election, he continued to be active in local and Democratic politics. After his defeat he became a member of the Board of Comptrollers of the Philadelphia public schools, and from 1841-1847 held the judicial office of Recorder for the city. Soon after his appointment as Recorder, the Whigs in the City Councils, in a partisan attack, abolished the fees and salary of the office, but Vaux stubbornly served on without compensation.

From 1839 to 1892 he served as an active member of the Board of Governors of the Eastern Penitentiary. His father had been a founder of this inhumane institution, which proved to be a misapplication of Quaker psychology. Richard, a believer in hereditary influence as the source of crime, continued his father's misguided advocacy of solitary confinement as a proper means of reforming criminals—despite mounting evidence that the system drove most prisoners into psychotic states or permanent insanity. A longstanding member of the Girard College board, Richard Vaux helped introduce vocational training into that school's curriculum.

19. Vaux's biography must be patched together from fragments. *Dictionary of American Biography;* Richard Vaux, *Address on the Anniversary of the Victory at New Orleans, January 8, 1840* (Philadelphia, 1840, pamphlet, University of Pennsylvania Law Library), 6; Richard Vaux, *Address to the Philadelphia Hose Company* (Philadelphia, 1851, pamphlet, Pennsylvania Historical Society), 18; Scharf and Westcott, *History of Philadelphia,* II 1542-1544; and the Pennsylvania Historical Society has some letters and odds and ends.

He was also an active Mason, eventually Pennsylvania Grand Master, and was a member of numerous organizations.

In politics Vaux was a gentleman champion of the common man and an upholder of the old radical animus against large merchant institutions. He made strong speeches against the "power of corporations," and the "Bank Party," and was always a good, orthodox supporter of President Jackson. Despite increasing criticism of the gang warfare among the fire companies, Vaux remained a staunch friend of these politically influential, working-class and lower-class groups. Indeed, while he was in politics municipal patronage was still too small to support many ward heelers, and as a result much of ward politics was organized around the fire companies. Though a friend of the common man, like most Philadelphians of his age, he was strongly prejudiced against Abolitionism and the Negro. Indeed, around the time of the Civil War he was nicknamed the "Bourbon War Horse" for his mildness towards the South.[20]

Although Vaux began in politics as a gentleman candidate who, the Democrats hoped, could attract votes of the well-to-do in the strongly Whig city, in the end he formed an alliance with Irish politicians and was elected mayor of the consolidated city as the leader of a coalition of local bosses. In style and manner, Vaux was a forerunner of such American gentleman-democrats as Theodore Roosevelt and John F. Kennedy. He favored the athletic image—took ice-cold showers, walked through the streets rather than take a streetcar, and went without a coat in rain and frost. The style suggested a man who would doff his coat, roll up his sleeves, and tackle the commonplace problems of his society.

Vaux's first campaign for mayor (1842) coincided with a nationwide, depression-inspired reaction to twelve years of Jacksonian hegemony in Washington. Moreover, in Philadelphia there had been bickering over the use of the King James Bible in the public schools and a summer race riot. Both these events favored the entrenched Whig party against the minority Democrats. The Democrats hoped that their gentleman candidate could attract some Whigs. His opponent was the incumbent mayor, John M. Scott (1789-1858), a lawyer, frequent city councilor, and the city's first

20. When Kansas exploded Vaux became a Douglas rather than an Buchanan Democrat, William Dusinberre, *Civil War Issues in Philadelphia* (Philadelphia, 1965), 68-69, 78-79, 86-89, 107.

popularly elected mayor. Scott carried all but three of the city's fifteen wards and won easily.[21]

In 1846 Vaux ran again. In this election he faced Philadelphia's perennial Whig mayor, John Swift (mayor 1832-1838, 1839-1841, 1845-1849), a lawyer, clubman, and supporter of Henry Clay who had won respect for his forthright, if not effective, action as leader of the city's watch and constables in past riots.[22] The rise of nativism and the violent anti-Irish riots of 1844 had given rise to a new Native American party and had split off a good number of artisan votes from the Democrats' party. Finally, the preparations and news of the Mexican War during the spring and summer of 1846 over-shadowed local issues. The incumbent was easily swept in again.[23]

For the next few years Vaux ceased to be a candidate. He was not well connected to the rising state Democratic faction of James Buchanan,[24] and within the city of Philadelphia no Democrat could expect to be elected until the city Democrats could be counted with their fellows in the outer districts of Philadelphia County.

The consolidation of all the boroughs and districts of Philadelphia County into one city in 1854 gave Vaux a new opportunity. By this time the national issues of slavery and free soil had subsided briefly and a general revival of nativism stood in their place. Within Philadelphia native Protestant artisans, unskilled workers, and members of the new middle class were in steady conflict with Catholics in general and with the Irish in particular. The Irish had been identified with the violent riots of earlier years, and they were the opponents of temperance reform.[25]

21. Scott 6,145 Vaux 5,137, *Public Ledger*, October 13, 1842. John M. Scott was a native of New York and Princeton graduate who came to Philadelphia in 1807 where he practiced law. He was a member of the Second City Troop, mayor 1841-1844, and had been President of the Common Council. John R. Young, *Memorial History of the City of Philadelphia* (N.Y., 1895), I, 499.

22. John Swift (1790-1873), biographical sketch in Thomas Willing Balch, "The Swift Family of Philadelphia," *Pennsylvania Magazine*, XXX (April, 1906), 150-152.

23. Swift, 5,562, Vaux 3,402, Peter A. Browne, Native American, 3,164, *Public Ledger*, October 15, 1846. Vaux carried only the Upper Delaware Ward, Browne took the North Mulberry Ward where Vaux had been strong in 1844.

24. Vaux and John M. Read had attempted to start a Democratic campaign for Gen. Zachary Taylor and when that failed they reluctantly supported Buchanan until the Kansas issue, Snyder, *Jacksonian Heritage*, 171, 209, 211.

25. Judges of the Quarter sessions had been complaining of "rum holes," while the commissioners of the Irish District of Moyamensing saw Sunday closings as the working of "the same fanatical, persecuting spirit . . . that prompted the Puritans of

The contest of 1854 was thus between Robert T. Conrad (1810-1858), Nativist and former Whig who regarded immigrant paupers as the source of disorder in the city,[26] and Vaux, gentleman democrat, friend of the lower-class fire companies, ally of neighborhood Irish bosses, and symbol of the old radical Revolutionary and Jacksonian tradition of a democratic society open to all. Conrad defeated Vaux 28,883 to 21,020.[27] The day after his defeat Vaux climbed the old State House steps to shout his intention to run again.

Mayor Conrad proved a conscientious mayor. He addressed himself to the administrative problems of uniting all the districts of Philadelphia County and established the consolidated police force. He appointed none but native-born Americans to the force, however, a policy which heightened the tensions between the police and the many Irish fire companies. Moreover, Conrad's strict enforcement of the Sunday liquor laws aroused widespread resentment from native-born and foreign alike. After one term he retired from office.[28]

In 1856 Richard Vaux and the Democrats faced a winning situation. The Native Americans had aligned themselves with the Temperance candidate in the election of county officers the year before and had been soundly defeated. The Whigs and Native Americans were splitting up under the pressure of national free soil and slavery debate. The Republican Party had just been established. Pennsylvania's leading Democrat, Buchanan, was on his way from England to the Democratic convention, where he would be nominated for President of the United States.

Vaux's opponent was Henry D. Moore (1817-1887), a former Whig congressman (1849-1853) who had been engaged in the mahogany and marble business and who was now running as the Native American candidate.[29] The Whigs at first nominated their own candidate and then withdrew, freeing their supporters to vote

---

Massachusetts . . . to maim, maltreat, and murder those who differed with them in religious belief." *Public Ledger*, December 7, 1847; prohibition, Oberholtzer, *History of Philadelphia*, II, 318; resurgence of nativism, Sister M. Theopane Geary, *A History of Third Parties in Pennsylvania 1840-1860* (Washington, 1938), 166-169; Erwin S. Bradley, *The Triumph of Militant Republicanism* (Philadelphia, 1964), 32-33.

26. Howard O. Sprogle, *The Philadelphia Police* (Philadelphia, 1887), 100.

27. *Public Ledger,* June 7, 1854.

28. Scharf and Westcott, *History of Philadelphia,* I, 718-720.

29. *Biographical Dictionary of American Congresses.*

as they wished. The issues of Vaux's campaign had an unpleasantly modern ring. As an old Jackson supporter, he would be a friend to the common man. The taxpayer would remember him well because there would be no luxury and extravagance in his administration, only the strictest economy. Finally, while some of his firehouse leaders and local bosses labored in his behalf, his supporters, to show Vaux's opposition to corrupt boss government, picked out a notorious saloon keeper, William McMullen (1826-1901) of Moyamensing as their target of attack. After his victory, lines of Vaux's supporters seeking jobs with the city filled the Chestnut street sidewalks.[30]

Vaux knew that he could do little as mayor beyond building up the police force. Many of the problems of municipal government lay beyond his reach in the ineffective management of semi-autonomous boards for water, gas, schools, and hospitals. He did try to keep his pledge of economy, but when the panic of 1857 struck in the fall, throwing thousands temporarily out of work, he took the traditional mayoral position of approving expenditures for relief and public works to counteract a winter of unemployment.[31]

Most of all Vaux enjoyed his police work, which had been the motive of consolidation and became the specialty of his administration. He abolished his predecessor's objectionable native-birth requirement for police employment and introduced a number of permanent reforms: a police and fire telegraph system, a police section to investigate fires, military drill for the force, a uniform blue coat for all the men, and close inspection of their appearance and work. Vaux acted out the role which journalists later made part of the Teddy Roosevelt legend. He prowled the streets at night checking on his officers, and he joined with them in their legalized war to disperse the gangs of Philadelphia. In later years a story was told about the vigilante methods of his police, in this case an evening's bout with the notorious Schuylkill Rangers.

30. McMullen, *Public Ledger*, obit, April 1, 1901; election, *Public Ledger*, May 7, 1856; Scharf and Westcott, *History of Philadelphia*, I, 721-722.

31. Mayor of Philadelphia, *Second Annual Message of the Honorable Richard Vaux* (Philadelphia, 1858), 6-13, 75-114; Benjamin J. Klebaner, "The Home Relief Controversy in Philadelphia, 1782-1861," *Pennsylvania Magazine*, LXXVIII (October, 1954), 421-423; Austin E. Hutcheson, "Philadelphia and the Panic of 1857," *Pennsylvania History*, III (July, 1936), 182-194; Scharf and Westcott, *History of Philadelphia*, I, 721-727.

There was no formal arrest, there were few prisoners in the dock in the mornings; the justices of the peace were not much troubled, but the fellow who was caught never forgot until his dying day the time he fell into the hands of Dick Vaux's police. I remember one night three of the Rangers were surprised, and jumped into the river and swam to a tug-boat in the middle of the stream. It was very cold, and they thought that Dick (I was there) and his men would not follow. They were never so much mistaken in all their lives. We got a boat and overtook them. The interview was more muscular than intellectual. The rascals were pretty well satisfied before it was over. So were we. They didn't trouble us again during the administration.[32]

Such a tale is hardly the story of a reformer of great thorough-ness; it is the tale of a sporting gentleman doing his best to deal with what was then the most dramatic problem of this city. Yet "Dick Vaux's police" did enjoy some success: they broke up some of the most troublesome criminal gangs; they confined most crime and violence to small areas of the city; they brought the frequent gang fighting of the firehouses under better control, and they began with the police force to make an institution which under a strong manage-ment during the Civil War prevented the sort of outbreaks which wracked New York.[33]

In his campaign for reelection in 1858 opponents questioned the effectiveness of his police management. There had been com-plaints throughout his administration of police inefficiency and of the failure of the mayor to discharge incompetent officers. Some felt that a full-time police force cost more than they wished to pay in taxes. The traditional methods of the sheriff's posse and the watch were, after all, much cheaper. More important than such com-plaints, was the fact that the anti-Democratic forces were recombin-ing in a more effective political grouping. In the spring of 1858, there was a fusion of Republicans and Native Americans on a com-promise platform which favored the tariff, free soil, restrained oppo-sition to foreign paupers, and mild opposition to Negroes. A Whig, Alexander Henry (1823-1883), defeated Vaux 33,159 to 29,120.[34]

On balance, Richard Vaux, though a professional who re-

32. Quotation from Sprogle, *Philadelphia Police*, 108.
33. Sprogle, *Philadelphia Police*, 105-113; Dusinberre, *Civil War Issues*, 177-190.
34. Dusinberre, *Civil War Issues*, 77-78; Scharf and Westcott, *History of Philadelphia*, I, 728; vote, *Public Ledger*, May 12, 1858; Alexander Henry as mayor, Winnifred K. McKay, "Philadelphia During the Civil War," *Pennsylvania Magazine*, LXX (January, 1946), 5-42.

mained active in politics, did not enjoy a successful career. Compared to such later gentlemen professionals as Boise Penrose (1860-1921), who was to dominate all of Pennsylvania, Vaux's years as Recorder, school board member, and one term as mayor seem modest in the extreme. His contributions to the city, however, were substantial. During the years of Philadelphia's most intense nativism and anti-Catholicism he steadfastly played his role of gentleman democrat, embodying by his candidacy and his actions as mayor his city's traditional goal of an open society. Though playing an old role, Vaux also was a creature of the transition to the new orientations of big-city politics. His active political years, from 1839 to 1858, coincided with the shift in ideology of Philadelphia politics from the old eighteenth and early nineteenth-century controversies over the representation of the mechanic and the laboring man in government to the new controversies over ethnic representation and ethnic power.

Vaux's career, like that of Joel Barlow Sutherland, also illustrates the growing constraints that professional politics were to impose on the city. Vaux's 1856 election resulted in large measure from a successful coalition of local bosses and firehouse gangs. To maintain such coalitions, lines of supporters seeking jobs had to be given work with the city. Neither Vaux nor his opponents could ignore that need. The price of such a pattern of professional politics is well known to American history: weak, corrupt, unimaginative municipal government. From the 1890's until the Great Depression reformers in every city in the nation labored against the consequences of this system of local government. As an old man Vaux himself led a group of citizens in an attempt to undo the then fully apparent disorders created by boss politics. A new charter was passed in 1885, but no basic reform resulted. No group of merchants came forward to lead the city. The new businessmen of the 1880's, like Jay Cooke before them, neither knew their city nor cared about it. Without such leadership, however, the voters of Philadelphia would not trust their government with large sums of money, big projects, or major innovations. Pinch-penny, corrupt, and unresponsive government ruled the city for the next sixty, if not one hundred, years.

6

Municipal Institutions

In responding to the pressures of rapid growth and the possibilities of industrialization, Philadelphians drew upon their town traditions. They began with the forms and goals as established by the Revolution. They expanded the old functions of street repair, wharf and market operation, hospitals and relief to modern proportions. In addition, they fashioned a number of new municipal institutions —water and gas works, dispensaries, police departments and free schools. By 1860 the institutions and activities of Philadelphia's municipal government were established and have remained virtually the same ever since. Thus, many of the city's twentieth-century successes and failures have been determined by the capabilities and limitations of these inherited arrangements.

The goals of the nineteenth-century municipality remained those of the Revolutionary era. The city was to be an environment for private money-making, and its government was to encourage private business. At the same time the city was to be an equalitarian society; its government should endeavor to maintain an open society where every citizen would have some chance, if not an equal chance, in the race for private wealth. These traditional goals worked upon the settled forms of the municipal corporation; they set the framework of the new municipal institutions, and they directed the attention and the efforts of the city's leaders, both the merchant amateurs and the new professionals.

The enduring effects of the interaction of these traditional goals with the demands of big city life can be summarized in the history of three institutions: the municipal corporation, the water-works, and the public schools. The history of the municipal corpora-tion is best known and therefore can be sketched briefly. The story of Philadelphia's pioneer municipal waterworks demands more at-tention since it shows the permanent constraints that the city's tradi-tion of privatism placed upon what was to be a universal public health program. The history of Philadelphia's public schools, like-wise, shows the enduring constraints of privatism upon a major in-stitution of urban social control.

MUNICIPAL CORPORATION

The Philadelphia municipal corporation grew directly out of the Revolution. The moderate merchant-artisan faction which had re-sumed control of the city and state at the end of the Revolution wrote the 1789 Philadelphia city charter, the first since independ-ence was gained. It blended the traditional offices of colonial munic-ipal government with the federalist fashion for bicameral legisla-tures. The taxpayer franchise established in 1776 by the radicals for all of Pennsylvania remained the electoral base of the city. The taxpayers of the city elected at-large both select and common coun-cils which, together, voted appropriations, levied taxes, and enacted local ordinances. The mayor, not popularly elected, but chosen by the councils, as in colonial times, was the chief executive officer. With the approval of the councils he appointed a board of commis-sioners and together the mayor and the board carried on the execu-tive business of the city government.

Despite domination by merchants, in the years following the 1789 charter, the demands of radical equalitarianism continued to press upon Philadelphia's corporation and thereby to hold it to a weak executive, to increase local control, and to expand both the franchise and the number of elected offices.[1] Philadelphia's munici-pal history, thus, ran directly counter to the trends of centralization and large-scale activity which characterized the contemporaneous in-dustrialization of the city.

The radical fears of strong executives, inherited from the con-flicts of the Revolution and continued by the Jacksonians in the nineteenth century, prevented the mayor and commissioners of the

1. Philadelphia's experience in these years appears to have been part of a general national trend, Ernest S. Griffith, *Modern Development of City Government in the United Kingdom and the United States* (London, 1927), I, 3-29.

Philadelphia corporation from exercising much independence of action. When new municipal functions were added, like responsibilities for municipal water and gas, the councils created independent committees which did not report to the mayor but to the councils themselves. The patronage of the new activities, thus, fell to the councilors, not to the mayor, and therefore the effectiveness of the municipal corporation throughout the first half of the nineteenth century depended on the quality of the elected councilors and the volunteers who served on the council's committees.

Localism also gained with successive reforms of the post-Revolutionary Philadelphia and Pennsylvania governments. In 1834, when the basic public school statute for Pennsylvania was enacted it stipulated that three citizens be elected from each ward of Philadelphia to serve as school directors. The colonial tradition of having resident tax collectors and assessors in each ward was continued on an elected basis until just before the Civil War. The pressures of neighborhood partisan politics upon these officials produced widely fluctuating assessments and ultimately great confusion in the tax rolls. In 1854, when all the boroughs and districts of Philadelphia County joined into one consolidated city, to preserve the strength of past localisms, the select and common councillors were hereafter chosen on a ward basis, not at-large as formerly.

State and municipal election reforms expanded the number of voters and the number of elected offices. In 1838, state judges became elected officials. At the same time the franchise, which had been restricted to all taxpayers, was redefined to include all white males who had reached the age of twenty-one. This franchise reform, one of the few genuinely popular accomplishments in a deeply divided constitutional convention (1837-1838), reflected an important current in American equalitarianism: An enthusiasm for the uniform political status of whites was often accompanied by a heavy prejudice against Negroes. By the time the state constitutional convention convened in Philadelphia the city had already experienced its first major race riot. In 1841 the mayorality became a popularly elected office, while the ballot for Philadelphia county positions grew steadily longer.[2]

2. The history of the municipal corporation is taken from Edward P. Allinson and Boies Penrose, *City Government of Philadelphia (Johns Hopkins Studies in Historical and Political Science,* Fifth Series, I-II, Baltimore, 1887), 33-61; J. Thomas Scharf and Thompson Westcott, *History of Philadelphia 1606-1884* (Philadelphia, 1884), III, 1703, 1737, 1936.

By mid-century the city of Philadelphia had grown to a big city and the functions of its government had kept pace with this growth. The cost of half a century of political change which ran against the trends of the city's industrialization now stood out clearly. The committee system of the councils, the extreme localism of politics, and the large number of elected offices appeared as handicaps to effective government. The consolidation of all the county into one municipal corporation in 1854 brought unity of management to the major functions of government, but it did not bring with it imagination or high quality of service.

The authors of the 1854 consolidation charter had voiced concern for effective control over municipal departments and sought devices for protecting the corporation from looting by predatory local political groups. To these ends they considerably enlarged the powers of the mayor at the expense of the councils' committees, and they created new executives in the offices of comptroller and receiver of taxes. So strong was the tradition of elected officials, however, that both these new executives had to be elected, not appointed by the mayor. Altogether, the reforms of 1854 could make but little progress. Bigness and industrialization had already destroyed both the source of competent leadership and the informed community which would have been necessary for the city to have enjoyed a future of strong, efficient, and imaginative government. Instead, a century of weakness and corruption lay ahead.[3]

DEVELOPMENT OF WATERWORKS

Philadelphia pioneered in building America's first municipal waterworks and thus operated for forty years an experimental water supply project for all other large cities in the nation. The success of Philadelphia's water program stands as a tribute to its old merchant-led committee system of government. Indeed, in the beginning, its success was as much a product of an aggressive committee as it was the result of sponsorship by the municipal corporation.[4]

The yellow fever epidemic of 1793 forced Philadelphians into

3. Eli K. Price, *The History of the Consolidation of the City of Philadelphia* (Philadelphia, 1873), 82-89. Compare with Lincoln Steffens, "Philadelphia: Corrupt and Contented," *The Shame of Cities* (N.Y., 1904, 1957 ed.), 134-161.

4. Public water supplies were established in Philadelphia in 1801, in New York in 1842, Boston 1848, Baltimore, a small private system in 1808, expanded in 1838, and a full public system in 1857.

their pioneering public water system. In that epidemic, the city's first major plague, one in twelve Philadelphians perished. More than 23,000 persons fled the city, and all business with the outside world ceased for a month.[5] It was clear to those who tasted the well water of different neighborhoods that in crowded blocks the contents of privies penetrated the wells.[6] Although doctors debated repeatedly the causes of the fever, all sides agreed that the cleansing of the streets, yards, and houses of filth and an abundant supply of cool, clear water for drinking were essential requirements if the city was to be preserved.

During these years a private company was digging a canal to connect the Schuylkill River to the Delaware River. It therefore seemed reasonable to add to these transportation plans a branch water supply canal through the center of the city. The canal company, however, soon went bankrupt. In 1797 another serious epidemic of yellow fever struck the city and carried away over 3,000 citizens. Extended negotiations between the canal company and the city were renewed, but satisfactory financial arrangements could not be worked out. The issue then moved to the state legislature, where the company proved a more powerful lobbyist than the municipal corporation. The fever returned in 1798.

In 1799 the immigrant English engineer and architect, Benjamin Latrobe (1764-1820), visited Philadelphia on a commission to design the Bank of Pennsylvania. While in town he heard of the problem and published a pamphlet proposing a quick solution. He suggested, as an alternative to the slow and expensive program of a dam and canals, that the city build two steam pumps, a culvert from the Schuylkill to the edge of the city's dense settlement (then Pennsylvania Square), and a distribution system of wooden pipes and street hydrants. To capture popular support he added the provision of free water to the poor at the street hydrants. The cost of construction and operation of the system, Latrobe maintained, could be met by rents charged to businesses and private homes that were directly

5. The first U.S. Census returned 44,096 persons for Philadelphia, the Liberties and Southwark. Therefore the population of the city on the eve of the plague must have been about 48,000. The epidemic is recounted in detail in John H. Powell, *Bring Out Your Dead: The Great Plague of Yellow Fever in Philadelphia in 1793* (Philadelphia, 1949).

6. Latrobe noted the seepage of wastes through the Philadelphia sand in his journal, Talbot Hamlin, *Benjamin Henry Latrobe* (New York, 1955), 157.

connected to the system. Although there had been a steam engine in Philadelphia before the Revolution, Latrobe's scheme was a bold innovation.[7]

At this point, as in the later expansion of Fairmount Dam, the strength of the city's merchant-led committee system of government proved itself. During the years from 1799 to 1837 very able leaders of the city served on the Watering Committee of the City Councils. Henry Drinker, Jr. (1757-1822), son of the well-known Quaker merchant and himself cashier of the Bank of North America, Thomas P. Cope (1768-1854), then at the beginning of his successful merchant career, and Samuel M. Fox (1763-1808) of the Bank of Pennsylvania led the campaign for the Latrobe plan. In subsequent years William Rush (1766-1833), the famous sculptor; Joseph S. Lewis (1778-1836), prominent attorney and son of a wealthy china merchant; and John P. Wetherill (1794-1853), of the old Philadelphia paint manufacturing company Wetherill and Brother, all served on the Watering Committee and directed its aggressive policies.[8]

The city councils and their watering committee fought free of the canal interests and arranged their own financing without state aid. Despite setbacks in construction and periodic shortages of funds which the committee sometimes met by the members' advancing money out of their own pockets, they pushed the project through to completion by 1801. Henceforth Philadelphians enjoyed a reasonably adequate supply of water to cleanse themselves and to fight fires. The trials of the watering committee, however, did not cease. It continued to suffer all the pains of innovation. Engineering problems hampered the Committee until the twenties, financial problems until the thirties. The steam engines for the pumps, though good examples of Watt's low-pressure engine, broke down frequently and consumed mountains of cordwood. After sixteen years of difficulty they were replaced with high-pressure engines but these, though steady and powerful, used even more fuel. The original hydrants rarely shut off completely and in the winter froze solid. After two seasons the hydrants had to be entirely replaced by a new de-

7. Hamlin, *Latrobe*, 134-135, 157-167; John A. Kouwenhoven, *Made in America* (New York, 1948), 41.

8. For the narrative of the Philadelphia waterworks I have relied on Nelson M. Blake, *Water for the Cities* (Syracuse, 1956), Ch. II, V.

sign. The hollow wooden logs used to distribute the water from the tank above the second pump leaked badly and after a few years a program of replacement by cast iron pipe was instituted.[9]

The original Latrobe scheme for financing the works was based on the assumption that many families would want direct water connections to their houses and that these private subscriptions would carry the cost of building and operating the system. Except for the boldest thinkers, however, Philadelphians in 1801 used water sparingly. By 1811 only 2,127 Philadelphians subscribed for water. Most of the city's 54,000 residents (city proper in 1810) depended for water on street hydrants or private wells. There were only two bathhouses in the entire city. As for home bathrooms, American inventors did not turn their attention to sanitary appliances until the 1830's. Thus over the first three decades of operation the watering committee struggled against heavy deficits while continuing to supply its product at a loss in advance of popular usage, for public health reasons.

Having established abundant clear water as part of the city's health services, the watering committee could not turn back even in the face of heavy financial deficits. During the second decade of the nineteenth century the city grew at the rate of about 2,200 persons per year. By 1820 Philadelphia and its immediate environs held a population of 114,000. The lawyer Joseph S. Lewis led the committee to seek a lasting solution to its problems of high operating costs and inadequate supply for the enlarging city. In 1819, in the midst of a severe depression, he proposed, and the City Councils accepted, a plan to invest another $400,000, this time in a dam across the Schuylkill and a series of water-powered pumps to raise the water to adjacent Fairmount Hill, where large reservoirs for a gravity-fed system could be built. The waterpowered pumps would cut the

9. There is some evidence that the Philadelphia waterworks may be a case of provincial technological backwardness caused by the imperfect communication of engineering technique in the Atlantic world. W. H. Chaloner, "John Wilkinson, Ironmaster," *History Today*, I (May, 1951), 67 reports shipments of cast iron water pipe from England to Paris in 1780-1781 but does not indicate whether these pipes were for a Paris waterworks or for the Versailles fountain system. Whichever the case it would seem that French engineering and specifications would have saved Philadelphia the grief it experienced with faulty hydrants and fittings. The changeover to cast iron pipe went slowly. Scharf and Westcott claim replacement did not begin until 1818 and that in 1822 there were still thirty-two miles of wooden pipe in the city, *History of Philadelphia*, I. 605.

operating costs to a mere fraction of the former steam costs. Also, the dam was to be constructed for eight water wheels, although only three would be needed immediately. Thus it was hoped that the Fairmount scheme afforded enough surplus capacity for years to come. Within four years the works were completed.

The Fairmount works met every economic and engineering expectation. They also stand as a lasting memorial to the era of Philadelphia's merchant-led committee government. The watering committee had sufficient taste, standing in the city, and pride in its accomplishment to finish the works and lay out the grounds as a beautiful park. Although only a beginning, like the works themselves, the park was an extremely valuable project. With its 1844 additions, it became the first large urban park in America, and, as such, was an essential link in the chain of outstanding landscapes that included Boston's Mt. Auburn Cemetery, New York's Central Park, and Chicago's lake front. Over the years Philadelphians expanded the original waterworks layout to create the greatest civic monument of Philadelphia, the Fairmount Park system.[10]

The excess capacity of the Fairmount works soon disappeared. Since public waterworks with their abundant supply of water for domestic and commercial users offered a novel product, there was no way to predict its future use. The growth of Philadelphia during the years 1830-1850 exceeded its rate for any other period (1820-1830 38 percent, 1830-1840 37 percent, 1840-1850 58 percent, Philadelphia only). Such a pace of growth, occurring for the first time in large American cities, likewise could not be expected to yield reliable future estimates. Both the sustained, rapid growth in Philadelphia's population and the increase in per capita consumption of water must have surprised contemporaries.[11]

10. Commissioners of Fairmount Park, *First Annual Report* (Philadelphia, 1869), 6-12; George B. Tatum, "The Origins of Fairmount Park," *Antiques*, LXXXII (November, 1962), 502-507.

11. Today planners struggle with the identical problem which faced the Philadelphia Watering Committee. How much extra capacity should be built into the works in the case when capital is in short supply and a city is growing at an indeterminate pace? The size of the Fairmount Works, and hence the amount of extra capacity for the entire system was set by a combination of engineering considerations and prior private property rights. The design of the dam and its wheels followed the plans of an English engineer who had formerly built mills along the nearby Brandywine River. He estimated the possible height of the dam and hence the available power at the site on the basis of contemporary rules of thumb. To guard against an underestimate on

In 1837 the committee issued a triumphant report. It had $100,000 in the bank, six wheels running at the dam, and the number of paying customers had jumped to 20,000. Of equal significance, consumption had begun its rise toward modern levels; doubling since 1823, it now equaled twenty gallons per person per day. The system as a whole—street hydrants, house and commercial connections—served a total population of 196,000. The report noted that 1,500 Philadelphians had installed bathrooms with running water. That critical moment in the history of any social innovation, the time when a fashion of the rich becomes an imperative for the middle class, seemed to have arrived.[12]

Though public enthusiasm for bathing and water closets grew apace, after 1837 the watering committee began to lose the imagination and largeness of view which had characterized its early performance. It seems reasonable to detect in this falling off of the quality of the committee the beginning of the decline in the quality of Philadelphia's municipal officers and a weakening of the committee system of government. Perhaps the very triumph of the Fairmount works in routinizing the water supply of the city, at least for a few years, made the watering committee unattractive to the most imaginative city leaders. Whatever the cause, the committee began to falter and in one way or another failed to keep pace with the growing needs of the city.

During the 1840's, spurred by immigration and industrial expansion, Philadelphia filled up rapidly and the towns and districts outside its boundaries grew at unprecedented rates. Spring Garden,

---

his part of the efficiency of the pumps the Watering Committee purchased additional upstream riparian rights so that the height of the dam could be raised to carry its lake to the Manyunk mills upstream. No further height was possible since to purchase the Manyunk mill rights would have been enormously expensive. Thus the efficiency of the overshot wheels at the Fairmount Dam and the presence of the Manyunk mills determined the capacity of the Philadelphia system for the next thirty years. Thomas Gilpin, "Fairmount Dam and Waterworks, Philadelphia," *Pennsylvania Magazine* XXXVII (October, 1913), 471-479; Select and Common Councils of Philadelphia, *Report of the Watering Committee on the Propriety of Raising the Dam at Fair Mount* (Philadelphia, 1820), 4-6.

12. A great enthusiasm for bathing seized the public at this moment and even suggested to an editorial writer that public bathhouses would improve the moral habits of the poor by lessening the jealousy between classes. *Public Ledger*, July 10, 1838. Purity of the water had not been entirely satisfactory. The same paper complained that the hydrant system meant impure water. It reported an "animal, like a centipede" in a glass of hydrant water, *Public Ledger*, October 6, 1836.

Kensington, and Northern Liberties, districts which had joined the Philadelphia system, now used water in enormous amounts and demanded an equalization of their rates with those of Philadelphia customers. In addition, Spring Garden requested a high-pressure reservoir to give more adequate service on its hills. The watering committee, forgetting the essential public health purpose of its undertaking, now responded like a short-sighted monopolist by refusing to lower its rates. Spring Garden countered by securing legislative authorization to build its own works. Negotiations continued for a time, and ultimately the rates were conceded by the watering committee, but no satisfactory long-term contract could be worked out among Philadelphia and its neighbors. Spring Garden, Northern Liberties, and Kensington joined together to build their own pumping station in 1844. Ironically, they drew their water from behind the Fairmount Dam. In 1850 Kensington set up its own station, drawing from the Delaware River.

By 1850 only Southwark remained connected to the Philadelphia system. Yet such had been the decade's increase in per capita consumption that with all eight wheels working at the dam, and all the reservoirs filled, only three day's supply of water could be stored. In the summer 160,000 people drew forty-four gallons per person per day. Fifteen thousand houses had water closets, and 3,500 had baths. Clearly, the middle class of Philadelphia had adopted modern plumbing as an essential in its standard of living. The modern urban rate of water usage had arrived.

The subsequent history of the Philadelphia Water Works is inglorious. In 1851 inadequate capacity forced the watering committee to refuse West Philadelphia's request for service. The consolidation of all Philadelphia County into one city government in 1854 reunited all the water systems of the city, but union did not revive the old policy of aggressive building to meet future needs and to popularize higher standards of consumption. In the 1870's the city erected new steam pumping stations, but droughts brought shortages. Increasing pollution of the Schuylkill and Delaware rivers destroyed the former quality of the water. Such were the popular priorities of the city that the citizens taxed themselves with disease and dirty drinking water in order to allow private pollution of the rivers to continue unabated. In the years from 1880 to 1910 the typhoid fever rate in Philadelphia exceeded that of New York and

Boston. Though filter systems had been demonstrated for over a decade, Philadelphia purchased its filters late and proceeded slowly. As late as 1906, 1,063 persons died of typhoid in Philadelphia in one season. In 1910-1911 filters and chlorine brought relief from these recurrent epidemics.[13]

The early history of the Philadelphia's water works does more than help to date the mid-nineteenth century decline in the effectiveness of its municipal government. Its history shows how the city's general culture of privatism stopped a universal public health program short of full realization. Fear of epidemics had created the water system, but once this fear had abated, little or no public support remained to bring the benefits of the new technology to those who could not afford them. The popular goal of the private city was a goal to make Philadelphia a moderately safe place for ordinary men and women to go about conducting their own business; the goal was never to help raise the level of living of the poor.

By the late 1840's water closets and baths had become a permanent part of, if not as yet an inevitable companion to, Philadelphia's middle class standard of living. The efficient use of a system of waterworks for maximum public health benefit to the city as a whole required that every person in the city have easy access to toilets and to running water. So far the public effort had brought water to the sidewalk of every built-up section of the city, although not into the crowded interior alleys of the poor. In effect, fifty years of public water had resulted in leveling all Philadelphians up to the standard enjoyed by the rich in the late eighteenth century. The street hydrant with pure water had been substituted for backyard and street wells. The new standard of personal cleanliness and the new technology of sanitary appliances, however, required moving beyond the street into the houses themselves.

A Philadelphia doctor conducting a survey for the American Medical Association wrote,

> . . . in most of the houses recently erected on the main streets, or now in progress, conveniences for bathing are furnished—and a bathhouse is considered indispensable for domestic comfort. There is, however, a gen-

13. Philadelphia Bureau of Water, *Description of the Filtration Works and History of Water Supply 1789-1900* (Philadelphia, 1909), 3-4, 50-51, 70-71; City of Philadelphia, *Third Annual Message of Mayor Harry A. Mackey* (Philadelphia, 1931), 388; pollution, Blake, *Water for the Cities*, 97-98, 255-256, 259-261.

eral absence of bathing apparatus, and even of hydrants, in the houses of the poorer classes, and especially in the confined courts and alleys of the populous districts of the city. This is a great evil, and calls loudly for public interference. A regulation, enforcing the introduction of water into·every house, would, it seems to us, fall within the power of municipal bodies. Upon this point . . . the Sanitary Committee of the (Philadelphia) Board of Health remark: 'the agents of municipal bodies execute the orders of the body they represent; but it is believed that a very short-sighted, circumscribed policy obtains too generally in the administration of local ordinances, with reference to public health in the *free use of water,* which it should be made obligatory to have introduced into every house erected, however small. By facilitating the means of frequent bathing in families—particularly the poor and laboring classes— the effect would soon be apparent, by removing a prominent cause of disease, and contribute to the moral, as well as physical improvement of the lower classes of society.'

But five public baths exist within the city limits, and one in the district of Spring Garden; and the entrance to these is at a cost which excludes a large proportion of the inhabitants who are without the facilities of bathing at their own houses.[14]

Contemporary sanitarians clearly saw the failure of the city to carry out the logic of the new waterworks' technology. Their remedy, characteristically, was a modest one: The city should require all *new* houses to have baths and toilets. Even they stopped short of the more logical reallocation of municipal resources—the establishment of a municipal program for bringing water into existing houses that lacked them. Their modest recommendations went unheeded. The ordinance requiring the installation of running water and baths in all new construction waited until the twentieth century; it was to wait, in fact, until the popular custom of builders and buyers had made such facilities the inevitable accompaniment of new construction. In this respect of regulation following popular norms for private construction, Philadelphia seems to have followed the national tide. Boston, New York, and Chicago also passed build-

14. Italics in the original, Isaac Parrish, "Report on the Sanitary Condition of Philadelphia," American Medical Association, *Transactions,* II (Philadelphia, 1849), 479. An earlier, 1833, inspection revealed that 253 persons living in thirty tenements in the Delaware Ward were without even privies, Mathew Carey, *A Plea for the Poor* (Philadelphia, 1837), 15. The labor leader William Heighton claimed in 1828 that even hydrants had not been brought into the workers' streets in Southwark, Louis H. Arky, "Mechanics' Union of Trade Associations," *Pennsylvania Magazine,* LXXVI (April, 1952), 166.

ing and sanitary codes only after the standards of the codes had become general practice in new construction.[15]

PUBLIC SCHOOLS

In the case of the waterworks, the traditions of private property forbade the reasonable extension of a public health program to poor citizens and thereby prevented the city from realizing the benefits of a universal improvement in its standards of living. The public schools present quite the opposite case. The very motive for the creation of Philadelphia's public schools was to aid the poor. From the beginning the schools were open to all whites, and in time compulsory education (1895) made school inescapable to all children.

The traditions of the city and circumstances under which the Philadelphia system first grew, however, confined the public schools permanently to low-cost, mass uniformity of instruction. The city's tradition of privatism set narrow goals for instruction, while the early nineteenth-century institutional division of educational labor between public and private schools further constrained the public schools from offering a variety of programs. Uniform acculturation for urban industrial life became the great specialty of the public schools, a specialty set before the Civil War and a task from which Philadelphia's schools never could extricate themselves.

The public schools of Philadelphia grew out of a failure of private schools to reach a large enough fraction of the city's children. The Philadelphia Directory of 1800 listed about two hundred school teachers, mostly women. Using their own front room, or a rented room, these teachers managed several programs: infant schools for children of six and under, elementary schools for reading, writing, and arithmetic, academies and "colleges" for girls and boys up to the ages of fourteen to sixteen. In addition to these

15. On May 7, 1855 the city of Philadelphia passed a comprehensive construction code. The first sanitary law was the state statute of 1895 (*Laws of Pennsylvania, Session of 1895*, 178-181) which required water closets for new and remodeled tenements.

Programs for the municipal enforcement of higher housing standards raise difficult economic issues. The program must not simply price standard-conforming housing out of the reach of the poor. Such was the case in Boston when sanitary and fireproofing regulations made conforming tenements too expensive for lower income families to occupy legally, Lloyd Rodwin, *Housing and Economic Progress* (Cambridge, 1961), 13-38. For the New York experience see Roy Lubove, *The Progressives and the Slums* (Pittsburgh, 1962); for Chicago, Edith Abbott and Sophonisba Breckinridge, *The Tenements of Chicago 1908-1935* (Chicago, 1936).

private money-making schools a number of the city's churches ran elementary schools, and the University of Pennsylvania continued to operate its academy.[16]

Although this collection of private schools offered a tolerable elementary education to artisans' and shopkeepers' children, many of the poor lived beyond these schools' reach. Both the Pennsylvania Constitutions of 1776 and 1790 had called for the state to establish free education for poor children, but rural and religious prejudice and the selfish outlook of taxpayers had forestalled action for many years. To meet the needs of the poor, Dr. Benjamin Rush (1745-1813), the Revolutionary leader, formed in 1790 a Society for the Establishment of Sunday Schools. The schools operated by his Society were not the later type of catechism schools, but were schools run on Sundays, a time when poor children were not working and therefore had time to learn to read and to write. Rush's poor schools found many imitators, the largest being the Philadelphia Society for the Free Instruction of Indigent Boys which had been formed by a junto of young clerks and shopkeepers.[17]

In 1802 Philadelphia educational reformers succeeded in getting the legislature to authorize Philadelphia County to pay tuition for children whose families had been certified by the assessors as too poor to pay the usual fees, but this pauper system never worked. Many families refused to accept the stigma of the certification process. Also, the system led to fraud. In one case the County Commissioners reported paying for the tuition of three hundred children when only thirty attended school.[18]

At about this time an English merchant and philanthropist who had retired to Philadelphia to participate in the new American republic brought an expert in the schooling of the poor from Paris to live and teach in the city. The expert was Joseph Neef (1770-1854), a disciple of the Swiss educational reformer Pestalozzi. Neef had been running a Pestalozzian school for orphans in Paris. After three years of preparation, of learning English and writing a book on the theory and practice of education, Neef and an assistant in

16. James P. Wickersham, *A History of Education in Pennsylvania* (Lancaster, 1886), 278-280.

17. Wickersham, *Education in Pennsylvania*, 261, 281-282; Scharf and Westcott, *History of Philadelphia*, III, 1924.

18. Scharf and Westcott, *History of Philadelphia*, III, 1924, 1926.

1809 opened a private boarding school for about one hundred boys on the banks of the Schuylkill, at the site of the later Fairmount waterworks. Historically, the importance of Neef's school lay in its early demonstration of alternative goals and methods of education to those adopted by the city's public and private schools.

Neef, an eighteenth-century romantic, stressed nature study, open-air classes, music, and oral instruction as devices to liberate the natural talent and interests of each child. Many of his techniques would be revived in the early twentieth century by the progressive school movement. Contemporary Philadelphia observers were wonderfully surprised to note that despite the unbusinesslike setting of Neef's school his pupils became lightning calculators and learned a great deal. Neef's secret does not seem to have been romanticism but rather warm personal contact between teacher and pupil, great variety of content, stress on self-discovery, boyish discipline, and the example of a teacher's enthusiasm for learning. His visitors saw none of this. Instead, like later Americans viewing progressive schools, they saw only the issue of discipline: The sentimental freedom of the child of nature versus the regular rows of children and the rods of the common schoolmaster. After four successful years training the children of wealthy Philadelphia families Neef moved his school farther into the country. The greater distance proved to be a mistake; he lost a good deal of his custom, and in 1816 was forced to start again in Louisville, Kentucky. Later he ran a famous school at the New Harmony experiment and successful schools in Ohio.[19]

As in the case of Bronson Alcott's radical school in Boston, the leaders of the city learned nothing from Neef's demonstration. They chose, as most Americans always have, the uniformity, the discipline, and the low-cost production methods that they themselves knew as children and which have characterized most of their adult lives.

Instead of Neef's methods the school reformers of Philadelphia decided to begin their public schools with the guidance of an English innovator, the inventor of the cheapest form of education ever

19. Joseph Neef, *Sketch of a Plan and a Method of Education Founded on an Analysis of the Human Faculties and Natural Reason: Suitable for the Offspring of a Free People, and for all Rational Beings* (Philadelphia, 1808), 6, 162, 165-166; Will S. Monroe, *History of the Pestalozzian Movement in the United States* (Syracuse, 1907), 61-107.

practiced. This beginning of public education in Philadelphia in 1818 opens a melancholy major theme in American educational history. The goals of democracy commit the nation to the task of educating all children; yet since elementary and secondary education do not inevitably create visible wealth and prosperity, the general public has always been reluctant to pay heavy taxes to support a good system of education. Assigned large numbers of children and insufficient funds, American educators have ever been prone to seek mass production methods with low per-unit costs.

Joseph Lancaster, (1778-1838) London Quaker, faced such modern problems, and found a modern solution. At the age of twenty he opened a school for poor children in his neighborhood. Since most of his pupils could pay nothing and Lancaster himself lacked a large fortune, he hit upon the idea of appointing his best students as monitors to instruct the rest. In time he devised a special classroom architecture which made it possible for one teacher to supervise one thousand children in a single classroom. In the Lancastrian room there were three classes, each subdivided into three groups. These nine groups moved simultaneously in production line rotation: first they formed into semicircles for recitation, then they moved into banks of desks for written work; then they passed to a rear gallery for group instruction; then back to the recitation semicircles, the desks, and so forth. At all times the three classes were supervised by student monitors; at all times their nine subdivisions filled the room's special instruction areas. The gratifying spectacle of hundreds of orderly pauper children receiving instruction at the cost of one large room and one school teacher's salary immediately captured the philanthropists' imagination. George III became a patron of Lancaster's school.[20] In 1818 Governor DeWitt Clinton in his inaugural speech to the New York legislature recommended New York City's Lancastrian schools to the state.

> Having participated in the first establishment of the Lancastrian system in this country, having carefully observed its progress, and witnessed its benefits, I can confidently recommend it as an invaluable improvement which by wonderful combination of economy in expense, and rapidity of instruction, has created a new era in education . . . As this system

---

20. *Dictionary of National Biography;* Joseph J. McCadden, "Joseph Lancaster and the Philadelphia Schools," *Pennsylvania History,* III, (October 1936), 225-239; Timothy L. Smith, "Protestant Schooling and American Nationality, 1800-1850," *Journal of American History,* LIII (March, 1967), 684-685.

operates with the same efficiency in education as labor-saving machinery does in the useful arts, it will be rapidly perceived that it is peculiarly adapted to this country.[21]

Lancaster was a visionary man, impressed with himself, whose successes made him very difficult for adults to deal with. He quarrelled with his supporters in England and in 1818 was sent by friends to America to attempt a fresh start. Meanwhile, a hard winter had jarred Philadelphia's leading citizens into taking steps to establish a permanent public school system.

The winter of 1816-17 had borne hard on Philadelphia's poor and, as often in the past, leading citizens formed a philanthropic society to give food and fuel to the needy. This group, however, did not stop at short-term measures, but determined to try to eliminate the enduring causes of such distress. Calling itself the Society for the Promotion of the Public Economy, it appointed a number of investigating committees. One dealt with education. Its chairman was Roberts Vaux (1786-1836), Quaker philanthropist, father of the later mayor Richard Vaux, and underwriter of a number of free infant schools. His committee, observing the lack of schooling among the destitute, concluded that universal education could be a powerful antidote to future poverty. His committee then examined existing charity schools in Philadelphia, including some using Lancastrian methods. It reported favorably on the system as the proper basis for public action.

Accordingly, the Society drew up the successful legislation of 1818 which authorized Philadelphia city and county to form one school district under a Board of Governors. This board received the essential power to use taxation to build school houses, train teachers, furnish textbooks, and give free education to indigent orphans or children of indigent parents. The ages to be taught were boys six to fourteen, girls five to thirteen. Although the state legislation of 1802 and 1809 had given Philadelphia authority to run charity schools, the unified district and systematic efforts of the Board of Governors begun in 1818 make this year the start of the city's public education system.[22]

In the fall of 1818, learning that Lancaster was in New York City, the Board invited him to come to Philadelphia to run a model

21. *Journal of the New York Senate and Assembly*, II (Albany, 1819), 903.
22. Wickersham, *Education in Pennsylvania*, 269, 286-287, 296.

school and to train other teachers in his methods. Lancaster accepted, and after a winter of bickering with the authorities he was fired in the spring of 1819. His teaching, however, had been successful and for the next thirteen years Philadelphia children continued to be instructed by his methods. Lancaster went on to Baltimore; then he accepted an invitation from Simon Bolívar to open a school in Venezuela which he tried for a year, and after drifting about he settled in Philadelphia once more. From 1834 until his death in 1838, he ran a private school in the city.[23]

Lancaster's system was clearly in the main current of American tradition. After some years of observing the experiment, however, the Philadelphia Board of Governors came to realize that their schools were mostly a system of military baby-sitting and very little was being learned. With the retirement in 1831 of the philanthropist and champion of Lancastrian methods, Roberts Vaux, from the presidency of the Board, the Lancastrian system was abolished and the city schools reverted to more intensive instruction by adult teachers.

From the 1818 Lancastrian school beginnings it took about twenty-five years before Philadelphia had established what would today be regarded as an approximation of a city-wide system of free public education. Irregular attendance by the children and enormous ungraded classes characterized the early years of Philadelphia's public schools. In 1819 the school district operated ten schools with as many teachers; 2,845 pupils attended that year. In 1834, the year the Pennsylvania legislature authorized all the state's cities and towns to establish general free education, Philadelphia had twenty public schools, thirty-one teachers, and 6,769 pupils. In fifteen years the pupil-teacher ratio had been reduced only from 285 to 218 pupils per teacher. Most of the primary classes were conducted in rented rooms scattered throughout the district.[24]

In this same year, 1834, the definitive statement of the goals of Philadelphia public education emerged from the campaign for statewide authorization for universal free tax-supported schools. Philadelphia educational reformers had led the campaign ever since 1827

23. Joseph J. McCadden, "Joseph Lancaster and Philadelphia," *Pennsylvania History,* IV (January, 1937), 6-20.

24. Samuel Breck, Diary 1838-1841, manuscript, Pennsylvania Historical Society, page 1; Wickersham, *Education in Pennsylvania,* 289.

when they formed the Pennsylvania Society for the Promotion of Public Schools.[25] One of their leaders, Samuel Breck (1771-1862), a lawyer and former Federalist Congressman, ran for state senator with the express purpose of proposing school legislation. His report for the Joint Committee on Education of the legislature was a classic statement of the union of privatism and equalitarianism which permanently set the goals of Philadelphia's and Pennsylvania's public schools.

> . . . your committee have taken care to exclude the word poor from the bill which will accompany this report, meaning to make the system general, that is to say, to form an educational association between the rich, the comparatively rich, and the destitute. Let them all fare alike in the primary schools, receive the same elementary instruction, imbibe the republican spirit and be animated by a feeling of perfect equality. In after life, he who is diligent at school will take his station accordingly, whether born to wealth or not. Common schools universally established will multiply the chances of success, perhaps brilliant success, among those who may otherwise forever continue ignorant. It is the duty of the State to promote and foster such establishments. That done, the career of each youth will depend upon himself. The State will have given the first impulse; good conduct and suitable application must do the rest. Among the indigent 'some flashing of a mounting genius' may be found; and among both rich and poor, in the course of nature, many no doubt will sink into mediocrity or beneath it. Yet let them all start with equal advantage, leaving no discrimination, then or thereafter, but such as study shall produce.[26]

Breck's report and bill were accepted almost unanimously. Free public education in Pennsylvania began that year. His statement of the goals of public schools was a brilliant condensation of Philadelphia's and America's tradition: the dramatic call for social equality, the fruition of the demands of Paine and the radicals of the Revolution; the total acceptance of a society of economic competition, a reiteration of the commercialism of Robert Morris and the moderates. The fusion of these two elements of the city's tradition into one program has ever since set the limits on the public schools of the city. This was the uniform culture of privatism which they must

25. Warren F. Hewitt, "Samuel Breck and the Pennsylvania School Law of 1834," *Pennsylvania History*, I (January, 1934), 63-75; Joseph J. McCadden, "Roberts Vaux and His Associates in the Pennsylvania Society for the Promotion of Public Schools," *Pennsylvania History*, III (January, 1936), 1-17.

26. Quoted in Wickersham, *Education in Pennsylvania*, 312.

teach. This same culture would also set a narrow budget within which the schools would have to operate.

Even after the successful state campaign of the 1830's public education came slowly to Pennsylvania. Philadelphia, however, remained the leader of the commonwealth. By dint of enormous effort over the next nine years the Board of Governors created a system which resembled a modern public school system. In 1843 the city ran 214 schools with 499 teachers and 33,130 pupils. This massive expansion brought the pupil-teacher ratio down to 66 children per teacher, with an average of 155 children per school. In that year there were still over two hundred rural school districts in Pennsylvania which, voting under the local option law of 1836, still refused to establish public schools.

Though in the 1840's Philadelphia's schools served as the model for the state they had yet to fully establish literacy in the city, or to reach all the poor. The 1850 U.S. Census revealed 15,186 adults in Philadelphia County who could not read or write in any language. Of these, 6,723 were native Americans, 8,463 foreign born. Also, since education was not compulsory many children stayed away. In 1867 the police took a census of the city's children only to discover that there were twenty thousand boys and girls age six to eighteen who were neither employed nor attending school. Finally, as in the case of the watering committee after the 1840's there appeared to have been a decline in the quality of leadership in public education. The Board failed to keep pace with the enormous growth of the city so that by 1883 it was attempting to educate 170,948 children with a load of seventy-eight pupils per teacher.[27]

Although the public education system of Philadelphia began to falter in the 1840's, private education continued to expand and to elaborate. By 1860 Philadelphia displayed the characteristic institutional division of educational effort which has marked the city and all other large American cities ever since. Private religious and secular schools multiplied. The Society of Friends established a number of new academies[28] and the Catholic Church tried to keep up with the demand for parochial schools and priests to serve the incoming

27. Scharf and Westcott, *History of Philadelphia*, III, 1934; Wickersham, *Education in Pennsylvania*, 289.

28. Friends Central 1845, Germantown Friends 1845, Greene Street Friends 1855.

waves of Irish and German immigrants and their children.[29] Private
teachers continued to found schools, but most of these were imper-
manent affairs lasting the lifetime or career of one or two teachers.
In general, these schools merely maintained or expanded a little the
old traditions of private, genteel education. They constituted a continuing parallel private network alongside the giant innovation of
public education.[30]

More important for the economic and cultural growth of the
city were the successive private innovations in advanced and technical education. In this case the public effort was the dwarf, the private effort the giant. The City Normal School, continued from
Lancaster's day, and the High School (1838) represent the sum of
the public effort. In contrast, the private technical and professional
schools of Philadelphia present a story of half a century of successful
innovation. In 1800 the old American Philosophical Society (1743)
and the University of Pennsylvania stood alone. In 1805 the Pennsylvania Academy of the Fine Arts was founded, and in 1812 the
Academy of Natural Sciences. In 1821 the Philadelphia College of
Pharmacy was established. In 1824 a group of artisans and young
businessmen consciously following the traditions of the eighteenth
century founded the Franklin Institute of the State of Pennsylvania
for the Promotion of the Mechanic Arts. A model for many later
institutions, it presented public lectures, held exhibits and competi-
tions for new inventions, built a library and laboratories, taught
classes in drafting, and in time published a research bulletin. The
scientific departments of the University of Pennsylvania grew directly from this pioneer applied-science institute,[31] and so did the
Philadelphia School of Design for Women (1844), now the Moore
Institute of Art and Science, and the Fels Planetarium (1933).

A split among the medical practitioners of Philadelphia resulted in the Jefferson Medical College (1825). In 1850, in response
to the movement for the emancipation of women, a number of
doctors joined together to establish the Women's Medical College of

29. Most notable as continuing institutions were the Theological Seminary of St.
Charles Borromeo, Overbrook 1832, Mt. St. Joseph, Chestnut Hill (now Chestnut Hill
Academy for Girls), 1858, St. Joseph's College 1851, and Villanova University, 1842.

30. Wickersham, *Education in Pennsylvania*, 484-485; Scharf and Westcott, *History of
Philadelphia*, III, 1949-1954.

31. Wickersham, *Education in Pennsylvania*, 430.

Philadelphia, the only enduring institution of its kind in the country. Reflecting the enormous growth of mechanical industries in Philadelphia and sustained public interest in such subjects, three more institutions came into being in the 1850's. Two of them, the Spring Garden Institute (1850) and the Wagner Free Institute of Science (1852), offered public lectures on science and both have continued to this day. The Spring Garden Institute maintained a training program in mechanical drawing and tool design in addition to the usual lyceum functions. In 1853 Dr. Alfred L. Kennedy, after viewing European schools, established his ambitious Polytechnic College of Pennsylvania, hoping to create a permanent technical college. He set up a state-wide board of trustees, but his effort was premature, and it died with him. Finally in response to the business patterns of the modern city, commercial colleges opened: Crittenden Commercial College (1844-1884), and Bryant and Stratton Business College (1857-   ).[32]

The consequences for the city of these early nineteenth-century institutional arrangements are clear enough. By the division of labor between private and public, private institutions preempted the role of innovation and preempted the fields of advanced and specialized education. Public institutions, on the other hand, were not expected to be innovators; rather the city depended upon them for mass low-cost education. Rigid uniformity, poor quality, and lack of inventiveness inevitably followed. This unending poverty of the public educational system meant a massive waste of the city's human resources. Year after year the city's schools saved the taxpayers' money while spending the human potential of their children with a prodigal hand.

The mass system of the public schools proved to be too cumbersome to fit the variety of human nature with which it had to deal. As the nineteenth century progressed, the problem of the unresponsiveness of the schools in respect to their pupils grew more and more serious because schools became more inclusive, and education more ambitious. Free primary education waxed to compulsory primary education in 1895, and in the twentieth century compulsory pri-

32. Wickersham, *Education in Pennsylvania*, 434-441; and there was a parallel growth of private libraries in the city, Lloyd P. Smith,"Public Libraries of Philadelphia," U.S. Department of Education, *Public Libraries of the United States of America*, pt. I (Washington, 1876), 952-977.

mary education waxed into near-compulsory twelve years of school. As the system reached down into the lower classes of Philadelphia and attempted to hold all pupils longer, its inherent rigidities became increasingly serious disorders. By the end of the nineteenth century these rigidities constituted major obstacles to the education of children.

For example, grades, a step toward better supervision of the large ungraded rooms of the early nineteenth century, proved to have an unfortunate consequence. They generated an annual pacing of children's learning in which the children of the city moved like biscuits through an automatic oven in batches of fifty. Together with the classroom the grades proved most effective in teaching the majority of the pupils the habits of office and industrial discipline they would need in later life. As environments for encouraging individual learning, or encouraging mastery of subject matter, this mass pacing can only be defended as a compromise required by economy of production.[33]

In the early twentieth century a unique confluence of events gave the city's public schools a moment when they could have begun to break out of the mold of uniform mass education by running a variety of elementary and secondary schools within the one system. In the years after World War I there was an oversupply of women candidates for teaching positions. The downtown businessmen, especially the Chamber of Commerce, fearful of alien radicalism vigorously supported programs for Americanization. The political bosses of the city, though requiring that new municipal programs be introduced in such a way that each ward they controlled got something, were not opposed to schools. In the 1920's, therefore, there was the possibility that the abundance of manpower, and the special interests of business and bosses could be brought together for an ambitious educational expansion. At .this very moment the Progressive education movement gave the Superintendent and his teachers the motive to try new kinds of schools and new kinds of classrooms.[34]

33. The tension in the 1850's between decent sized classrooms and mass education is nicely demonstrated in, "Samuel Sloane and the 'Philadelphia Plan'," *Journal of the Society of Architectural Historians,* XXIII (October, 1964), 151-154.

34. Oversupply of women candidates for teaching positions, *Annual Report of the Superintendent of Schools for the Year Ending June, 1928* (Philadelphia, 1928), 22; Philadelphia Chamber of Commerce, Americanization Committee, *Americanization in Philadelphia* (Philadelphia, 1923); just before World War I the bosses, educational

Spurred by these events, Philadelphia's schools attempted to become truly universal. Night classes were offered for drop-outs; Navy Yard apprentices were given English and mathematics on the job; night Americanization classes met for immigrants; special programs went forward at the Art Museum; the district high schools fielded a full array of teams for the new school stadia, and for the sick and handicapped there were fresh-air schools and many special programs. The Superintendent of Schools, Edwin C. Broome (1874-1950), prided himself on his system's wide reach.[35] He also repeatedly stressed that within the regular classrooms the goal was to educate each individual child to his own capacity, not just to carry classes of children through an acculturation mill which would enable them to compete reasonably successfully in the adult economic world. This latter goal he could not fulfill.[36]

The habits of the city and its educational system had too long been set in the low-level equalitarian and commercial mold into which the reformers of the 1830's had first cast it. Superintendent Broome could not generate the financial and cultural support necessary even to begin to build a truly flexible system of public education which would train each child to the limit of his own abilities. He could not even keep pace with his modest goal of building enough schools so that every child in Philadelphia would be taught in a room of fifty or less pupils.

The failure of Broome's fifty-seat classroom program and the scale of the physical plant of the Philadelphia public schools expressed the system's rigidity. In the 1920's the public schools handled about 300,000 pupils a year in school units which averaged 4,000 for high schools, and 1,300 for elementary schools.[37] Though

reformers, and the superintendent joined forces to push through a program for district high schools and to destroy the special position of the elite college preparatory Central High School, William H. Cornog, *School of the Republic; A Half Century of the Central High School of Philadelphia* (Philadelphia, 1952), 224-232. The case is a fascinating example of problems of maintaining a variety of institutions in an equalitarian school system.

35. Broome, a Columbia University Ph.D. had been superintendent of schools at Mt. Vernon, New York 1909-1913, and at East Orange, N.J. 1913-1921 before coming to Philadelphia. He was superintendent in Philadelphia from 1921 to 1938.

36. Spread of school activities, *Annual Report of the Superintendent* . . . 1925 (Philadelphia, 1925) 17-102; the superintendent's philosophy, "Expression vs. Repression," *Annual Report of the Superintendent* . . . 1927 (Philadelphia, 1927), 5-7, 20.

37. *Annual Report of the Superintendent of Schools* . . . 1925 (Philadelphia, 1925), 11; in 1929 the system was still struggling to get all classes below fifty pupils per class, *Annual Report of the Superintendent* . . . 1929 (Philadelphia, 1929), 30.

within these schools there were four different tracks for students to pass along—college, general, commercial, and industrial—and some special classes, the buildings, tracks, and classes of the public schools appear limited indeed when compared to the private possibilities of the same era.

The *haut bourgeois* of Philadelphia, like their counterparts in all Eastern cities, have never accepted the mass-production economy education of the public schools. They have continually maintained and expanded their private school network to get just that variety of education and individualized pace which has been denied the majority. In the 1920's for private pupils there were small neighborhood nursery schools, kindergartens, and elementary schools, in-town elementary and secondary day schools, schools for boys, schools for girls, country day schools, coeducational schools, day and boarding English-style schools, progressive schools, parochial schools, military schools, and more besides for children with special problems. By contrast, when some of his teachers tried to imitate a then fashionable experiment in self-directed education at the South Philadelphia School for Girls, Superintendent Broome could not even back them up with the changes in rooms and teaching assignments they would have needed to continue the program.[38] It is an unpleasant irony of the history of Philadelphia and of the nation's other cities that such class variations in opportunities for education were the very evils which the Philadelphia school reformers of the early nineteenth century hoped to avoid.

38. Faculty of the South Philadelphia High School for Girls, *Educating for Responsibility, the Dalton Laboratory Plan in Secondary School* (Philadelphia, 1926), ix-6, 24-33.

7

Riots and the Restoration of Public Order

The successive riots from 1834 to 1849 show in a series of brief dramatic episodes the interaction of most of the important elements of the big-city era: industrialization, immigration, mixed patterns of settlement, changing styles of leadership, weakness of municipal institutions, and shifting orientations of politics. The series of riots that began in 1834 rose in intensity to a peak of violence in 1844 and then abated as organized politics assumed the place of fragmentary outbursts of frustration, prejudice, and anger. These outbursts both locate the stresses of the period and offer a crude measure of public attitudes. They are thus an important record and summary of the transitions of the first big-city era.

The occasions for rioting, the composition of the mobs, and the targets for attack shifted frequently. The series opened with an attack upon Negroes and fights between Whigs and Democrats; then abolitionists, non-strikers, and finally Irish Catholics were singled out. Each riot of the series thus records the shifting groups who felt threatened by the changes of rapid growth and industrialization. Because no large body of professional police existed to quell the mobs, each riot also forced many of Philadelphia's leaders and ordinary citizens to show their feelings toward the rioters and the victims. Major riots which imperiled many lives and substantial property, often for days at a time, pressed every class and ethnic group into some kind of action—as members of militia troops or fire companies, as deputies in the sheriff's posse, as municipal officials, or as sullen, cheering, or disapproving onlookers.

Before 1834 the city had known election-day disorders, Protestant-Catholic Irish brawling, and sporadic harassment of Negroes.[1] But the anti-Negro fracas of August 1834 took on a special significance because it was the first in a series of riots of ascending violence and duration. In respect to Negro caste practices, Philadelphia was a southern city. It had many trade connections to the South and the customs of the adjacent slave states of Maryland and Delaware seem to have influenced Philadelphians. With the exception of four Friends Meetings and one Unitarian church, the city's congregations steadfastly avoided the slavery issue.[2]

Philadelphia Negroes "knew their place." In the eighteenth century they had been relegated to special galleries in the Methodist churches, but over the years segregation within church buildings had given way to segregated churches and segregated missions and segregated Sunday schools. Although several thousand Negroes were scattered throughout the city as domestic servants in white families, the bulk of Philadelphia's Negroes in 1830 lived in a shanty town on the south side of the city in the Cedar, Locust, New Market and Pine wards of Philadelphia and adjacent Moyamensing and Southwark. (Table X). The location of this ghetto proved unfortunate. It straddled the municipal boundaries of Philadelphia, Moyamensing, and Southwark. Thus when trouble broke out in one part of the ghetto, the watchmen and constables of all three jurisdictions were slow to arrive, presumably excusing themselves on the basis of

1. Riot on Fifth street near Walnut, Philadelphia Mayor's Court, *A Full Report on the Trial for Riot . . . on the Thirteenth of October, 1831 Arising Out of a Protestant Procession on the Twelfth of July* . . . (Philadelphia, 1831). Fire companies were often organized around Orange and Green gangs, which then used the occasion of fires for brawling.

2. Elizabeth M. Geffen, "Philadelphia Protestantism Reacts to Social Reform Movements Before the Civil War," *Pennsylvania History*, XXX (April, 1963), 192-202. It is sometimes said, without justice, that Philadelphia's racial attitudes were caused by large proportions of Southerners living in the city. The 1850 statistics show the leading birthplaces of native-born Philadelphians to have been as follows: Pennsylvania 242,681, New Jersey 15,570, Delaware 8,678, Maryland 5,760, New York 4,858, Virginia 2,602. This same year there were 121,699 foreign-born in a total population of 408,762 (1854 city boundaries). Thirty-third Congress, 2nd session, House of Representatives, *Executive Document #98, Mortality Statistics of the Seventh Census of the U.S.* (Washington, 1855), 41-42.

the confused boundaries within the ghetto. Neither Philadelphia, nor Southwark or Moyamensing had police in the modern sense; yet even by 1830 standards the south Philadelphia Negro ghetto was ill-protected.[3]

TABLE X

PHILADELPHIA WHITES AND NEGROES IN 1830

Ward or District	Whites	Slaves	Free Negroes	Total
Cedar	5,110		1,212	6,322
Chestnut	3,881		234	4,115
High Street	4,235	1	191	4,427
Locust	5,404	1	1,711	7,116
Dock	4,689		689	5,378
Lower Delaware	6,566	2	295	6,863
Middle	3,378		254	3,632
New Market	5,568	1	1,875	7,444
North	5,371	2	418	5,791
N. Mulberry	5,514		219	5,805
Pine	4,510	3	1,027	5,540
South	3,017		449	3,466
S. Mulberry	4,843		529	5,372
Upper Delaware	5,482	1	280	5,763
Walnut	3,088		340	3,428
Sub-Total, City of Philadelphia	70,656	11	9,795	80,462
Kensington	13,171		223	13,394
Moyamensing	5,171		1,651	6,822
Northern Liberties	27,868	2	1,002	28,872
Spring Garden	10,707		433	11,140
Southwark	19,225		1,356	20,581
Total, Philadelphia & Suburbs	146,798	13	14,460	161,271

Source:

   U.S. Fifth Census: 1830 (Duff Green, 1832), 64-65.

   3. Sixty-one percent of the city's 14,473 Negroes lived in the Cedar, Locust, New Market, and Pine wards of Philadelphia and the adjacent districts of Southwark and Moyamensing. The poorest Negroes lived in a core ghetto bounded by Pine, Fitzwater, Fifth and Tenth streets. The adjacent Pine ward was the tough tavern district of Philadelphia. Philadelphia Society of Friends, A Statistical Inquiry into the Condition of the People of Color (Philadelphia, 1849), 6, 31-41. The best general accounts of Negro life and conditions are: Edward R. Turner, The Negro in Pennsylvania (Washington, 1911), 109-205; Leon F. Litwack, North of Slavery: The Negro in the Free States, 1790-1860 (Chicago, 1961).

The bombardment of Philadelphia with abolitionist propaganda and southern protests during the years 1831-1833 pinpointed the Negro ghetto as a target for socially acceptable violence.[4] The anxious avoidance of all slavery issues by Philadelphia churches and the attacks by leading citizens upon abolitionists as subversives revealed the strength and popularity of caste feelings among most white citizens.

In August 1834, someone set up a carrousel in a vacant building on the edge of the Negro ghetto on South Street near Seventh. On Monday night, the eleventh, some whites and Negroes got into an argument which apparently came to a quick end. The next day, however, a rumor spread through some taverns and gangs that whites had been insulted by Negroes. On Tuesday night, the twelfth, a large group of toughs descended on the carrousel, began fighting with those there, presumably both whites and Negroes, and ended their evening's pleasure by totally wrecking the carrousel. No watchman or constable appeared on either night, so the gang went home unmolested.

Who and what transformed one night's fist fight and a second night's brawl into a full-fledged race riot remains unclear.[5] The next evening, large numbers of boys and young men armed with sticks and clubs assembled on Seventh Street near the downtown. They marched down Seventh to a vacant lot on the edge of the ghetto. From here they moved across the city line into the alleys of the Moyamensing quarter, smashing windows, breaking down doors, throwing furniture into the street, and mercilessly beating any stray

4. William Lloyd Garrison's *Liberator* first appeared in January 1831. By the end of 1831 the New England Anti-Slavery Society had been founded and southern congressmen were protesting abolitionist attacks on the slave trade in Washington, D.C. In October 1833 the New York Anti-Slavery Society was founded, and on December 4, 1833, Garrison of Boston, Arthur Tappan of New York, Benjamin Lundy of Baltimore, and fifty other delegates met in Philadelphia to found the American Anti-Slavery Society. Some of these delegates were Negroes. Earliest attacks on Negroes, William E. B. DuBois, *The Philadelphia Negro* (Philadelphia, 1899), 26-29.

5. J. Thomas Scharf and Thompson Westcott, *History of Philadelphia*, I, 637. Scharf and Westcott give complete but often over-dramatic accounts of all the city riots. Their details sometimes vary with newspaper accounts. Westcott was until 1846, when he joined the *Public Ledger*, practicing law and writing occasional pieces for newspapers and magazines. In 1844 he ran unsuccessfully for the state Assembly as a Native American, *Public Ledger*, October 10, 1844. I have tried to check Westcott's accounts with those of the *Public Ledger* and where there is conflict I have followed the *Ledger* or sources other than Westcott.

Negro they caught. The Moyamensing watch was helpless. The mayor of Philadelphia, John Swift, the city constables, and a large body of the city's watchmen arrived and charged the rioters, taking twenty prisoners and dispersing the mob which was apparently small by comparison to later riots. Curiously enough, the whites of the area protected themselves by lighting candles in their windows. This response seems to have been a folk continuation of the custom of the days of the Revolution when Philadelphians lit candles in their windows to celebrate the Continental victories while gangs roamed the streets smashing the dark windows of the disapproving Quakers.[6]

The next and final night of the riots (Thursday, August 14) the mayor of Philadelphia assembled at 8 o'clock on the Seventh Street vacant lot two troops of militia and a posse of three hundred freshly sworn constables. Soon a rumor reached him that an attack would be made on the African Grand Lodge of Masons Hall a few blocks to the south. The mayor's men marched down Seventh Street to South Street to find a crowd of armed Negroes on one side of the street and a threatening crowd of whites facing them from across the way. The mayor addressed the crowd which then slowly dispersed. Meanwhile, farther to the south, a crowd gathered before a small Negro church which it had threatened the night before, and acting on the rumor that shots had been fired from the church at two white boys, they pulled the church to the ground. When the mayor's forces arrived at the scene no one remained on the street. At midnight the posse and militia retired and no further rioting broke out.

Despite the inevitable slowness and inefficiency of a mixed force composed of a citizen-posse, militia, and a band of watchmen, the police power of the city bore more strongly and effectively upon these first riots than on any that followed in the decade of violence. The number of active rioters must have been few; city-wide support for the rioters seems not to have manifested itself, and even in the immediate neighborhood, composed as it was of artisans and unskilled workers, most of the citizens seem to have remained in their houses rather than pouring out onto the streets. Moreover, there were none of the incidents of incendiarism or the direct attacks upon the mayor and posse which typified later outbreaks.[7]

6. The custom of lighting candles as protection against a mob was also followed in eighteenth-century London.

7. Scharf and Westcott, *History of Philadelphia*, I, 637-638.

The following autumn, on the night of October 14, a southside election riot raised the level of violence to a new pitch. In the evening's fighting between the Democratic supporters of Congressman Joel Barlow Sutherland and the attacking Whigs, guns were used, one man killed, and fifteen to twenty wounded (Chapter V). The Moyamensing authorities made no attempt at restoring order. After the volunteer fire companies had been driven off by the mob, six buildings burned all night with no further attempts to extinguish the flames. The mob was left at the scene to disperse at its own pleasure.

During the next two years the Negro ghetto suffered some minor violence, but the attentions of the city were caught up with the great Ten-Hour movement of 1835-1836. Except for some fighting between dockworkers and scabs in the first strike, the movement swept forward by repeated successful strikes and workers' parades all of which were peaceable. Boom times made concessions to workers easy, while Jackson's war with the U.S. Bank held Philadelphians to their traditional political arguments over privilege and egalitarian democracy. On July 14, 1835, Mayor Swift had to assemble a large group of watchmen to protect the ghetto when news of a Negro apprentice's murder of his white master broke in the newspapers. In this case the fire companies fought their way through the gangs of toughs to put out the fires that had been set.[8]

Unfortunately for the city's later peace, the next month some of the young business leaders of the city gave notice to the general public of their approval of anti-Negro, anti-abolitionist feelings. Since a December 1833 meeting in Philadelphia at which the American Anti-Slavery Society had been formed, the city's abolitionists had grown increasingly active. Southerners had reacted violently against circulation of anti-slavery tracts in the South, and in Congress southerners protested abolitionists' petitions for the halting of the slave trade in Washington, D.C. To allay the fears of Philadelphia's southern customers, a town meeting had been organized on August 24, 1835. A popular young playwright, journalist, and lawyer, Joseph T. Conrad, led the assembly. After speeches condemning the "incendiarism" of the abolitionists, resolutions were

---

8. Scharf and Westcott, *History of Philadelphia*, I, 641-642.

passed opposing the formation of abolition societies and the circulation of abolitionist tracts as threatening the peace and harmony of
the nation.[9]

The next day, longshoremen accidentally broke open a box
bulging with abolition literature. Conrad and the officer's of the
town meeting called on the addressee, who denied any knowledge of
the shipment or its contents. The officers then went to the pier,
loaded the box upon a small boat, and, with official decorum, sank
the box in the middle of the Delaware River. The next day, newspaper reports were highly approving. The next year, young Conrad
was appointed judge in the Philadelphia Court of Criminal Sessions.
Twenty years later Judge Conrad was to be elected as a nativist
mayor of the consolidated City of Philadelphia.

Abolitionism in Philadelphia, however, continued to grow.
The following year Benjamin Lundy moved from Baltimore to
begin publishing in Philadelphia his *National Enquirer* (August,
1836). Philadelphians began to organize the state. In the city they
announced boycotts of merchants carrying southern goods, and set
up "free goods" stores of their own.[10]

Aside from disrupting the customary modes of Philadelphia's
business and politics, abolitionism was a constant threat to the city's
caste lines. Many of the early abolitionists went beyond political
philanthropy. Wanting more than to help the Negro gain his freedom and political rights, they practiced integration. Also, the abolition movement captured the imagination of women; indeed, in this
campaign, women appeared for the first time in public as political
activists, circulating petitions from door to door, attending meetings, and even addressing all-male audiences. It is not hard today
after the recent years of civil rights struggles in the North and South
to imagine the intensity of feeling which accompanied these depar-
tures from centuries of established custom.

Philadelphia's abolitionists first gathered at the Friends meeting houses on the north side of the city in the prosperous working-
class and middle-class wards west of Third Street and north of Market Street. Every assemblage was a threat to the established norms of
the city and the neighborhood. Women like Philadelphia's Lucretia

9. Scharf and Westcott, *History of Philadelphia*, I, 642.
10. *National Enquirer*, August 24, October 22, November 26, 1836, March 18, 1837.

Mott addressed mixed audiences of whites and Negroes, men and women, while the easy social interaction of the races deeply offended the caste sentiments of the city.

In the winter and spring of 1837 the social tensions of the city began to rise as a severe depression wiped out the gains of the previous boom and Ten-Hour movement. There was unemployment in the winter and news of demonstrations and bread riots in New York. In March the price of cotton fell by half at New Orleans, and in May the banks of Philadelphia, New York, Boston, and Baltimore stopped making specie payments. A hard, worldwide, six-year depression set in. In March and April, Mayor Swift twice had to defend the Negro ghetto. In the second outbreak, the members of the Robert Morris Hose Company of Moyamensing were identified as participants in the attack on the blacks. Their action was an ominous sign of a transition of these important clubs of unskilled workers and artisans from defenders of the public order to sympathizers with the attackers—or attackers themselves—of the city's scapegoats.[11] During the summer of 1837 the Pennsylvania Constitutional Convention deliberated in Philadelphia. This convention altered the customs of the state so as to exclude Negroes from voting.

The burning of the abolitionists' hall the following spring showed the effects of a year's weakening of the city's defenses for public order. Because Philadelphia's abolitionists often had trouble hiring halls for their meetings, and they wanted to publicize their cause, they formed a joint stock company to build a hall of their own. This was to be Pennsylvania Hall. The project was a large and ambitious one, intended to serve as the headquarters for publishing newspapers and tracts, as well as to provide a hall for abolitionist, temperance, and lyceum meetings. The managers chose a good site, Sixth Street near Franklin Square, on the north side of the downtown next to the settlements of heaviest support for the abolition movement. While construction was underway there had been some mutterings about such a building's disgracing the city, but no incidents occurred.[12]

11. *National Enquirer*, March 18, May 6, 1837.
12. For a general account of the burning of Pennsylvania Hall I have relied upon the stories published in the *Public Ledger*, May 18, 19, 21, and the official report of the Police Committee of the Common Council published July 18, 1838. The *Ledger*

To celebrate the opening of the hall such national abolition leaders as William Lloyd Garrison, Angelina and Sarah Grimke, and Mrs. Maria Chapman came to Philadelphia to participate in a three-day series of meetings. The newspapers on Monday, May 14, 1838, carried advertisements announcing the program and listing the temperance, women's rights, and lyceum lectures and meetings which were to be interspersed with the abolitionist assemblies.

Monday and Tuesday passed without incident. The mayor, at the request of the managers of the hall, had assigned two members of the watch to stand at the doorway to prevent small boys from running in and out and making noise during the meetings. The fashionable lawyer David Paul Brown delivered a dedicatory oration which was so mild and equivocal on the issue of abolition that it offended many in the audience. The streets next to the hall were crowded during the day with those attending the lectures and many curious Philadelphians who had come to see the newest and largest hall in the city.

On Tuesday night an unidentified group posted placards throughout the city calling for a mob to assemble before Pennsylvania Hall the next evening. The placards read in part:

> A convention to effect the immediate emancipation of the slaves throughout the country is in session in this city, and it is the duty of citizens who entertain a proper respect for the Constitution of the Union and the right of property to interfere.[13]

On Wednesday evening, the 16th, Angelina M. Grimke addressed the national delegates of the Female Anti-Slavery Society. An opposition crowd of unknown size apparently gathered slowly. Some moved into the back of the hall to hiss the speaker; outside, others threw stones through the windows. The Mayor was not in his office at the time and there were only two watchmen on duty in the hall. For some unknown reason the attackers dispersed of their own accord. The audience, mostly women, had been frightened, how-

---

was the city's largest penny daily and was non-partisan. Its steady tone lends credibility to its accounts. A brief comment on its history, Elwyn B. Robinson, "The Public Ledger: An Independent Newspaper," *Pennsylvania Magazine*, LXIV (January, 1940), 43-55. There is also useful comment on the city's attitude toward abolition and Negroes in William Dusinberre, *Civil War Issues in Philadelphia 1856-1865* (Philadelphia, 1965). These riots are recounted in somewhat different form than I have given in Scharf and Westcott, *History of Philadelphia*, I, 651-652.

13. Quoted in Scharf and Westcott, *History of Philadelphia*, I, 651.

ever, so the program was cut short and the meeting closed early. No further incidents occurred that night.[14]

On Thursday, the managers of the hall called on the mayor to request protection for their meetings. Mayor Swift urged them to close the hall for a few days, saying he lacked the legal power and police force necessary to protect them. The managers at first insisted upon continuing their meetings, but in the late afternoon, observing a crowd of men and boys gathering outside the hall, they decided to cancel the evening program of the Methodist Anti-Slavery Society. They summoned the Mayor and gave him the keys. Mayor Swift then stepped outside to deal with the crowd. He arrested one man who was haranguing the group and asked the crowd to disperse. After applause they began to move off and the Mayor returned to his office. The managers were especially instructed by the mayor to post people some distance from the hall to turn back any Negroes who might be coming to the cancelled meeting.

At nightfall a crowd poured into the neighborhood filling the streets and alleys around the hall. By 10 o'clock, the crowd was estimated at three thousand. The street lights were extinguished, the doors of the hall battered down, the blinds broken up, the gas turned on, and the fire set. When the mayor arrived with a crew of watchmen he shouted for the support of the law, but the crowd only parted sullenly to let him through. On the first floor some of the crowd were throwing abolitionist books and literature into the street. When the volunteer fire companies arrived they restricted their work to wetting down adjacent buildings. The evidence is not clear as to whether the firemen refused to fight the blaze or whether they feared the anger of the mob if they tried to put it out. In any event, Pennsylvania Hall burned undisturbed and was completely destroyed. For several years its charred ruins stood as a monument to Philadelphia's racial prejudice and political weakness.[15]

The next evening, Friday night, the Mayor had taken no special precautions against rioting. A small crowd attacked the Friends

14. The most information on this Wednesday evening May 16 molestation appears in the Police Committee investigation, *Public Ledger*, July 18, 1838.

15. The *Ledger's* account of May 18 strongly suggests that the fire companies were happy to see the hall burn. The official report puts the blame on the crowd, saying that this was the first time in remembrance that the firemen "whose zeal and undaunted courage have long been the boast of our city" failed to play upon a fire. *Public Ledger*, July 18, 1838.

TABLE XI

APPROXIMATE LOCATION OF MAJOR OCCUPATIONS BY CORE AND RING, 1840

Core		Ring						All Philadelphia	
Old City	%	South	%	Northeast	%	Northwest	%	Core & Ring	%
Merchant	13.3	Female, o.n.s.	9.7	Cordwainer	6.6	Carpenter	11.7	Female, o.n.s.	6.6
Female, o.n.s.	5.6	Laborer	6.5	Carpenter	4.9	Laborer	7.4	Merchant	6.0
Gentleman	3.4	Shoemaker	4.1	Grocer	4.5	Female, o.n.s.	5.3	Laborer	4.5
Grocer	2.9	Tavern	3.7	Female, o.n.s.	4.1	Merchant	5.3	Carpenter	3.9
Male, o.n.s.	2.9	Grocer	3.2	Laborer	4.1	Victualler	5.3	Cordwainer	3.5
Dry Goods	2.1	Male, o.n.s.	3.2	Male, o.n.s.	2.9			Male, o.n.s.	3.4
Laborer	2.1	Carpenter	2.8	Weaver	2.9			Grocer	3.3
Attorney	1.9	Cordwainer	2.8	Tavern	2.5			Gentleman	2.1
Carpenter	1.9	Tailor	2.8	Cabinetmaker	2.1			Tailor	1.9
Cordwainer	1.9	Weaver	2.8	Morocco Dr.	2.1			Carter	1.8
M.D.	1.9	Carter	2.3	Tailor	2.1			Tavern	1.8
Tailor	1.9			Tobacconist	2.1			Shoemaker	1.6
Boardinghouse	1.6							Weaver	1.6
Shoemaker	1.3							Cabinetmaker	1.2
								Dry Goods	1.1
								M.D.	0.9
								Victualler	0.9
								Boardinghouse	0.8
								Tobacconist	0.7
								Attorney	0.6
								Morocco Dr.	0.4
Major Occupations	44.7	Major Occupations	43.9	Major Occupations	40.9	Major Occupations	35.0	Major Occupations	48.6
Other Occupations No. in	55.3	Other Occupations No. in	56.1	Other Occupations No. in	59.1	Other Occupations No. in	65.0	Other Occupations No. in	51.4
Sample	377	Sample	217	Sample	243	Sample	94	Sample	1,126

Shelter for Colored Orphans on Thirteenth Street near Callowhill. Here they were in the heart of the abolitionist section, the Spring Garden, native-American and German, skilled-artisan, merchant and shopkeeper northwest district (Table XI). The previous night's mob may well have frightened the neighborhood. The attackers broke into the building and set it afire, and then, when the Good Will Fire Company arrived, the attackers stood between the fire company and the building. At this moment the local police magistrate, Morton McMichael, rallied the firemen and with another citizen and the chief engineer of the company led a charge which drove off the arsonists and the orphanage was saved.

On Saturday, May 19th, the *Public Ledger,* the city's penny daily, published an editorial condemning these mob attacks. This condemnation by the newspaper so offended some that for several days a large detachment of constables had to be posted to protect the *Ledger's* downtown office at Second and Dock streets. Saturday night, too, Mayor Swift, all Philadelphia's watch and constables, and several troops of militia spent a busy night patrolling the city. They arrested a group of men attacking a Negro church, and several times arrested bystanders who jeered at the officers.

In a long editorial on Monday, May 21, the *Public Ledger* reviewed the previous days' riots and disturbances. It concluded that the fault lay with the Mayor, who had been so slow to take action. Why had the Mayor not called out the militia to protect Pennsylvania Hall? The year before, the editor noted, Swift had called out the troops to protect the banks when they were refusing to pay their notes in specie.

The slowness of the Mayor to make preparations, despite the advance notice of the placards and the previous evening's disturbance was part of the ambivalence caused by the deep prejudice of the day. Such ambivalence about violence against Negroes and abolitionists crept into the thinking of all Philadelphians on the subject. A few weeks later the city councils ordered the committee on police to investigate the affair. This committee's report, given July 5, 1838, expressed the city's conflict between desire for order and antipathy for violation of its caste rules.

> However much it may be a subject of regret to this Committee, it can be
> no matter of surprise to them, that the mass of the community, without
> distinction of political or religious opinions, could ill brook the erection

of an edifice in this city, for the encouragement of practices believed by many to be subversive of the established orders of society, and even viewed by some as repugnant to that separation and distinction which it has pleased the great Author of nature to establish among the various races of man . . . perhaps, even, if the active participation in this dedicatory celebration had been confined to residents of our own city, well known, and endeared to many by private wealth and respectable character, the feelings of those opposed to them in opinion, might have been repressed by the general regard of the community; but when it was found that our city had been selected as a rallying point of men known among us only as restless agitators and disturbers of the peace elsewhere; and when on the arrival of these strangers in Philadelphia, and during their sojourn here, our streets presented, for the first time since the days of William Penn, the unusual union of black and white walking arm in arm in social intercourse it is a matter of no great surprise, however it should be of deep reprobation, that any individuals should have so far forgotten what was due the character of the city, and to the supremacy of the law, as publicly to give vent to that indignation which ought never to have been felt, or if felt, should have been repressed within their bosoms.[16]

For the next four years the city remained relatively quiet, falling back upon a regular pattern of fire company gang fights and occasional threats to renew attacks on the Negro ghetto. The problems of police control of everyday crime, gang fights, and mob violence of a big city, however, had been made completely clear to the editors of the *Public Ledger*. They called for the consolidation of all the cities and districts of Philadelphia county so that there could be effective law enforcement without respect to the petty boundaries which then obstructed police movement and law courts.[17]

Financial panic and depression ruled the next few years. Banks closed; some failed. In 1842 the largest in the nation, the Bank of the United States, closed, bringing the state of Pennsylvania into temporary bankruptcy. The city of Philadelphia had to issue shinplasters to pay its bills. Unions and union wage gains died with the passing of prosperity. Slack work and periodic hard times broke the prices of piecework, and men took what they could get.

Worse conditions in Europe, however, drove more and more immigrants into American cities. In 1835 only 1,890 immigrants

16. *Public Ledger*, July 18, 1838.
17. Editorial, *Public Ledger*, July 18, 1838.

had debarked at Philadelphia's wharves; in 1840 4,079 debarked.[18]
Similar numbers of immigrants presumably came to the city via
New York. The largest proportion of these newcomers were Irish
Catholics. The available 1860 statistics suggest that the Irish of the
1840's were settling evenly all over Philadelphia except for the native American and German section in the northside districts. The
artisan-unskilled Northern Liberties and Kensington riverside wards
nearest the city proper (1860 wards 11, 12, 16, 18) and the middle
class, artisan, and commuters' wards between Sixth Street and Broad
Street (1860 wards 13, 14, 20) had very light proportions of Irish
foreign-born in 1860 (Table XII). Since the Irish settled into the
alleys, basements, and upstairs rooms of every other ward and district, this light concentration can only be attributed to hostility on
the part of the other residents. As the 1838 riots showed, these anti-
Irish wards of the northside were the wards of greatest abolitionist
support. They were also the wards where Protestant Native American clubs first appeared in December 1843.

Thus as the Depression years from 1837 to 1843 wore on, the
city's prejudices and tensions began to build up, one upon another.
Although no official realized it at the time, the conditions for citizen
control of public order were eroded, one by one, by a tide of fears.
By 1842, no large group in the city remained untouched. Abolitionism, with its explicit behavior pressing for social integration, chal-
lenged the long-cherished caste feelings of Philadelphians of all
classes. The influx of Irish Catholics aroused artisans and middle-
class Protestants with immediate controversy over the use of the
Bible in the public schools, and over the future prospect that their
ancient enemy, the popish church, would rise again in the New
World. Unskilled workers faced direct competition from Irish immigrants. For the first time in the history of American labor, workingmen's groups began to complain of immigrants driving down
their wages.[19] Finally, the Depression itself made all classes tense and
fearful.

Looking back from the vantage point of an historian it is clear

18. Immigrant landing continued to rise sharply in the forties and early fifties: 1845
5,767; 1850 10,515; 1855 7,581. Thus the Philadelphia Nativist response preceded the
heaviest waves of Irish immigration to the city, William J. Bromwell, *History of
Immigration* (New York, 1856), 61-177.

19. John R. Commons ed., *History of Labor*, I, 488-492.

TABLE XII

Location of Foreign Born Irish by Ward and Approximate District, 1860

District & 1860 Ward #	No. of Irish	% of Ward's Population
Southwark and Moyamensing		
Ward # 1	6,224	19.5
2	5,076	17.9
3	4,310	22.2
4	5,911	25.5
Old City of Philadelphia		
5	4,381	18.2
6	2,855	19.3
7	8,117	26.3
8	7,103	26.0
9	4,746	27.6
10	3,085	17.5
Northern Liberties and Kensington		
11	1,604	9.7
12	1,087	6.5
16	1,327	6.6
17	5,431	23.3
18	1,160	5.7
19	7,069	18.2
23	2,517	10.6
Spring Garden, Penn Township and Germantown		
13	1,546	7.8
14	2,108	8.7
15	6,661	20.7
20	2,732	9.2
21	2,565	14.9
22	2,440	14.2
West Philadelphia		
24	4,334	18.0
All Philadelphia	94,989	16.9

that the ambivalence and animosities which had manifested themselves among the authorities and the crowd at the burning of Pennsylvania Hall would manifest themselves again in the mid-forties. No strong institution, like a professional army or professional police, existed in the city to prevent a repetition of such events. All that remained to cause the collapse of public order was for the Irish to be identified as a legitimate target for violence. Another race riot provided the transition by bringing the Irish and the city's officials into conflict.

On Monday morning, August 1, 1842, a group of young men of a Negro temperance society began a parade through the streets of south Philadelphia intending to wind up on the banks of the Schuylkill for a celebration of Jamaican Emancipation Day. A banner, showing a colored man breaking his chains and depicting the rising sun of freedom, attracted the attention of some bystanders who misread it as a representation of a Negro triumphing over the massacre of whites at St. Domingo. Perhaps the bystanders were only spoiling for a fight. In any case, as the parade reached the public market stalls at Shippen street, near Fourth, boys began throwing fruit and vegetables and a general melee ensued. The neighborhood of the market was a district of poor Irish and native workers.[20]

A crowd soon broke up the parade and chased the marchers into the heart of the Negro ghetto where fighting between Negroes and whites continued. A sheriff's posse and mayor's watch arrived and arrested about twenty fighters, mostly Negroes. Some of the whites, who had been seized by the police, were snatched by the crowd before the officers could hustle them to a stationhouse. By midday the streets had become quieter, and the crowd broke up into small gangs who contented themselves with chasing and beating with sticks, staves, and iron bars any stray Negro who had the misfortune to come into the district unaware of the morning's conflict.

That afternoon a volley of gunshots fired from the Negro quarter wounded three boys. The rumor of the incident spread and soon a crowd of angry whites estimated at one thousand was milling around St. Mary's and neighboring streets. The police gave up all attempts to arrest white men. The mayor, two attorneys general, and two judges came down to the neighborhood to try to bring the crowd to order. The newspaper the next day reported that, "the active rioters, as usual, constituted only a small portion of the people assembled . . ." and the mayor sometimes succeeded in getting

20. Southwark third ward had a low proportion in the marine trades, high in manufacturing, *Hazard's Register*, IV (January-July, 1841), 394; 1860 Philadelphia ward 4 was roughly the same area and had by then a very high proportion of foreign-born Irish, Table X.

the large body of spectators to stop a call to break down a door, or to halt the attack upon a trapped Negro victim. Despite the efforts of the mayor, the other officials, and the watch, the crowd burned to the ground a hall rumored to have been used by Negroes for abolitionist meetings, and it set fire to the Negro Presbyterian Church on St. Mary's street.

The next day, Tuesday, while curious sight-seers walked through the district, many Negroes packed up their possessions and fled the city. By evening the central police station was crowded with Negroes seeking refuge from attack. Meanwhile on the southwest edge of town, the gangs in the poor Schuylkill, Irish weavers', and coal heavers' district became restless. Groups of men armed with clubs and shillelaghs chased and beat stray Negroes who reported for work in the neighborhood. The sheriff sent a posse of sixty men out to the area; each man in the contingent identified himself by wearing a green ribbon. Instead of calming the neighborhood, the posse brought on an attack against the sheriff's men by the Schuylkill gangs; spectators poured out into the streets, and a crowd of hundreds sent the posse running for safety back to downtown Philadelphia. This incident was the first in a series that placed native law officers and their deputies against the Irish. That evening the mayor ordered seven companies of militia out on duty and with such heavy patrols the city slowly quieted down. There were, to be sure, a few "light skirmishes" between gangs and the militia, and the mayor was knocked down, but by midnight all was calm, and at 3 a.m. the militia were discharged.

The following day the Negro banner that had given offense was exhibited in the mayor's court.

> "How grand in age, how fair in truth
> Are holy Friendship, Love, and Truth.
>
> Young Men's Vigilant Association of Philadelphia
>
> Instituted July 23, 1841"[21]

The "Nannygoat Market" riot in which a mob of Irish weavers drove off a posse, and then beat up the sheriff of Philadelphia county and two men and a boy who stood by him, turned the Irish into legitimate targets for violence. After several weeks during

21. This riot and the legend on the banner is given in the *Public Ledger*, August 2-4, 1842.

which some journeymen weavers had refused work and others accepted it, about three hundred men turned out in force in the poor, Irish weavers' district of Moyamensing to enforce their strike. The strikers' complaints were classic grievances associated with American industrialization: Rates for piecework had been reduced; pay was delayed and not in cash but in storekeeper's vouchers, and the men suspected that the employers conspired with the storekeepers for a rake-off on all the goods sold for the vouchers.

Reports of the first day's turnout, Monday, January 9, 1843, said the south side, Moyamensing, crowd was led by weavers from Kensington, the larger textile concentration on the north side of the city. Kensington itself was quiet Monday except for a small group who attacked a couple of houses of working weavers. In Moyamensing a large mob paraded the streets, breaking into non-complying weaver's houses, tearing out the webs which had been set on the looms by the bosses who dispensed the jobs to the weavers. A few men were beaten up, and in one house all the weaver's belongings were thrown into the street. The mayor of Philadelphia assembled a large posse next to the Moyamensing-Philadelphia line, thereby keeping order in his city. No watch or posse disturbed the strikers in Moyamensing.

On Tuesday, the Moyamensing weavers paraded through the streets with the webs and chains of yarn they had cut off the day before, but attacked no other weavers. In Kensington, however, the weavers turned out in large groups, roving the streets of Kensington and nearby Northern Liberties to stop all work. An alderman of the Northern Liberties district, a Mr. Potts, swore out a warrant against one Thomas Lynch, a strike leader who had broken into several homes. In arresting Lynch the constable was beaten, though he captured his man successfully. The weavers then threatened to burn Potts's and the constable's house. The sheriff of Philadelphia county, anticipating a night of trouble, deputized a small posse at the Kensington Commissioner's Hall. The striking weavers assembled at the Nannygoat Market (near the intersection of Master and Cadwallader, on American street, Kensington). As the sheriff's posse approached the market, they were attacked with bricks and boards torn from the stalls. The posse fled, leaving the sheriff surrounded by a hundred-odd angry weavers who beat him severely, as well as two men and a boy who stood by him. The next day, Wednesday, the weavers gathered at the market and drove off a carter who had been sent to clean up the mess. That evening the sheriff, being confined to his home by his wounds, was replaced by the deputy sheriff, who called out four companies of city and county militia, and eight more companies stood by at their armories. The weavers' district quieted down. Thursday, a committee of five weavers and five employers who hired weavers was established to discuss grievances. Eight men were arrested for rioting and beating up the sheriff. All but one had an Irish name.[22]

The incident promised ill for the future. Next to the Nannygoat Market stood the Hibernial Hose Company, citadel of the future Irish, native-American warfare. A few blocks to the east, in a neighborhood of Methodist churches, lay one of Philadelphia's greatest concentrations of native-born citizens. Kensington thus contained one of the city's highest concentrations of Irish and one of its largest native districts. The entire district also was the heart of the city's handloom weaving, an industry which remained active and troubled until after the Civil War. Mixed into both neighborhoods was some unknown quantity of Orangemen.[23] The local danger was clear, while the tensions throughout the city left it unprepared for more general conflict.

Any year in the early 1840's could have been the year of prolonged rioting. The organization of Native American Clubs (American-Republicans they called themselves in these years) throughout the city, however, made the spring of 1844 explosive. As early as 1837 a native-American meeting had been held in Germantown and a society established there, but it had met with little support elsewhere in the city. Beginning in December, 1843, however, full-fledged native-Americanism moved into Philadelphia. The

22. Strike and Nannygoat Market riot, *Public Ledger*, January 10–14, 1843; Scharf and Westcott, *History of Philadelphia*, I, 661, 664.

23. The first, fourth, and eastern half of the fifth wards of Kensington in the 1854 consolidation became Philadelphia ward 18. This ward was heavily native-born and voted strongly against the Democratic candidate, Richard Vaux, in 1854, 1856, and 1858 (Table XIII). Vaux then was allied with the Irish local bosses. Kensington's third ward, containing the Nannygoat Market, was heavily Irish. Most of it was absorbed into Philadelphia's ward 17, which voted strongly for Vaux. The narrative of John H. Lee, *The Origin and Progress of the American Party in Politics* (Philadelphia, 1855) should be read in conjunction with the 1850 U.S. Census tabulations of John H. Kane, "The Irish Immigrant in Philadelphia 1840–1880" (unpublished Ph.D. thesis, University of Pennsylvania, 1950).

first meeting convened in Spring Garden, a section of well-paid artisans, tradesmen, and downtown white-collar workers. This ward, site of the first meeting, was probably second only to the Kensington native district for having the highest proportion of native-born residents.[24] The subject of the meeting was the undue political influence of foreigners and their rapid, even fraudulent, naturalization as voters.

An organization calling itself the American Republican Association of the second ward, Spring Garden, was formed, and in the ensuing months similar associations were organized in many parts of the city. The platforms of these associations called for the lengthening of the waiting period for naturalization to twenty-one years, the restriction of public office to citizens born in the United States, and teaching from the Protestant version of the Bible in the public schools. By March 15 the movement had gained sufficient popularity for candidates to enter the spring ward elections for Constable and Assessor as "Native Americans." Before the May riots, however, it was thought that the clubs had only 500 members altogether. After the riots 4,500 Native American club members marched in the giant Fourth of July parade.[25]

Around six p.m. on Friday evening, May 3, about one hundred people gathered on a vacant lot at Master and Second streets one block from the Nannygoat Market for a meeting called by the Native Americans of Kensington. At the edge of the crowd, hecklers, men and boys, constantly interrupted the speaker until fights started and the meeting was broken up.[26]

After this local fiasco the Native Americans called for a mass meeting in retaliation for the following Monday, May 6, in the early afternoon. Supporters came from all parts of the city. The meeting began auspiciously, a large crowd having turned out to hear

24. In 1860 the Spring Garden ward 14 was 80.8 percent native born, the Kensington ward 18 was then 83.3 percent native born, author's transcription from the U.S. Eighth Census: 1860.

25. Elections, *Public Ledger*, March 15-18; clubs, Scharf and Westcott, *History of Philadelphia*, I, 663-664, 668.

26. For the basic account of the Native American riots I have again followed the reports of the *Public Ledger*, May 4-9, 1844. This account is confirmed by that given by Sister Geary, who had access to pamphlets that I did not. Sister M. Theopane Geary, *A History of Third Parties in Pennsylvania 1840-1860* (Washington, 1938), 69-92. The official Native American version is Lee, *Origin and Progress*, 49-102.

the speeches by city leaders of the party. Then a cloudburst sent the crowd running for shelter. There was considerable confusion for a time, and as the meeting seemed about to be reorganized under the cover of the Nannygoat Market, fighting broke out at the edge of the crowd and pistol shots were heard. Soon hails of bricks and stones were exchanged between Native Americans and their Irish attackers, and sporadic firing began from windows of houses and behind fences. George Shiffler, a boy of nineteen, fell first, and became the martyr of the ensuing riots.[27] Subsequently a kind of skirmish line formed starting at the Native American's stronghold at the market, extending up Master street into the Irish territory. Irish gangs charged down the street, and the Native Americans made forays up it, breaking into houses, throwing the furniture into the street, and setting fire to a few homes.

News of the fighting spread through the city and groups of men, many boys, and perhaps some firehouse gangs came running into the Nannygoat Market district. The Irish disappeared from the streets, although they kept sniping from alleys and houses until at least 10 o'clock in the evening. The sheriff called for the militia, but the militia officers refused to call out their men. This reluctance of the militia, in contrast to their previous response for patrol during the weaver's strike, can probably be interpreted as a sign of sympathy with the mob. At best, it was a weary reluctance to make much effort to stop fighting between Irish and Native American gangs. An attack on a nearby Catholic school was halted for the night by a volley from an upper floor which killed two men, but the next afternoon the crowd returned and burned the school building to the ground.

On Tuesday, handbills appeared throughout the city announcing a Native-American meeting in the State House yard at 3:30 p.m. The last line read: "Let Every Man Come Prepared to Defend Himself." That same morning many Irish families gathered their possessions and fled the Kensington riot district. Householders displayed flags to get protection from the Native American mob, much as they had formerly placed burning candles in their windows. A

27. A nagging issue in all riots involving Irish in this period is the question of the degree of involvement of Orange vs. Green conflict. Among the first wounded with Shiffler were several Native American supporters with Irish names, perhaps Irish Protestants, Lee, *Origin and Progress*, 56.

large crowd (the Native Americans claimed six thousand) gathered that afternoon to hear two Protestant ministers and other Native American leaders address them on the need for political action to stop "aggression by foreigners." Despite the notice of the handbills no posse or militia stood by to restrain the meeting. On a resolution to adjourn someone shouted: "Adjourn to Second and Master street," and soon, raising their flags, the crowd marched up Second street, out of the downtown, through the Northern Liberties toward the Nannygoat Market.

Apparently armed men joined the marchers as they proceeded up Second street through the Northern Liberties industrial district. When the parade arrived at the market about 5 o'clock in the evening, the Native Americans raised a flag and began some sort of ceremony in honor of George Shiffler. At that moment, firing from nearby houses and the Hibernia Hose Company was renewed and full rioting began again. The crowd sacked the Hose Company and broke into and burned thirty houses around the market square. No fire companies dared enter the district. As in the Negro riots, except for short periods, most of the fighting took the form of sporadic attacks by gangs of men and boys on houses, or after a shot was fired. Apparently boys added to the confusion by firing off guns throughout many neighborhoods of the city as they did on the Fourth of July. Lists of dead and wounded indicated that many of the fighters came from Southwark, but no attempt was made by the Philadelphia city militia to prevent the crowds from running north and south along the streets from Southwark through the downtown and Northern Liberties to Kensington.

The sheriff declared himself overwhelmed by the rioters, and said no city posse could control the situation. At dark, after an afternoon of intermittent fighting and burning, militia companies were called out and moved into the market area. By midnight the area was quiet.

Tuesday proved to be the last day of fighting, but not the last day of destruction. On Wednesday, the Irish had been so terrorized that they had fled from Kensington or barricaded themselves in their houses. While the militia patrolled the area, huge crowds of curiosity seekers moved into the district. Despite the militia patrols, several houses were set afire in Kensington until large bodies of militia dispersed the crowds in the evening. The evening papers carried the announcement of the mayor's call for a town meeting of citizens to restore order to the city. Meanwhile, at 6:30 in the evening, a rumor was reported to the mayor that St. Augustine's church on the north-south route (Fourth street near Vine) of the rioters would be burned down. He immediately dispatched a posse and some police, who arrived to find a large crowd of curiosity seekers surrounding the church. When Mayor Scott himself came at 8:30 to urge the crowd to disperse, the mob stoned the mayor and his volunteers, broke down the gates to the church yard, and burned the church and parsonage to the ground.

That same evening, the city councils, by now highly alarmed by the riots, appropriated $20,000 to pay for the militia service. On Thursday, May 9, 1844, the city managed to restore law and order. A large turnout of citizens attended the mayor's town meeting, where they were urged to join the ward police in protecting the law, order and property of the city. All the county militia companies were called out and the governor of Pennsylvania came to Philadelphia in time to announce that he had sent for two companies of troops, scheduled to arrive that evening from Harrisburg. Battle headquarters were established at the Girard Bank. That night the militia, the crew from the frigate, the *U.S.S. Princeton*, and the ward police guarded the Catholic churches of Philadelphia. The city was at last quiet.

Although order had been restored, the peace of the city remained precarious. The May rioting in Kensington and on the north side of town seemed to show that the city would act slowly to protect its Catholic Irish. The Irish themselves, though numerous, and a growing segment of Philadelphia's population, were dispersed throughout the city, and in no place were they so strongly concentrated for defense as were the Negroes of the south-side ghetto.[28] Catholic churches, standing in all parts of town, were easy targets for mob destruction. The lack of coordination in May between the sheriff and the militia and the reluctance of the militia officers to call out their men for riot duty suggested that a large mob could enjoy a night's foray without interference. Although there had been

28. In 1850 there were 72,312 foreign born Irish (from North and South Ireland) living in Philadelphia County. They were thus 17.7 percent of the population of the city according to its consolidated 1854 boundaries. Thirty-third Congress, second session, House of Representatives, *Executive Document #98*, 41.

arrests, there were no convictions as yet for crimes arising out of the four days of violence.[29]

What no one could predict, however, was the attitude of the militia companies, once assembled. As yet these artisan and workingclass groups had been sympathetic to the rioters. During a decade of street violence there had been no serious fighting between militia and rioters. No clash of that time had even been as vigorous as today's police action against a college football riot. The militia had never fired on rioters, although rioters had been shooting at each other in the past several outbreaks.

For politicians the lessons of May stood out clearly enough. Hostility between Protestant and Catholic had proved to be an enormously popular issue to which thousands would respond. Native Americanism would have a political future. Four and a half thousand marched with banners and floats on the Fourth of July, 1844, while a crowd estimated at fifty thousand lined the parade route. No incident marred the occasion.

Catholic priests and their parishes, however, were naturally fearful. The Grand Jury of Philadelphia had issued its presentment on the riots favorable to the Native Americans and future protection by Philadelphia officials seemed uncertain at best. Some laymen of the Church of St. Philip de Neri on Queen street, between Second and Third streets, Southwark, approached the governor to request firearms, and he had authorized them to draw muskets from the Philadelphia arsenal. During May it had been rumored that this church was to be a target for burning. The neighborhood of the church was a poor district of dock and downtown factory workers with many Irish. But, as in Kensington, it was situated near a concentration of Native Americans to the South.[30]

On Saturday, July 5, someone in the neighborhood noticed a dozen muskets (which were being returned after repairs) being taken into the church. The rumor soon spread in the district that the church was an armed Catholic fortress. First, small knots of people came to look at the church. By evening, a large crowd began to gather. Two aldermen of Southwark called for the sheriff, who

29. Lee, *Origin and Progress,* 134.

30. The church was in what became, at consolidation, Ward 3. In 1860 ward 3 was 68 percent native-born, 22.2 percent foreign-born Irish. This area corresponded to the old Southwark wards 1-3, a section of sailors and marine trades workers, *Hazard's Register,* IV (January 1841-July 1841), 394.

rushed to the scene. Together the aldermen and sheriff searched the church and found the twelve unloaded muskets. After showing them to the crowd, they ordered the populace to go home and then went off to the Southwark Commissioners Hall to impound the muskets. General George Cadwalader (1805–1872) of the militia, on this occasion, was quick to support the sheriff.[31] Soon after the sheriff had left, a militia company arrived to take possession of the church. By eleven in the evening, the crowd had dispersed quietly. At 2 a.m., the militia found a large cache of arms hidden in the church.[32]

On Saturday afternoon, a large crowd again gathered before the church having heard news of the discovery of arms. They refused to be dispersed and hissed General Cadwalader. Occupants of nearby houses abandoned their households, and American flags began to appear in the windows of neighborhood homes, placed there for protection against the mob. At 7 p.m., the sheriff, with a posse of men, arrived to help defend the church. Supplementing his posse, five more companies of militia accompanied him. The militia also took the unusual step of bringing three cannon. Together, the sheriff's men and the militia began to clear the streets adjacent to the church, the sheriff's posse working in front, between the soldiers and the crowd. At Third Street the crowd grew balky and a number of arrests were made. The crowd then began throwing stones at the militia officers, and General Cadwalader, perhaps smarting from the gibes of the mob that afternoon, or over-reacting from his experience in May, ordered a cannon leveled at the crowd. A former Whig congressman, Charles Naylor (1806–1872), leapt before the cannon and ordered the militia not to fire. Naylor was thereupon arrested, but the crowd, intimidated by the incident, fell back and Naylor was confined to the church. By daylight Sunday, all the troops had left the neighborhood except three companies, one of which was the Hibernia Greens. The company perhaps had been left behind because of its assumed interest in protecting a Catholic church.

At 11 o'clock Sunday morning, a group of men wheeled up a

31. Cadwalader was a lawyer and a soldier. During the riots he commanded the 1st Brigade, 1st Division, Pennsylvania Militia (based in Philadelphia proper). He later served in the Mexican War (1861–65) (*National Cyclopedia of American Biography*, XII, 269).

32. Narrative of the riot, *Public Ledger*, July 6–9, 1844; and Scharf and Westcott, *History of Philadelphia*, I, 669–673. The Native American account, Lee, *Origin and Progress*, 162–194.

cannon and demanded that the militia free Naylor. The cannon was not fired, but instead another group brought a beam and battered down a side door of the church. The militia released Naylor to the crowd without further resistance. Addressing the cheering crowd, he asked them to follow his example by going home.

After the Naylor incident, the gang with the cannon opened an intermittent bombardment of the church. They loaded the cannon at a nearby wharf, rolled it several blocks up to the church, and discharged it, filling the air with miscellaneous bolts and hardware. Although it terrorized the neighborhood, little damage was done to the church. They repeated this performance several times before leaders of the Native American Party arrived and succeeded in mollifying the crowd with an agreement that the Hibernia Greens should quit the church. The Greens left with another company marching outside them. The crowd pelted the Greens with stones and after two and one-half blocks the company fired into the crowd, broke and ran. One member was caught by the crowd and severely beaten but no one else was hurt.

The sound of the firing excited the crowd that was still standing before the church and they demanded to see the inside of the building. Despite the pleas of the Native American leaders, who now attempted to protect the church by lining up before the church doors, the mob broke in. A group brought a large timber and battered a hole through the wall of the church. The Native American leaders at that point gave up and allowed the crowd to mill through the church for the next few hours. After a time, however, they succeeded in stopping newcomers from entering, and the church slowly emptied; the crowd seemed to be quieting down. It was now about 7 p.m.

At that moment, perhaps in response to the attack on the Hibernia Greens, but more likely because the militia were being sent in anticipation of the formation of a more dangerous night mob, a large body of militia, perhaps two hundred men, came marching down Second street. The militiamen turned the corner of Second and Queen streets and started down Queen to clear the crowd from the area in front of the church. The crowd, however, stood fast and this time no sheriff's posse stood between the soldiers and the crowd. Someone grabbed a soldier's sword and the soldier fell to the street; someone else began to throw stones. The officers ordered their troops to fire. The first volley killed one man and wounded several others. The crowd fell back and dispersed, leaving the militia posted before the church on Queen Street and at the intersections of Queen and Second and Queen and Third streets.

At 8:30, however, a mob of armed men assembled at the Wharton Market a few blocks to the south. Pushing a cannon, with its wheels muffled, they moved slowly toward the unsuspecting militia. In their first firing of the cannon down Third street they killed two of the Germantown Blues. Screened by darkness, they fired several times more before the cavalry captured the cannon when it misfired. Snipers on the roofs of houses kept taking shots at the militia until well after midnight.

The next day the Governor ordered militia companies from nearby Pennsylvania towns to report to Philadelphia, and the cavalry rushed more ammunition to the units in Southwark. It was a riot, however, not the beginning of a revolution or a civil war. There were no more clashes on Monday. Although, counting both sides, fourteen men had been killed and many more wounded, no roundup of Southwark mob leaders or troublemakers followed the restoration of order. Only those captured by the police and militia during the event faced court charges.

This Southwark riot, with its head-on clash between the militia and the crowd, differed in quality from all the preceding decade's outbursts. Former riots had been brutal street plays in which gangs of toughs had acted out the fears and enmities of the ordinary citizens by attacking their scapegoats. When the militia and the crowd turned on each other the ordinary citizen found himself fighting with his own kind. Laborer, clerk, artisan, and shopkeeper faced laborer, clerk, artisan, and shopkeeper. At that moment the audience merged with the actors and thereby destroyed the play. Such an experience, following as it did the terrible four-day riots of May, so frightened most Philadelphians that no large sympathetic audience ever again flocked to the scene of neighborhood outbursts. Street violence continued at a high level for many years, but with declining size and power.[33]

33. Fire company fights, *Public Ledger*, December 9, 1844, December 17, 1847, June 4, 1849; criminal gangs, "the bouncers," "the killers," "the rats," Grand Jury presentment, *Public Ledger*, December 10, 1846; the notorious "Schuylkill Rangers," *Public Ledger*, June 25, 1849, *Cummings Evening Bulletin*, August 13, 1850.

The shock to the city of the collapse of public order in the days of violence of May and July 1844 brought two basic changes to the structure of Philadelphia. First, the shock gave rise to the successful campaign for consolidation of all the twenty-nine jurisdictions of Philadelphia County into one municipal corporation. Second the shock caused the reorientation of the city's politics from the merchant vs. mechanic issues inherited from the Revolution to new ethnic and racial issues. Both changes were essential ingredients in the system of social control of the nineteenth-century big city and the early twentieth-century industrial metropolis. The creation of a large professional police force which could control riots had been the major demand and was the first product of consolidated government in Philadelphia. The shift to ethnic politics, campaigns explicitly against Catholic Irish, native Protestants, Negroes, and Abolitionists, repugnant though they were to a democratic society, yet had the effect of bringing professional boss control, and therefore institutionalization, of the expression of conflicts which formerly could seek only fragmentary, irregular, and violent expression.

The consolidation movement began in the fall of 1844 after the national elections. A committee of Philadelphians held a well-attended meeting in a downtown courtroom at which it was resolved to petition the legislature for consolidation. This group made an important contribution to consolidation strategy. They gave public notice that they intended to leave the politically influential and ethnically organized volunteer fire companies untouched, and that they planned to concentrate on the demand for a professional, civilian police.

Leading Philadelphia lawyers, however, were shocked by such a radical measure as consolidation. They formed a committee of important Whigs and Democrats from the city of Philadelphia to oppose the suggestion. Their motive seems to have been partly pure conservatism; they wished to continue to run the city of Philadelphia as they had in the past. Partly their opposition seems to have been based on a reluctance to assume the problems, and potentially the tax burdens, of the poorer outside districts. This lawyers' group, instead, petitioned the legislature for police reforms. Their measure of 1846 required a kind of federation of local police units; a later scheme (1850) established an emergency police force. After a few years' trial neither reform proved adequate for the protection of the city.[34]

Over the next five years consolidation made little progress. Significant for the ultimate passage of the measure, however, Whigs and Native Americans in the city and the county began to cooperate in endorsing a number of common candidates. No union of the two groups resulted, but it must have been clear to many Whig politicians, as it was by no means clear just after the riots, that Whig-Native American collaboration could help the Whigs where they were weakest, in the outside, Philadelphia County, districts beyond the city limits.

In the late 1840's the enthusiasms of the Mexican War for a time buried local Nativist fears. Then, as the slave status of the territories captured from Mexico became burning national issues Philadelphia politics again became intensely racial and ethnic. The Democrats became identified as pro-slave and Catholic, the Whigs and Nativists as pro-Negro, pro-Abolitionist. Party politics in Philadelphia in the fifties organized itself around these stereotypes.[35]

Fortunately for the consolidation movement, the division of the county between the Democrats and their opponents was so even that politicians of either camp could imagine themselves as benefiting by the unification. An analysis of the ward pattern of voting for mayor in the consolidated elections of 1854, 1856, and 1858 shows that the traditional city vs. outside county division, a division in which the Whigs controlled the city and the Democrats controlled the outside county, had broken down into a very balanced political situation throughout the entire Philadelphia County.

If one calculates as a Whig or Native American politician might have tallied the wards then of the twenty-four wards of the consolidated city, there were nine which would surely vote anti-Democratic, six variable, and nine Democratic (Table XIII). Of the anti-Democratic wards two were to the south of the old munici-

---

34. *Public Ledger*, November 12, 13, December 19, 1844; Scharf and Westcott, *History of Philadelphia*, I, 674.

35. The politics of the late forties and fifties is related in Sister Geary, *A History of Third Parties*, 123-151. I am indebted to William Dusinberre's, *Civil War Issues in Philadelphia* (Philadelphia, 1965) for my interpretation of the effects of anti-Negro sentiment on everyday politics.

TABLE XIII

VOTE FOR THE DEMOCRAT RICHARD VAUX FOR MAYOR, BY WARD
AND PERCENT, 1854-1858

Ward	Vaux vs. Conrad	Vaux vs. Moore	Vaux vs. Henry
1	40.9	53.4	46.2
2	43.3	55.7	48.3
3	48.5	58.4	54.2
4	52.2	72.7	67.2
5	43.9	59.3	56.5
6	39.8	55.0	47.2
7	31.2	57.3	39.2
8	41.8	52.0	47.1
9	36.4	51.5	46.7
10	29.4	39.2	32.6
11	50.9	58.8	57.8
12	40.2	52.9	49.0
13	41.6	39.9	32.8
14	36.3	42.4	31.5
15	43.7	55.5	44.3
16	41.0	50.8	47.6
17	59.0	56.7	65.0
18	31.5	38.6	35.9
19	54.7	60.3	51.6
20	46.2	54.0	48.1
21	43.6	55.9	46.0
22	32.7	49.7	34.8
23	41.5	54.7	50.6
24	44.3	51.8	48.4
Total for Vaux	21,020	29,504	29,120
% Total Vote	42.1%	53.2%	46.8%

Source:

Election statistics published in the *Public Ledger,* June 7, 1854; May 7, 1856; May 12, 1858.

pal boundaries of Philadelphia, three within the old city, and four in the north; of the variable wards two lay to the south, two in the old city, two in the north. This scattering of anti-Democratic wards throughout the city and county, and the general evenness of the political situation must have been sensed by contemporary politicians. If one calculates as a Democratic politician might have tallied the wards then, two of the anti-Democratic wards would have been moved into the variable column. The distribution of these wards' post-consolidation voting patterns suggests why neither Whig, Native American, nor Democrat felt particularly threatened by consolidation.[36]

A race riot the night after the October 9, 1849, elections carried consolidation into its final phase. A gang of southside toughs attacked the Negro ghetto; in the night of fighting Negroes and fire companies three men were killed by guns and a couple of dozen wounded. A large body of militia had to be assembled and stationed in the district to protect the firemen and to restore order. Tempers of respectable Philadelphians seemed frayed by the event. The governor of Pennsylvania took the hitherto unprecedented step of offering a reward for the arrest and conviction of any rioters, and the Philadelphia County Grand Jury opened a full investigation.[37]

All opposition by leading Philadelphians melted away, and within a month a committee of the city's businessmen and lawyers held a Town Meeting calling for consolidation. Former Mayor John Swift, himself a veteran of several race riots, was chosen chairman, and addressed the crowd. "We have a common interest to protect life and property. Matters have arrived at such a pitch that even our lives are not safe. This has been made manifest by recent events; and it has also been made manifest that our property is not secure . . . property is rendered valueless, comparatively speaking by popular outbreaks and riots."[38]

It took several years of maneuvering against the opposition of the petty office holders of the county before consolidation could be effected. In the end the consolidation committee adopted the mode of merchant leadership and the strategy used by the school reformers of 1834. Eli K. Price was elected from the city of Philadelphia to the state Senate and Mathias W. Baldwin and William C. Patterson to the Assembly to guide the consolidation bill through the legislature.[39] The measure carried easily and in June 1854 Philadelphia

36. See Election Table XIII. In all elections Richard Vaux was the Democratic candidate for mayor. The anti-Democratic wards were on the southwide, wards 1 and 2 in the old city, wards 7, 9, and 10; on the northside, wards 13, 14, 18, and 22; the variable wards were on the southside, wards 3 and 5; in the old city, wards 6 and 8; on the northside, wards 16 and 24.

37. "The California House" race riot centered about the issue of a Negro innkeeper and his white wife, *Public Ledger*, October 10, 11, 1849.

38. *Public Ledger*, November 17, 1849.

39. *Public Ledger*, August 29, 1850.

held its first consolidated election for mayor. A Native American won.[40]

The immediate political history of consolidated Philadelphia was that of ethnic politics. The conservative gentleman Democrat, Richard Vaux, aided by an alliance with local Irish bosses ran against a succession of Whig-Nativist candidates (Chapter V). The results in terms of social control of the city were immediately beneficial. The first mayors organized a mixed native and Irish police force which maintained order. By contrast, in New York street violence continued unchecked in the fifties[41] only to reach its terrible climax in the four-day Irish Draft Riots of 1863. In Philadelphia the gangs of toughs and criminals were penned into small red light districts and civil order maintained. At the same time, for most Philadelphians, the political expression of anti-Negro, anti-Catholic, anti-Protestant fears and animosities proved an adequate substitute for the violence of street rioting.

In the long run municipal politicians working in a climate of ethnic politics became promoters of neighborhood ethnic leaders and loyalties within the city. Again in terms of social control and public order, these contributions to neighborhood clubs, saloon entertainments, political picnics and dances, and parish charities may well have helped big-city residents to orient themselves in a manageable small community setting. One of the remarkable features of the American big city and later industrial metropolis was the abundance of small-scale ties and loyalties. Though it was a giant, it was not, typically, a place of isolated individuals and mass anomie. The growth of ethnic politics in the mid-nineteenth century must thus be considered a major social event in the history of the city, as important an event as the growth of work groups by the process of industrialization. Both events furnished the big city and its successor, the industrial metropolis, with numerous small-scale loyalties and linkages.

Of course, the new ethnic style of politics could not restore strong democratic government to the city. For the moment it ob-

40. The story of consolidation is told in Eli K. Price, *The History of Consolidation in the City of Philadelphia* (Philadelphia, 1873); and more briefly in Henry Leffmann, "The Consolidation of Philadelphia," *Philadelphia History*, I (Philadelphia, 1908), 26-40.

41. Max Berger, "The Irish Emigrant and American Nativism as Seen by British Visitors, 1836-1860," *Pennsylvania Magazine*, LXX (April, 1946), 146-160.

scured the slow breakdown of city government which had commenced in the 1840's. But in the long run it contributed nothing to the vital issues of the maldistribution of personal income, physical growth, and need for new high-quality municipal institutions which were the major problems of the city for the next century. The big city of 1860 had regained public order, but as a meaningful democratic society it was out of control.

Part Three

THE INDUSTRIAL METROPOLIS

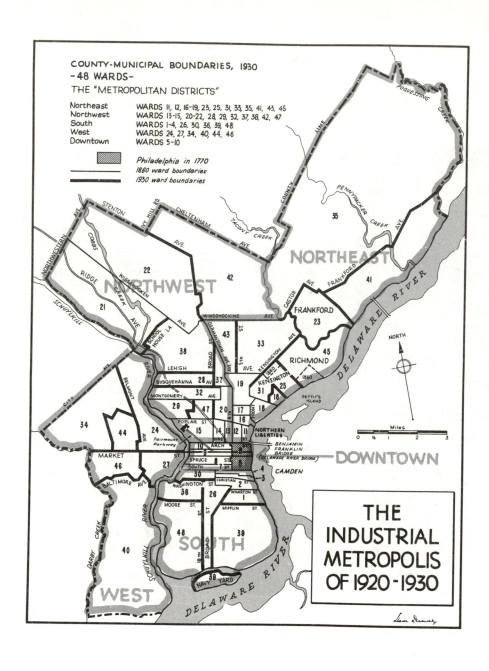

COUNTY-MUNICIPAL BOUNDARIES, 1930
-48 WARDS-
THE "METROPOLITAN DISTRICTS"

Northeast	WARDS 11, 12, 16-19, 23, 25, 31, 33, 35, 41, 43, 45
Northwest	WARDS 13-15, 20-22, 28, 29, 32, 37, 38, 42, 47
South	WARDS 1-4, 26, 30, 36, 39, 48
West	WARDS 24, 27, 34, 40, 44, 46
Downtown	WARDS 5-10

Philadelphia in 1770
1860 ward boundaries
1930 ward boundaries

THE
INDUSTRIAL
METROPOLIS
OF 1920-1930

8

The Structure of the Metropolis

Now that America's largest cities are growing into regional metropolises, it is possible to appreciate the early twentieth-century industrial metropolis as an historical event in its own right. This latest urban form, the regional metropolis, can be seen both in the spread of a new city like Los Angeles and in the dispersal of old cities like Philadelphia and New York. The industrial metropolis was not just the nineteenth-century big city grown larger; neither was it today's megalopolis constricted. It had a unique social and spatial organization.

In 1930 Philadelphia was the third metropolis in the nation, one of ten whose population exceeded one million inhabitants. The metropolitan region as defined by the U.S. Census held a population of 2,847,000; of these residents 1,951,000 lived in the city of Philadelphia itself; 896,000 lived in seven adjacent counties of Pennsylvania and New Jersey. In the twentieth century the growth of the metropolis had slowed substantially, but its size had become so great that even small annual increments to its population meant thousands of new families, jobs, and houses.[1]

1. To reduce the burden of research the analysis of the metropolis has been limited to 68.5 percent of the total Philadelphia metropolitan region, that is the businesses and residences situated within the boundaries of Philadelphia itself. This restriction somewhat distorts the proportions of elements present in the region, but neglects none. The Philadelphia municipal boundaries were so long that they encompassed every kind of activity and every kind of social and economic structure from slum sweatshops to exurban farms and forest. In respect to city and metropolitan propor-

The sheer size of the industrial metropolis of the early twentieth century makes it difficult for the historian to describe. The
important issues of the quality of everyday life upon which any final
assessment of this stage of urbanization must rest defy easy reconstruction. The metropolis was composed of hundreds upon hundreds of offices, shops, mills, and neighborhoods, each one an important element in the urban environment of some Philadelphia
residents. Only a few of these environments have been studied, and
those studied have received only partial and fragmentary treatment.
Nevertheless, even the briefest survey reveals two special qualities of
the industrial metropolis: its organization of most of the population
into work groups and its widespread use of residential segregation.

THE GROUP ORGANIZATION OF WORK

By the early decades of the twentieth century the process of industrialization had advanced so far that three-quarters of all manufacturing workers (Table XIV), and probably a majority of all other
workers, labored in industrially organized work groups. The new
mode stretched far beyond just factories. Philadelphia's nineteen
department stores employed an average of 1,465 employees per company. They were bureaucratically arranged into layers of managers,
buyers and salesladies, supervisors and clerks, foremen and ware-
housemen. Most downtown banks, brokerage houses, insurance
offices, finance companies, some warehouses and some women's ap-
parel stores had attained a size appropriate to group work organization. The major exceptions to the ubiquitous work group were the
small retail storekeepers and domestics, who still labored alone, with
one or two helpers, or in families as in the eighteenth and early
nineteenth centuries.[2]

---

tions of population types the city markedly lacked children under fourteen as compared to its metropolitan environs. The difference in non-white population, on the
other hand, was not startling; Philadelphia in 1930 had 11.4 percent of its population
non-white, the environs 6.7 percent. Simon S. Kuznets, *Population of Philadelphia and
Environs in 1950* (Philadelphia, Institute of Local and State Government, 1956), 20, 24.
The population of Philadelphia and its metropolitan districts was given in *Fifteenth
Census of the U.S.: Metropolitan Districts* (Washington, 1932), 10-12, 158-162.

2. A comparison of William M. Hench, *Trends in the Size of Industrial Companies
in Philadelphia for 1915-1930* (Philadelphia, 1938), 7-8, 21-23, with the *Fourteenth U.S.
Census: 1920*, IX *Manufactures*, 1277 shows a manufacturing structure in which 88.6
percent of all wage earners worked in the 21.3 percent of the establishments which
employed more than twenty hands. The average size establishment employed 31.0

TABLE XIV

AVERAGE SIZE OF ESTABLISHMENTS IN MAJOR LINES
OF MANUFACTURE, PHILADELPHIA 1930

Total Persons Employed		Average No. Persons Per Establishment
292,616	All lines of manufacture	52.6
1,986	Sugar refining	662.0
3,103	Iron and steel mills	443.3
20,280	Electrical machinery	375.6
1,535	Paper	307.0
5,105	Leather	204.2
8,321	Worsted goods	180.9
8,564	Cigars and cigarettes	161.6
26,693	Knit goods	134.1
1,861	Chemicals	124.1
1,245	Dental goods and equipment	113.2
13,806	Printing and publishing, newspaper and magazine	99.3
3,479	Silk and rayon manufacture	94.0
2,219	Cotton, small wares	92.5
1,829	Druggists preparations	91.5
5,692	Cotton goods	79.1
3,002	Woolen goods	73.2
3,327	Shirts	72.3
1,840	Meatpacking, wholesale	59.4
13,083	Foundry and machine shop products	59.2
3,227	Boxes, paper	50.4
4,056	Dyeing and finishing textiles	41.4
4,676	Furniture, incl. store fixtures	41.0
11,680	Clothing, men and boys	39.6
3,884	Confectionery	39.2
2,070	Paints and varnishes	37.6
1,432	Ice cream	36.7
1,114	Structural and ornamental iron	35.9
9,304	Clothing, women's	31.3
1,464	Fancy and miscellaneous articles	30.5
1,463	Planing mill products	28.7
1,513	Non-ferrous metals	28.0
1,293	Copper, tin, sheet iron work	21.9
8,413	Bread and bakery products	16.5
7,319	Printing and publishing, book and job	15.2
189,878		

The new mode of economic life in the metropolis called for groups of workers, roughly between four and twenty members, set as cells in a hierarchically arranged larger institution. Although the statistics of the 1920's do not yield precise information on the social modes of urban economic life, it seems reasonable to assume the presence of the group organization of work in all institutions of more than twenty employees. Certainly at that scale, and often perhaps in smaller organizations, it becomes impossible for one man to supervise all his workers. It also becomes impossible for him to channel through himself the daily flow of information, socialization, and psychological orientation needed by his workers. Thus, at this scale the crew must be broken down into smaller groups for effective supervision, for the independence and specialization complicated work requires, and to allow adequate intensity of socialization amongst the workers. If small groups are not provided by the industrial process itself—as in the case of large, noisy spinning rooms, big office clerical pools, or in the case of a long line of assemblers all doing the same thing at the same time, some sort of small groupings will form about the lunch break, the water cooler, or the washroom.[3]

The industrial plan of work groups did not require uniformity of arrangement. In Philadelphia in the 1920's observers reported a wide variety of groups. There were knitting teams of four in the

wage earners. Hench's analysis shows that in Philadelphia the number of firms was two-thirds the number of establishments, and that their size distribution was like that of the establishments. The *Fifteenth Census: 1930, Manufactures*, III, 444 gives Pennsylvania figures only. In this case 33.9 percent of the total establishments had more than twenty employees and they hired 93.7 percent of the state's wage earners.

Such information about manufacturing leads one to interpret the statistics on average size of non-manufacturing establishments as revealing a preponderance of the group organization of work in all lines except small retail stores and domestic service. In 1930 the average sizes of establishments for Pennsylvania were: construction 44.1, wholesaling 12.1, banks 19.1, brokers 10.7, installment finance companies 10.7, insurance companies, home and branch offices 25.1 and 27.1 respectively. *Fifteenth Census, Wholesale Distribution*, II, 1262-1267, *Retail Distribution*, I, pt. 3, 785-787, *Construction Industry*, 1058; *Census of American Business: 1935*, "Banks, U.S. Summary," 1, "Financial Institutions Other Than Banks," 3-14, "Insurance," 1, 9, 26; *Pennsylvania Department of Labor and Industry*, "Employment Fluctuations in Pennsylvania 1921-1927," *Special Bulletin, #24* (J. Frederic Dewhurst, ed., Harrisburg, 1928), 30.

3. The definitive analysis of industrial work groups was built upon 1927-1934 observations at the Hawthorne Works of the Western Electric Co. in Chicago, Illinois. Fritz J. Roethlisberger, William J. Dickson, and Harold A. Wright, *Management and the Worker* (Cambridge, 1939), 493-524.

hosiery mills where the operator of one machine depended directly on the work of the others; there were the much more individualized rooms of the toolmakers where the workman often faced new tasks and could determine many of his own methods; there were workers in carpet mills whose intermittent labor gave them time to chat with friends; there were garment workers cramped together in griping groups in a back room; and there were a hundred silk underwear workers who stitched in a sunny room at the top of a loft building in apparent easy sociability.[4]

Two cases of isolation have been reported. One, an embittered girl who worked alone stitching overalls in a corner of a factory; the other, a fascinating 1923-1924 case of forty mule spinners who failed to form a group because of the noise of the machinery, the wide spacing of their posts, and the unremitting need to tend their machinery. The manager of the plant brought in a group of industrial engineers led by Elton Mayo, then of the Wharton School of the University of Pennsylvania, to seek the cause of the spinners' low production and high rate of turnover. The spinners troubles turned out to be caused by fatigue and social isolation. Short rest periods overcame both difficulties. After a year of observation Mayo concluded that one of the most important causes of his success with the spinners was the transformation of "a hoard of 'solitaries' into a social group."[5]

The informal sociability of the shop and office could grow to be important elements in workers' lives because mature workers stayed as long as possible with one employer. Although their motive was to seek seniority against the danger of layoffs and slack time, their long

4. Dorothea de Schweinitz, *How Workers Find Jobs, A Study of Four Thousand Hosiery Workers in Philadelphia* (Philadelphia, 1932) 67-68; quotations from the "toolmakers' study," of the Wharton School in Hummel La Rue Frain, *Earnings in Standard Machine Occupations.* (Philadelphia, 1929), 78-81; Anne Bezanson et al, *Earnings and Working Opportunity in the Upholstery Weavers' Trade in Twenty-five Plants in Philadelphia* (Philadelphia, 1928), 118-120; essays by those who seemed to be Philadelphia workers at the Bryn Mawr Summer School, Andria T. Hourwich and Gladys L. Palmer, *I Am a Woman Worker; A Scrapbook of Autobiographies* (mimeo, New York, The Affiliated Schools for Workers, Inc., 1936, copy in University of Pennsylvania Library); U.S. Bureau of Labor Statistics, *Bulletin #399, Labor Relations in the Lace and Lace Curtain Industries of the U.S.* (Gladys L. Palmer ed., November, 1925), 21.

5. Elton Mayo, *The Social Problems of an Industrial Organization* (Boston, 1945), 67; "Revery and Industrial Fatigue," *Journal of Personnel Research*, III (December, 1924), 273-281.

tenure had the added effect of making the job relations important to their personal lives, culture, and discipline. A study of textile, metal working, ship building, chemical, and some miscellaneous firms showed that despite variations in level of skill and variations in the rules of apprenticeship, within five to ten years after first entering the labor force workers settled down for extended periods in one shop. Among the firms studied the majority of the workers had appeared on the payrolls for five years or more. These men and women constituted the core crews of experienced help whom the firm tried to carry in slack times or seasonal slumps. They, in their turn, jealously guarded their places against newcomers.[6]

Out of such habits came two uniformities which characterized all the work groups of Philadelphia firms, despite variations among them in degree of mechanization, steadiness of the pace, amount of supervision, the discretion of the worker, or the nature of the clerical or industrial task. The two uniformities of work organization were, first, the dual control of the worker by his work group and his supervisor, and second, the displacement of a large measure of the personal responsibility from the worker up the hierarchy of the firm to some known or unknown authority.

Under ordinary conditions Philadelphia workers had to respond successfully to the social norms and work expectations of their peers in the work group and they had, as individuals, and members of the group, to take direct supervision from a foreman or supervisor who represented the hierarchy of control of the larger organization. The flexibility of this dual control gave it an effectiveness far superior to the old indirect controls of the response of the market place or the rumored reputation of the maker. In the early nineteenth century, individual producers or small shops worked only with the quality control of custom and the vague reputation of the artisan. The pacing varied with the temperament of the artisan or his need for cash. Moreover, similar outputs did not always earn the

6. Anne Bezanson et al, *Four Years of Labor Mobility, A Study of Labor Turnover in a Group of Selected Plants in Philadelphia 1921-1924* (Philadelphia, 1925), 7-9, 66-67, 96. The building trades also suffered from seasonal unemployment, and from lost days owing to bad coordination of subcontractors; yet they had core crews who worked through most of the year, William Haber, *Industrial Relations in the Building Industry* (Cambridge, 1930), 97-100; *Fifteenth Census: 1930, Construction Industry*, 1058.

same rewards. The number of customers and the prices of work fluctuated widely from year to year, regardless of the quality of the artisan's work.

In the typical work group of the industrial metropolis dual supervision went on continuously, in discrete amounts, and rewards became much steadier than formerly. By its approval or disapproval, the group could teach a wide variety of skills and habits, the tricks of the production process, its sense of fair pace, its definition of punctuality, its games and codes of loyalty. The individual's work did not have to be received or rejected on an all-or-nothing basis as in the earlier market system of independent workmen, but could be corrected as he worked. Unlike the isolated artisan, or the men in the three-man shop, the individual could in some narrow degree make appeals to his peers against his supervisor, or make appeals to his supervisor against his peers. Finally, and perhaps most important of all, the worker could seek friendships and protection within the sub-groups of the workroom.

The possibilities of the social structure of work groups in large firms did not escape the observation of Philadelphia's efficiency engineers of the 1920's. Philadelphia had been the home of the pioneer engineer Frederick W. Taylor, and although his vision had concentrated on the teaching, discipline, and reward of the individual worker, by 1920 his followers became much more group-oriented.[7] They experimented with various programs of group incentives to replace past, individual, competitive piece work in the hope that production would rise from stimulation of cooperation among work group members.[8]

All the work groups in large organizations offered a good measure of relief from responsibility for the task at hand. Large organizations, by sheer size, created a "they," others who set the group's tasks, determined the hours and wages, approved the piece-work rates, allowed the vacations, called the layoffs and short weeks. The "they" presumably were the ones who profited by the group's labors.

7. Samuel Haber, *Efficiency and Uplift, Scientific Management in the Progressive Era* (Chicago, 1964), 22-27, 160-167.

8. C. Canby Balderson, *Group Incentives, Some Variations in the Use of Group Bonus and Gang Piece Work* (Philadelphia, 1930), 24-42.

This displacement and movement of important responsibilities in an adult's life up the power hierarchy of the firm protected the individual and the group from some of the conflict, guilt, and uncertainties which inevitably attended free-enterprise employment: the competitive pay scale, the hazard of unemployment, the uncertainties of fluctuating paychecks, and the inability to find openings at the level of skill and experience which one had attained. The industrial metropolis' work environment was more a world of officers and enlisted men than of aspiring entrepreneurs, petty shopkeepers, and thrifty artisans. At the lowest levels of work the displacement of responsibility made work just a job; at the top bureaucratic levels work was a career, a calling. Along the whole job continuum, although more so at the bottom than the top, the large, modern, industrial organization offered a "they" who held ultimate responsibility.[9]

Thus for the ordinary citizen the twentieth-century metropolis added a lattice of loyalties to the older connections of family and neighborhood. This addition of a whole new set of social units helps explain one of the paradoxes of the industrial metropolis. To many observers, novelists, and sociologists of the early twentieth century, the metropolis seemed so large, so fast-changing, and made up of so many varieties of people, all pursuing different ends, that social disorder, even explosion seemed the logical next event.[10] Yet no explosion occurred. No riots disturbed Philadelphia in the decade before or after World War I. There was labor unrest, strikes by both unskilled and skilled workers, organizing by the revolutionary International Workers of the World, outbursts of superheated patriotism, and bitter feeling against radicals and foreigners; yet the daily newspapers report little more than a bloody nose and gangster shootings. The contrast between the peace of this era and the riots of Philadelphia during the first era of industrialization of the 1830's and 1840's is compelling. Equally compelling is the contrast between Philadelphia's slow-changing industrial districts of the 1920's and the riot-torn large ghettos of unskilled Negro migrants of East St. Louis in 1917 or of Detroit in 1943 or in 1967.

9. Marc Fried, "Work and Mobility," *Planning for a Nation of Cities* (Sam Bass Warner, Jr. ed., Cambridge, 1966), 81-104.

10. The contemporary American view of the industrial metropolis as a place of weakened social contacts might be summed up by Theodore Dreiser, *Sister Carrie* (1900), Robert E. Park, "The City: Suggestions for the Investigation of Human Behav-

The whole subject of the relationship between work groups and the social order of cities calls out for systematic study by historians, but a first examination of the most available Philadelphia evidence suggests that the industrial metropolis was more peaceful and better able to absorb conflict and variety than any of its predecessors. The answer to those who saw a future of social disorder seems to have been the replacement of weakened extended family and neighborhood relations with strengthened work associations. If an historian may hazard an estimate of such a vast process as the rise of the urban work group then it seems reasonable to say that Philadelphia in 1930 offered more social relationships to its citizens than it had ever offered before.

RESIDENTIAL SEGREGATION

The second major innovation in the structure of the twentieth-century industrial metropolis was its widespread use of residential segregation. During the seventy years from 1860 to 1930 the residential areas of Philadelphia shifted from mild to pronounced segregation by income and ethnicity. Whereas earlier the clustering of skilled workers had contributed significantly to the residential patterns of the city, now most skilled workers settled about the city in much the same proportions as the rest of the population. Unskilled workers, on the other hand, became ghettoized. The settlement habits of the workers in some industries can be compared between 1860 and 1930. With a few significant exceptions most of the workers in comparable industries became less intensely clustered. Specifically, the degree of clustering declined for those in baking, paper and printing, metal working other than iron and steel, iron, steel and shipbuilding, professions, building trades, and wholesaling and retailing (Table XV).

The method of large-firm organization which prevailed in most of these industries during the late nineteenth and early twentieth centuries, and the new street railway transportation of the same era, allowed substantial proportions of workers to settle outside the neighborhoods of their work. Particularly the white-collar and high-skilled members of these industrial groupings chose the modern pattern of living at some remove from their office or plant.

ior in the City Environment," *American Journal of Sociology*, XX (March, 1915), 577-612; Robert A. Woods and Albert J. Kennedy, *The Zone of Emergence* (c. 1915); John Dos Passos, *Manhattan Transfer* (1925); Lewis Mumford, *The Culture of Cities* (1938).

TABLE XV

INDEX OF DISSIMILARITY, PHILADELPHIA 1860, 1930

1860	Index No.	1930	Index No.
Negro, free, native born	47.3	Rental under $15 per month	56.0
Miscellaneous textiles	40.3	Italy, foreign born	50.7
German, foreign born	34.1	Negro, native and foreign	50.7
Bakeries	30.7	Rental $100 and up	50.2
Iron, steel and shipbuilding	29.0	Russia, foreign born	44.4
Hotels, laundries and		Poland, foreign born	44.0
domestic	25.9	Miscellaneous textiles	42.3
Metalworking, ex. iron and		Rental $15-29	35.3
steel	25.6	Germany, foreign born	32.4
Professional, ex.		Rental $50-99	31.5
entertainment	25.4	Hotels, laundries and	
Laborers	21.9	domestics	30.8
Clothing	21.8	Clothing	27.7
Ireland, N and S,		Transport, ex. rail and	
foreign born	19.8	transit	27.2
Transport, ex. rail and		Britain, ex. N. Ireland, f.b.	26.6
transit	19.6	Professional, ex.	
Paper and printing	19.0	entertainment	23.1
Building trades	16.4	Owned occupied home	22.6
Pennsylvania, native born	10.1	Ireland, foreign born	21.5
Wholesale and retail	9.6	Iron, steel and shipbuilding	20.8
		Rental $30-49 (the median)	17.7
		Metalworking, ex. iron and	
		steel	16.4
		Bakeries	15.2
		Paper and printing	11.4
		Building	10.4
		Wholesale and retail	5.3

In 1860 machinists, shipyard workers, bakers, professionals, and textile operatives had clustered in blocks near their work places, partly to avoid costly transportation, partly to benefit from the external economies of the hive of many small operators. Streetcars, telephones, big mills and offices had freed the skilled worker to use residential criteria in choosing his home neighborhood.

The only category which represented a good many skilled workers and which still showed very high residential clustering in 1930 was, "miscellaneous textiles," (lace, lace curtains, trimmings, rugs, upholstery fabrics, cotton goods). These specialties had located in the northeast and northern sections of Philadelphia since before the Civil War and as new specialties like lace curtain manufacture were imported from England the new mills settled near the city's pool of skilled textile workers. Indeed, the residential and mill clustering of Philadelphia's entire textile industry continued the pattern of the pre-Civil War era. Seasonality, dependence on style changes, and irregular work schedules seemed to have held this industry to clustering even though the sizes of the mills had grown quite large.[11]

The other industrial categories which increased their residential clustering between 1860 and 1930 were all characterized by heavy use of low-paid, low-skill, or unskilled workers: hotels, laundries, domestic service, clothing, trucking, express, taxis, postal clerks, and marine transport.

The increased clustering of the homes of these workers derived directly from income, racial, and ethnic segregation. New immigrants, disfavored groups, low skills, and low incomes more and more clustered in those sections of the city with an abundance of cheap and old housing. The relaxation of the clustering needs of industry allowed this shift in residential patterns. As the organization of large firms (more than twenty workers per establishment) brought coordination of separate workers under one roof, instead of coordination of scattered workers in a neighborhood, the old pattern of skilled workers and proprietors living on the front streets and the unskilled in the alleys and back streets disappeared. As the nineteenth century wore on, the skilled and well-paid abandoned the old office and mill districts to seek at the outer, growing edge of the city the amenities of new houses, more light and air, larger yards, new schools, and income homogeneity. The result by 1930 was a core city of poverty, low skills, and low status surrounded by a ring of working-class and middle-class homes.[12]

This trend to income segregation is familiar enough today since

11. The entire textile industry of the city of Philadelphia employed 61,322 men and women in 1930, or 6.9 percent of the work force. For an interesting discussion of the reasons for the clustering of the textile workers near their mills, de Schweinitz, *How Workers Find Jobs*, 27-33, 55-61.

12. In Table XV and Table VII the foreign-born stand as proxies for ethnic segregation and the laborers, professionals, and rental categories stand as proxies for income and class segregation.

the pace of income segregation has accelerated with the automobile suburb and post-World War II patterns of decentralized business location. Even the slow pace of growth which took place within the municipal boundaries of Philadelphia during the 1920's sustained a strong trend of differentiation between core and ring. With but minor exception, all the inner wards of the city lost population between 1920 and 1930. The eleven wards of the ring, however, gathered all the growth of the city and presumably were the destination of many of the Philadelphians who had left the core.[13] The ring, as opposed to the core, was the place of higher incomes, higher proportions of home ownership, more members of the older ethnic groups, less members of the disfavored new immigrants and Negroes (Table VII).

In the trend to income and ethnic segregation the industrial metropolis was the passive victim of its building process. Building went forward year after year, by the accumulation of thousands of individual decisions. No dramatic event drove the middle class or well-paid working class from their old neighborhoods. Rather, the metropolis segregated itself as it grew, quietly and steadily. The poor could not afford to follow the new paths because they were unable to pay the rents for new housing. Moreover, for the newly successful no vacant land existed in the old districts for builders to put new houses on. If one wanted to trade up, one had to move out. So the building process went, the differential wage structure of the metropolis being transformed from millions of pay envelopes and checks into streets of slums, blocks upon blocks of drab houses, and miles of new suburban rows.[14]

The ethnic and racial consequences of the increasing division of metropolitan space between those who could afford new housing and those who could not are also reflected in the Index of Dissimi-

13. The 1920-1930 growth of the ring wards was: the northeast (wards 23, 35, 41) 75,441; the south (ward 48) 4,248; the west (wards 34, 46, 40) 62,284; the northwest (wards 38, 21, 22, 42) 102,701. The only other wards that grew were ward 8 (downtown apartments) 227; ward 47 (conversion of old housing) 603; ward 33 (near edge of ring) 889. *Fourteenth Census: 1920, Population*, III, 896-899; *Fifteenth Census: 1930, Population*, III, pt. 2, 750.

14. For a graphic representation of this process, Philadelphia City Planning Commission, Map Series 2, Population and Housing, Philadelphia, 1950, "Part B: Characteristics of Housing by Census Tracts," (Philadelphia, 1955), two maps, Dwellings Built 1920-1939, and Dwellings Built 1919 and Earlier; and Works Progress Administration, *Report of Philadelphia Real Property Survey, 1934* (Philadelphia, 1935), xxi-xiv.

larity (Table XV). All the disfavored racial and ethnic groups—the Negroes, Italians, Russian and Polish Jews—were crowded into those areas of old housing and low-paying industries. In fact, such had been the trend to income segregation, that in 1930 all the disfavored immigrants suffered the same degree of segregation that the Negroes had in 1860. In 1860 the Irish had been the major disfavored ethnic group. They had been an army of peasants and low skills. They were the object of violent prejudice, rioting, and continuous political attack. Yet in 1860 the Irish were slightly less segregated than professionals and clothing workers and much less so than German immigrants. Although the poor Irish had been strongly concentrated in a few wards, they also lived in large numbers scattered in poor housing throughout the city. In 1930 Italians, Russians, and Poles were three times as segregated as the Irish of 1860. Even twentieth-century Irish immigrants themselves had become more segregated than their predecessors.

The general shift in settlement patterns from 1860 to 1930, from the early big city to the late industrial metropolis, had a number of serious consequences. Within the context of Philadelphia's slow suburban growth segregation probably had a short-run pacifying effect. Income segregation held groups in conflict apart. The middle class and prosperous working class of the northwest and parts of west Philadelphia were separated from the ghettos of south Philadelphia or the ethnically integrated inner areas of their own districts. Moreover, segregation had a supportive effect. The new detached, middle-class modes of family life and child care could not have been maintained with so little supervision as existed in the new suburbs had not strong income, and hence class, segregation existed. At all levels of the society a rough neighborhood homogeneity gave a sense of place and continuity.[15]

The long-run cost to the city of this segregated settlement pattern proved to be the total loss of control over the metropolitan environment. The loss was both social and political.

Socially, city dwellers lost the manners and habits of living in

15. Even the patterns of marriage tended to perpetuate the social geography of Philadelphia's segregated districts. The majority of Philadelphians in 1905, 1915, and 1931 married partners who lived within twenty blocks of their own home address. Ray H. Abrams, "Residential Propinquity as a Factor in Marriage Selection," *American Sociological Review*, VIII (June, 1943), 288-294.

mixed-class districts. That combination of privacy, police, and toleration which must exist in mixed neighborhoods came to be regarded as a burden by middle-class city dwellers. As those who have returned to the inner city in the 1950's and 1960's have recently learned, mixed neighborhoods, to be habitable, require the restraints of locked doors, and walled yards; they require that adults discipline any children who are misbehaving in the streets and alleys of the neighborhood; they require a watchfulness against strangers and the presence of a policeman; they require a toleration of some class warfare among the children and some respect for different goals and values in the neighborhood and the neighborhood school.

These demands ran counter to the possibilities and needs of the new early twentieth-century, middle-class and working-class family. The discipline of the mixed neighborhood, its requirement of investing attention and energy on the block and nearby streets, stood in opposition to the spatial freedom of the suburban way of life. In the 1920's the family's pleasure was taken by automobile, over the entire metropolitan region and beyond, away from the constraints and discipline of the inner city. The hope of the new homeowner, or prosperous tenant, was to be free from responsibilities and demands. The suburbanite wanted to live informally among his equals, not to have to maintain his family's position in a neighborhood microcosm of the social and economic hierarchy of the daily business world. Finally, the middle-class and working-class family, a husband, a wife, and one or two children, could not draw upon the resources of servants or relatives as much as it had in the past, and, therefore, depended more upon the passive assistance of the income-segregated neighborhood. At the very least it needed a place where children could be left to run safely, at the most it expected neighborhood, school, and church to supply a cultural milieu.

Such needs and expectations could not be met by any amount of short-run political action. One had to purchase the neighborhood with the needed services and segregation already in being. Middle-class and prosperous working-class families did just that. With the full use of the automobile since World War II the pace and scale of metropolitan segregation has further accelerated. In pace it heightened the rate of mass suburban building to a Levittown and to inner-city block busting. In scale it reached out to the entire tri-state metropolis, far beyond any possibility of Philadelphia municipal control. Thus, habits of settlement which have precipitated Philadelphia's Negro crisis today—the specter of the black city and the white metropolitan ring—had been acquired long before Negroes made up an important fraction of the city's population. They were the habits of income segregation in the industrial metropolis.

Politically, the pattern of segregated residences increased the demands made upon the municipal government while further withdrawing active popular support for local government. Just as the wealthy businessman of the mid-nineteenth century withdrew from city politics, so with the habit of purchasing neighborhoods more and more the middle-class and working-class retired into the role of passive voters and spectators of national party contests. Symbolic loyalties oriented toward national issues came to be the key factors in party alignments and voter interests in Philadelphia.[16]

The trend to a narrow specialization of activists in municipal politics begun before the Civil War continued into the twentieth century. Knowledge of and interest in municipal government came to be the property of three groups only: first, downtown businessmen who needed city services; second, those who dealt with the municipal corporation, real estate dealers, lawyers, contractors, and the like; and third, those who had made a business or career of politics, court clerks, aspiring city councilors, or state and federal officials seeking local support. Municipal politics in twentieth-century Philadelphia can be summarized as a series of rapidly shifting coalitions of downtown, ward, and state political groups seeking to control that small fraction of the Philadelphia patronage and budget which could be varied during one term of the mayor's office. Such an era was not, nor could it have been, marked by major undertakings of great novelty or broad social concern.

Despite its weakened condition, the municipal corporation faced mounting demands for service. The new suburbs stood for higher, and therefore more expensive, levels of environmental, police, and educational services. The growing slums of the inner city also proved very costly in direct and indirect welfare charges like relief, hospital and public health services, and special educational facilities. Moreover, downtown businessmen and the indus-

---

16. Charles E. Gilbert, "National Political Alignments in the Politics of Large Cities," *Political Science Quarterly*, LXXIX (March, 1964), 25-51, shows the trend to the alignment of voters in cities by national not local issues.

tries of the city continued as they had in the past to demand heavy expenditures for transportation services, new wharves, railroad yards, bridges, and now surfaced streets and highways. Vaguely countering these demands stood an amorphous popular sentiment that taxes should be kept low.

In general the municipal corporation responded to its predicament of costly demands and weakened power by meeting the requests of business and industry and by attempting a cheap uniform service to all the neighborhoods of the city. This low-cost solution hastened the decay of both slum and suburb by failing to keep up with their expensive needs. The same compromise cast a dreary uniformity over the public services and amenities of the large working-class and lower-middle-class tracts of the city, thereby encouraging the escape of their more prosperous residents. Although some contemporary businessmen, planners, and educators saw the necessity for Philadelphia to take a very active role in shaping the social and physical environments of the city, the municipal corporation was helpless to do so. Neither popular support nor municipal power could be created out of the segregated and specialized structure of the industrial metropolis.

9

Some Metropolitan Districts

Despite the ubiquity of the industrial organization of urban life in the early twentieth-century metropolis, the city was not composed of uniform environments. Rather, the clustering of economic activities, and the segregation of classes, ethnic and racial groups, created a considerable variety of specialized districts. Indeed the presence of vast tracts of distinctive character, ethnic ghettos, bedroom suburbs, a downtown, and so forth, distinguished the industrial metropolis from its more jumbled predecessor, the nineteenth-century big city.

It is impossible in a brief canvass to survey all the variations of neighborhood which existed in Philadelphia in 1930, but by dividing the city into five large districts the most important variations can be observed and discussed. By approximate reckoning, the old city from Vine street to South street became the downtown; the northern industrial suburbs east of Sixth Street grew to be a vast mill town; the peninsula of south Philadelphia became a port and refuge for newcomers; across the Schuylkill to the west began the vast tracts of bedroom suburbs, and to the northwest new bedroom suburbs spread out beyond the old mills and decaying residences of the pre-Civil War era. These districts, radiating as they did from a common downtown center, reflected the general directions of growth already established in the 1830-1860 years. Rich and poor, factories and suburbs still occupied in 1930 the same points of the compass as they had almost a century previous. All districts had grown rapidly in population since 1860 except for the downtown, which was fast ceasing to be an important place of residence in the city. By 1920 south Philadelphia had been fully built up and those who were prosperous enough were moving out. Philadelphia in the 1920's was growing in the new suburbs beyond the municipal boundaries on the west and within the municipality on the northwest (Table XVI).

TABLE XVI

POPULATION OF THE DISTRICTS OF PHILADELPHIA
1860, 1930

| | Population | | Net Change | |
	1860	*1930*	*1860-1930*	*1920-1930*
Downtown	137,756	55,859	−81,897	−17,819
% Total Pop.	24.3	2.9		
Northeast	159,947	479,317	+319,370	+39,781
% Total Pop.	28.3	24.6		
South	103,399	357,755	+254,365	−17,694
% Total Pop.	18.3	18.3		
West	23,738	411,636	+378,898	+52,035
% Total Pop.	4.2	21.1		
Northwest	140,689	646,394	+505,705	+70,879
% Total Pop.	24.9	33.1		
Total	565,529	1,950,961	+1,385,432	+127,182
	100.0	100.0		

Note:
    The 1930 wards which made up the districts were: Downtown, the old city from Vine to South streets, wards 5-10; Northeast, wards 11, 12, 16-19, 23, 25, 31, 33, 35, 41, 43, 45; South, wards 1-4, 26, 30, 36, 48; West, wards 24, 27, 34, 40, 44, 46; Northwest, wards 13-15, 20-22, 28, 29, 32, 37, 38, 42, 47.

Source:
    U.S. Eighth, Fourteenth, and Fifteenth Census of Population.

THE NORTHEAST, A MILL TOWN

By 1930 Philadelphia's Northeast had grown to enormous proportions: an industrial district of 479,000 inhabitants and two thousand-odd factories (Table XXI). Like parts of Brooklyn, New York; Cambridge and Somerville, Massachusetts; south Chicago, Illinois;

or south St. Louis, Missouri, it was a giant mill town set down in the midst of a metropolis. As such, it served the metropolis in a number of ways. Its wharves, yards, and warehouses along the Delaware River constituted an important segment of the Port of Philadelphia. These same facilities made it, like south Philadelphia, a good location for heavy industry—foundries, paper, paint, and chemical plants. Finally, the northeast offered something uniquely urban, something no other district of the metropolis could supply; it offered the economies and efficiencies of the densest concentration of manufacturing plants and skilled labor in the metropolis. Along the old streets of the Northern Liberties, Kensington, Richmond, and Frankford and next to the tracks and yards of the Reading and the Pennsylvania railroads, the clustering of shops and factories of every size and kind provided that encyclopedia of supplies and services which make highly specialized manufacturing possible. The northeast was, *par excellence,* a place offering what economists call "economies external to the firm." A machinist could send his electroplating around the corner; the plater could get his vats repaired nearby; the vat maker could get his stock milled in the district, and so the chain of interdependencies and efficiencies went. This was Philadelphia's workshop.

The mere clustering of the factories, however, did not give the northeast its mill town quality. Its mills might have been staffed with commuters, like downtown offices, or as the mills themselves have increasingly been staffed since World War II. Rather, the presence of large numbers of mill workers' houses, set near the factories, gave the district the look, and something of the internal social organization, of the mill town. Far from being a place of a mass of isolated and alienated metropolitan workers, the residents of the northeast had more habits of organized activity than those of any other district. Northeast Philadelphia was the home of benefit associations, craft unions, fraternal orders, and ethnic clubs. It also enjoyed some of the street life and neighboring qualities generally associated with lower-class, immigrant districts like parts of south Philadelphia.[1]

1. At Frankford High School, the only high school used solely by children of the northeast, there was a very active and politically effective Father's Association which lobbied for the school before the Philadelphia School Board, and acted like a PTA. It seems to have been closely linked with the fraternal organizations of the area. Francis C. Truxell, *Twenty-year History of the Frankford High School* (Philadelphia, 1931), 38. The district also had its own chamber of commerce, Northeast Philadelphia

The high degree of group-structured life in the northeast had emerged from long interaction of industrial and housing conditions. On the industrial side large textile, boot and shoe, and metal-working establishments had moved into the district in the decades just before and after the Civil War. The young men went into the mills, and the new factory organization of work swept all before it. Residents of the northeast became fully trained and habituated to the rhythms and disciplines of factory work. The old artisans and their shops died out together.[2] The group discipline, plus the passage of time, quieted the violent Protestant-Catholic conflict of the 1830's and 1840's. The Irish, English, German, and native American workers of the northeast settled into the orderly ways of the mill town.

Groups and organizations of all kinds flourished in the Northeast. Skilled English workers continued to be imported for the textile trades throughout the late nineteenth century, and each new group of specialists brought its own unions. The first Philadelphia textile union was a local in a British international. Also, the German workers of the district had fostered a succession of benefit associations and building and loan societies, and the newly arrived Poles imitated the Germans in this respect. The Irish supported athletic and ethnic clubs as well as building and loan associations, while the old Americans maintained their enthusiasm for fraternal organizations. For all ethnic groups, churches provided an important social organization.

Complementary habits thus characterized the life of the skilled factory workers of the northeast. The mill taught group work and discipline; unions, benefit associations, ethnic clubs, building and loan associations, and fraternal orders, continued these habits. The abundance of cheap housing in the district, the necessity to cope with the irregular hours of slack and busy seasons, and the job benefits of being close to shop gossip combined to give the social habits

Chamber of Commerce, *The Great Northeast* (University of Pennsylvania Library, Philadelphia, 1928). Also, *Kensington: A City Within A City* (Philadelphia, Kensington Printing House, 1891).

2. Many of the British textile immigrants to Philadelphia were skilled artisans who were fleeing modern methods in England. In Philadelphia they were able to continue, sometimes for the balance of their lifetimes, to practice their old craft before the new ways caught up to them again. Rowland T. Berthoff, *British Immigrants in Industrial America* (Cambridge, 1953), Ch. III.

of the skilled worker a spatial concentration. A large proportion of the workers in the northeast mills lived within the district and walked to work (Table XXII).

In the early nineteenth century, when it sheltered many of the city's artisans, the inner parts of the northeast had been built up with cheap housing. Contractors ran up the infamous "Father-Son-Holy Ghost" three-room house on narrow lots in the district. Row houses on twelve-front-foot lots were not uncommon, and in general much of the building went forward on a narrow and cramped basis. As such housing aged it became one of the city's pools of cheap rentals. The old Northern Liberties part, next to the downtown, had been fully built up by the time of the Civil War (wards 11, 12, 16, 17); Kensington and Richmond filled by 1900 (to Lehigh Avenue, wards 18, 19, 31); the outer area filled in the years from 1910 to 1930 as far as Wingohocking Avenue and Tacony Creek (wards 25, 45, 33, 43).[3]

The abundance of cheap housing held many workers near the mills, as did the rhythms of the mill worker's life. In the two largest industrial groupings, textiles and metal working, the normal year advanced by a succession of short weeks, overtime weeks, seasonal layoffs, and calls for extra hands. Some workers, like the upholstery weavers, possessed skills which allowed them to work on other machines when times were slow. When long stretches of short days or layoffs came, many workers sought fill-in jobs to tide them over until their old place opened up again. These adjustments depended upon shop and tavern friendships and gossip. In the northeast, neighborhood methods, not the more formal devices of union hiring halls nor the Pennsylvania Employment Service, dominated job seeking and job adjustments. Finally, union apprenticeship rules, and the mere proximity to factories of mill workers' children gave those in the mills some ability to favor residents of the northeast over residents of other districts for new openings. Most workers got their jobs because someone they knew, "spoke for them," or told them on what day to apply at the mill gate.[4]

3. Years of peak population are given in, Philadelphia City Planning Commission, *Population Peaks by Wards, Public Information Bulletin Number Five* (June, 1952), Table One.

4. Hummel LaRue Frain, *An Examination of Earnings in Certain Standard Machine-Tool Occupations in Philadelphia* (Philadelphia, 1929), 78-81; Anne Bezanson and Robert Gray, *Trends in Foundry Production in the Philadelphia Area* (Philadelphia,

This local control of entry into the jobs of the district manifested itself in a mixture of preference and prejudice which gave the
population of the northeast a unique ethnic and racial composition.
Poles had moved into the area in large numbers, despite some prejudice against them. Unlike all other districts of Philadelphia, Russian Jews and Negroes in 1930 were notable for their relative
absence. The only Negroes lived in the decaying streets next to the
downtown slum. They had not advanced past Poplar Street. Jews
were scarce throughout the entire district (Table XVII).

TABLE XVII

NEGROES AND FOREIGN BORN,
BY DISTRICTS, 1930

		Percent of Group Living in a District				
	Negro	*Italian*	*Russian*	*German*	*Irish*	*British*
Downtown	5.7	0.6	2.4	1.5	3.6	2.1
Northeast	5.5	10.6	9.3	43.8	17.8	41.4
South	26.4	63.7	28.1	4.2	12.0	5.0
West	23.3	13.0	24.2	9.2	26.2	18.0
Northwest	39.1	12.1	36.0	41.3	40.0	33.5
	100.0%	100.0%	100.0%	100.0%	100.0%	100.0%

Number Living in the City of Philadelphia

222,504	68,156	80,968	38,066	31,359	36,593

Source:
Statistics compiled from unpublished U.S. Fifteenth Census tract data.

Altogether the northeast had a somewhat old-fashioned quality.
It seemed almost to be a nineteenth-century adjustment to a 1930
metropolis. The active neighborhood life, the craft unions, the fraternal organizations, the taverns, seemed quite disciplined, quite out

1929), 56-7; C. Canby Balderson, *Philadelphia Upholstery Weaving Industry* (Philadelphia, 1932), 13-16; Ann Bezanson et al, *Four Years of Labor Mobility, a Study of
Labor Turnover from a Group of Selected Plants in Philadelphia, 1921-4* (Philadelphia, 1925), 70-96; Dorothea de Schweinitz, *How Workers Find Jobs, a Study of 4,000
Hosiery Workers in Philadelphia* (Philadelphia, 1932), 58, 85-89; *Contra,* When work
was steady, and pay good, as in the hosiery business, workers sought suburban locations in the manner of white-collar groups, William W. Jeanes, *Housing of Families of
the American Federation of Full-Fashioned Hosiery Workers* (New York, 1933), 49, 60.

of step with the greater freedom and greater isolation of the contemporary white-collar commuter's style. The northeast was the worker's contribution to Philadelphia's popular reputation as a city of contented home owners and long-settled neighborhoods.

South Philadelphia, Ghetto and Refuge

The southern district served some of the same roles for the Philadelphia metropolis as the northeast. Its wharves and terminals constituted the largest fraction of the Port of Philadelphia. Ever since before the Civil War factories had been built near the Delaware and Schuylkill river wharves and along the transverse railroad at Washington Avenue. In the 1920's a new rail loop circled the end of the southern peninsula opening up this land for freight yards, a new Navy Yard, and the booming oil refineries. Thus, in some of its functions, south Philadelphia remained what it had been since the early nineteenth century—a home of sailors, longshoremen, artisans, and mill hands. In the 1930's the more prosperous members of this working-class group clustered into the new residential areas of the extreme southern wards of the district.[5]

South Philadelphia's unique social role in the metropolis was to serve as a port of entry for poor immigrants and Negroes and as a refuge for the poor of the city in general. It was the home of Philadelphia's ghettos. Although large numbers of south Philadelphia's immigrants and poor worked in the service trades and loft manufacturing establishments on the edge of the downtown, the district was screened off from the downtown by its northern margin of sin and slums. The cramped streets and alley housing of the blocks between Spruce and South Streets had served as the Negro ghetto and a white slum for a century. Here, and on adjacent downtown streets, the police concentrated the gambling, prostitution, and speakeasies of the city. Moreover, because south Philadelphia was a peninsula, no middle-class commuters passed through the district on their way to outer suburbs. Indeed, the entire district, as well as its colorful street markets of the Italians, Jews, and Negroes, became a discovery for the newspaper feature writer or the suburban tourist.[6]

5. Wards 48, 26, and 33, especially south of Moore street. J. Frederic Dewhurst and Ernest A. Tupper, "Social and Economic Character of Unemployment in Philadelphia in April 1929," *Bulletin of the Bureau of Labor Statistics #520* (June, 1930), 43-44.
6. Christopher Morley, *Travels in Philadelphia* (Philadelphia, 1920), 15-20, 81-87.

Isolation from the main flow of Philadelphia life, however, helped the neighborhoods of south Philadelphia maintain a separate identity. Isolation bred parochialism and the shelter of insulated ghettos within which, at least when he returned home at night, the newcomer could learn American urban culture while living among his fellow beginners with whom he shared a common experience, language, and church. Similarly, the active street and neighborhood life of the district's ghettos offered support to the acculturated who remained in the district—the second generation of immigrants, the caste-isolated Negroes, and the old-stock American poor and working class who did not want to, or could not afford to, move to the new working-class and lower-middle-class districts of the west and northwest.

South Philadelphia, a district of 358,000 inhabitants in 1930, did not function as one giant neighborhood. Rather, it was a place characterized by many neighborhoods, each one with an active street life, a good deal of dependence upon neighbors, relatives, ethnic societies, and churches. The highly organized group life of the northeast did not exist here because the industrial patterns of the district did not encourage complementary neighborhoods, union and club organizations. Most south Philadelphia workers were not well paid or highly skilled and many worked in service trades. Few, thus, were union members.

The only unity of south Philadelphia, beyond its geographical isolation, had been imposed by the Republican machine of the native-born Vare brothers. Like all big-city machines of this period, the Vares offered strong equalitarian and patriotic rhetoric, token charity, jobs for some of their supporters, intervention with the police and city officials, some protection against the enforcement of the Prohibition laws, and a chance for ambitious and hard-working boys to get ahead through politics. In short, south Philadelphia, and its machine, followed the classic patterns of the American working-class district and immigrant port of entry.[7]

The role of south Philadelphia as a place where poor people and working-class people could make a stable family life and a stable

7. Marc Fried and Peggy Gleicher, "Some Sources of Satisfaction in a Residential Slum," *Journal of the American Institute of Planners*, XXVII (November, 1961), 305-315; Milton M. Gordon, *Assimilation in American Life: the Role of Race, Religion, and National Origins* (New York, 1964), Ch. III.

set of neighborhood relationships was reflected in the settled residence patterns of its inhabitants. In comparison to the other districts of the city, it had the smallest population of people who changed their homes within a year (22.5 percent), and the largest proportion of those who had lived in the same house for five years or longer (57.8 percent, Table XVIII).

Stability, parochialism, famliy ties of mutual demands, the friendships and loyalties of the gang, the street, and the saloon, all were necessities to help bolster the families and individuals of south Philadelphia against the successive crises of poverty. South Philadelphia was poor; only the downtown slums and a decayed corner of the northeast were poorer. Heavy proportions of the district's workers labored in low-skill, low-paid marine and transport jobs, in the low-pay and seasonal garment industry, in the irregular work of the building trades, and the unrewarding service jobs. For many families some unemployment each year was a fact of life.[8]

Statistics do not tell how many south Philadelphians found comfort, aid and a satisfactory sense of identity in its neighborhoods as opposed to how many remained isolated, pinched by the city's narrowness, or degraded by its poverty, but the general residental structure and function of the district was clear. South Philadelphia was the place where many were introduced to the life of the modern industrial metropolis; it was the place where many found a poor man's accommodation to that life; and it was, perhaps, a place where many found refuge from that life.

THE DOWNTOWN

Three districts of the industrial metropolis should be considered as linked together, the downtown, West Philadelphia, and the northwest. Each harbored a considerable variety of residents and jobs, and each varied from the other in age of its buildings, local employment,

---

8. The statement of the industrial specialization of the residents of south Philadelphia rests on the observation that in 1930 several of its wards were in the top quartile of the city's wards containing residences of particular industrial groupings. In all cases the top quartile reflected strong concentrations above and beyond mere variations in the total population of the wards. South Philadelphia wards were in the first quartile in the Building Industry, wards 26, 36, 39; Clothing, wards 1, 26, 36, 39; Other Transport, wards 2, 36, 39, 48; Hotels and Domestic, wards 30, 36. The statements of low income and unemployment appear in Dewhurst and Tupper, "Social and Economic Character of Unemployment in Philadelphia, April, 1929," 43-45.

TABLE XVIII

SOCIAL STATISTICS OF HOUSING, BY DISTRICT 1935

	Percent of Districts' Families Who Have Lived In Present Accommodations				No. of Family Accommodations	% of Accommodations Crowded
	1 Year and Less	2-4 Years	5 Years and More	Unspecified		
Center	34.7	23.1	37.9	4.3	49,127	21.3
Northeast	24.4	19.7	55.6	0.3	123,215	12.2
South	22.5	19.7	57.8	0.0	53,300	22.2
West	28.5	21.0	49.6	0.9	100,099	15.6
Northwest	26.5	20.1	52.3	1.1	182,151	9.3
All City	26.8	20.5	51.7	1.0	457,902	14.2

classes, and ethnic groups. But the dominant characteristic of all three districts lay in the daily rhythm of commuting to work and shopping and returning to suburban homes. Although for convenience of description each district will be dealt with separately, it should be borne in mind that the three constituted a characteristic system of the industrial metropolis—the arrangement of large segments of the middle class and working class by a central work core and peripheral residential suburbs.

The downtown was the most powerful and widely recognized symbol of the American industrial metropolis. Indeed, in ordinary conversation, or in everyday journalism, the downtown passed as an acceptable metaphor for the metropolis itself. It is what we recall today as the essence of the past American city, and although it has outlived most of its usefulness it remains the subject for concentrated civic action.

In the 1920's the downtown streets of Philadelphia gave the visitor a sense of experiencing the entire city within a concentrated space. Within a block or two the stroller could see the suburban shopper carrying her parcels to the Reading Railroad station, a Negro woman from the adjacent poor neighborhood picking through the sidewalk racks of clothes, second-story hash houses crowded at noon with men from the offices, workmen in overalls, and Kitty Foyles in short skirts. Moreover, in these years before the Great Depression and the post-World War II dispersal of the metropolis the downtown was full of life. It had not yet sickened into being an inanimate patient for federal and municipal reform. Little houses, old stores, and small hotels stood jammed next to the new skyscrapers, and their tenants filled the streets with life.[9] The characteristic post-World War II downtown, with its islands of big stores and office buildings surrounded by wastelands of parking lots, derelict houses and hotels, and vacant and half-used rows of stores had yet to come. The sheer variety of shapes and sizes of structures as well as the patchwork of signs of the tenants crammed within gave the downtown of the industrial metropolis the look of being the microcosm of the metropolis beyond.

The downtown, however, was not a microcosm of the metropolis. Instead it was a special environment composed by grouping

9. For a good sense of the architecture and feeling of the downtown in the teens and twenties, Joseph Pennell, *Pictures of Philadelphia* (Philadelphia, 1926).

those functions of the city which depended for their existence on being in the largest central place. It was an island of sixty crowded blocks (Fifth Street to Sixteenth Street, Arch Street to Walnut Street) in the midst of a metropolis of at least one thousand square miles. Far from being a representative sample of the metropolis, it was the monument of the middle class, the theater of its work and shopping.

Like the rest of the metropolis the downtown developed from the continuing process of bidding in the private market for land. Only those functions with the greatest need and profit from locating at the principal communications node of Philadelphia could afford to rent space there. Since 1860 the downtown had grown at its western edge where old houses could be purchased and torn down for stores and offices, rather than at its eastern edge where existing warehouses made the land expensive. In the seventy-year process of migration from Fifth Street to Fifteenth Street many firms had been left behind, or elbowed to one side, and the most central locations seized by newcomers. Giant new hotels, department stores, and multi-story office buildings had pushed most wholesalers and manufacturers to the fringes of the downtown. There at the edge, especially on the north side, stood the factory lofts and warehouses walling in the retail and office core by a heavy deposit of expensive real estate. Such a wall could be pierced only with the greatest difficulty. It was broken once for Fairmount Parkway in 1907, and then not pierced again until breached by federal funds in the 1950's.

Three kinds of activities dominated the downtown core:

First, the offices of Philadelphia's largest manufacturing, banking, insurance, transportation, and distribution companies. These were the firms which did a regional or a national business and which depended on a wide range of ancillary services from downtown professionals and business service firms.

Second, brokers, lawyers, engineers, accountants, architects, advertising agencies, public relations men, promoters of all kinds, hotels, restaurants, law courts and government offices, and stores which sold such a variety of specialties as books, office supplies, legal forms, pianos, exotic pets, antique furniture, and imported foods. Altogether a long list of persons, firms and institutions which both serviced the largest firms of the downtown itself and which located in the central place to be of moderate convenience to a wide metropolitan clientele.

Third, department stores, clothing stores, theaters, and large restaurants. Such activities depended upon masses of customers or mass audiences and had therefore to locate at the center of the metropolitan public transportation system.

Considered by its functions, the downtown advertised the centralizing tendencies of advanced industrialization. It also measured the state of late industrial communications. By centralizing functions the downtown gained power to handle large and intricate multi-stage transactions. In this sense the downtown was a geographical analog to the large corporation. The corporation by its coordinated bureaucracy could gather capital from thousands of individual bond and stockholders, buy and sell in hundreds of separate markets, and carefully supervise the thousands of workers and tasks which constituted the operations of a large modern factory. Where the large corporation coordinated activities within one institution, the downtown coordinated separate institutions by clustering them in one limited space.

Since the 1860's the scale of business had so enlarged, and the articulation of sales and production so improved, that all major firms maintained downtown office locations. Typical of the late industrial downtown mix were such old Philadelphia institutions as: J. B. Lippincott, publishers (1792); Baldwin-Lima-Hamilton Locomotive Works (1831); Armstrong Cork Co. (1836); Hardwick and McGee, rugs (1837); Smith, Klein and French, chemicals (1841). These firms shared downtown office buildings with branches of national organizations like Jones and Laughlin, steel; International Paper Company; Brown Brothers, Harriman, bankers; Metropolitan Life Insurance Company; and U.S. Rubber.[10]

In all these companies the sales and supply areas had grown so extensive that they depended on rapid inter-city communication by mail, telephone, and telegraph to carry on their business. The Philadelphia downtown core of the 1920's held the central Post Office, and the main offices and exchanges of the telegraph and telephone companies. It also offered two terminal stations for passenger service

10. Philadelphia Evening Bulletin, *Almanac: 1959,* "Philadelphia Centenary Firms," 286-287; and *Boyd's Philadelphia Directory: 1924.*

to New York, Pittsburgh, Chicago, and Washington, and hotels for those visiting on business.

As important to big offices as the inter-city communications node were ancillary services of the downtown cluster. As yet, none of these offices had grown large enough to provide most of its own needs within the corporation itself. Outside banks, insurance companies, law firms, advertising agencies, accountants, engineers, printers, and office suppliers made the downtown location the most efficient place for central offices of these corporations. At the same time the centralized street railway and transit system, and the presence of the retail stores assured the offices of a larger supply of clerks and female help than could be hired elsewhere in the metropolis.

This downtown pattern of large inter-city corporate office location in the late industrial era was not, of course, a permanent adjustment. In the years since the Great Depression increasing size of firms, the mobility of an auto-borne labor force, and the general improvement in communications have allowed firms to internalize many of the ancillary functions formerly performed in the downtown and thereby relocate the functions of management and supervision.

Since World War II Philadelphia firms have either enlarged their old downtown offices or taken advantage of two new business possibilities. Some have simply settled at the periphery of the metropolis where they can serve the entire region by automobile and telephone. Others have merged with huge national corporations. These new giants have abandoned old downtowns for internally oriented and managed central office buildings in New York City. This national office is then supplemented with automobile and airport-oriented branch offices in the regional cities throughout the nation. The net effect of these post-World War II locational shifts has been to destroy the rationale of the late industrial downtown and its symbiotic relationship of large corporate offices and ancillary services.

The most popularly recognized activities of the late industrial downtown were the mass shopping and entertainment units—the department stores, theaters, movie houses, and their complementary small stores and restaurants. The sixty blocks of the Philadelphia's downtown of the 1920's served the metropolis as the eighteenth-century central market had served its town. It concentrated a few retail functions: general merchandise and clothing, and to a lesser extent furniture, drugs, and a host of specialty items (Table XIX).

This mass shopping and entertainment downtown was fed by a public system of streetcars, subways, and to a much lesser degree it also depended on commuter railways. The largest stores bunched together on six blocks of Market Street from Litt Brothers on the east at Seventh Street to Wanamaker's on the west at Thirteenth Street. So situated, these giants straddled the city's first subway, the Market Street line to West Philadelphia, they abutted the Reading Railway terminal, and lacked but two blocks to reach the Pennsylvania Railway station at Fifteenth Street. In general, the subway and surface streetcar lines carried the mass of middle-class and working-class shoppers, office, store and downtown factory workers; the railroads carried the upper-middle-class buyers and workers from the outer suburbs.

TABLE XIX

THE DOWNTOWN'S PERCENT SHARE OF PHILADELPHIA'S
TOTAL RETAIL SALES, 1935

	Inner 60 Blocks
Food Stores	4.1
Automotive	2.1
Filling Stations	-
General Merchandise	71.1
Apparel	58.4
Household Furniture	25.2
Lumber and Building Hardware	10.7
Restaurants	28.6
Drug Stores	19.2
Other Retail	28.0

Source:

U.S. Census of Business: 1935, Intra-City Census Statistics for Philadelphia, Pennsylvania (Malcolm J. Proudfoot, geographer, processed May, 1937, deposited in the Philadelphia Free Library.)

The twentieth-century transit system grew directly out of the omnibus lines of the 1830's and the horsecar lines of the 1850's. By 1900 every major street in inner Philadelphia carried an electric streetcar line, and traffic jams and slow service plagued the long hauls from West Philadelphia and the northwest. In 1908 a private syndicate constructed the Market Street subway to link the downtown with the fast-growing commuter suburbs of West Philadelphia. This first transit line, like the later public construction of the twenties and thirties, was clearly designed to profit from and maintain the specialized character of the downtown. These were public facilities whose principal beneficiaries were downtown real estate owners and middle-class office workers and shoppers.

A 1912 traffic survey of all streetcar and subway lines showed who was using the downtown and its transit system (Table XX). The relatively light traffic from nearby south Philadelphia as compared to the heavy flows from West Philadelphia and the north side showed that the downtown was not only the world of the white-collar worker, but also the world of the white-collar worker's wife. Neither the residents of the poor ghettos of south Philadelphia nor the more distant mill workers of outer south Philadelphia, Kensington, and the northeast used the downtown frequently.

TABLE XX

STREETCAR AND RAPID TRANSIT TRAFFIC, 1912

Percentage of Traffic Arriving in the Downtown Whose Origin Was:	
South Philadelphia	17.0
West Philadelphia	27.4
North Philadelphia	25.1
Outer Northeast	4.7
Outer North Suburbs	7.1
Downtown	18.7

Transit construction programs, however, were not unpopular. Any call for enlargement of the system could count on at least three groups. First, the downtown office managers, storekeepers, and real estate owners, all of whom wanted to extend the transportation reach of the downtown. Second, real estate developers at the outer edges of the city and storekeepers along the proposed routes who expected a big growth in their neighborhood businesses. Finally, any appeal for enlargement met an enthusiastic response from the daily riders of the crowded rush-hour cars. Such a combination of business interest and public sentiment propelled the enormous investment Philadelphia made in transit during the years 1916-1934.

A 1916 study set the transit plans for the metropolis. Following this plan, the Frankford Elevated to the northeast opened for service in 1922, the North Broad Street Subway opened in 1928, and the South Broad Street and Ridge Avenue Connector opened during the years 1934-1936. The latter projects had been financed in part with federal aid under the Public Works Administration program. These additions, and the construction of the Delaware Bridge which brought bus service from Camden to the Philadelphia downtown, vastly increased the ease of mass movement to and from the inner sixty blocks of the metropolis. The process of speeding up commuting to the downtown, however, had an unlooked for consequence. The lengthened lines of fast transit supplemented the automobile's outward thrust of metropolitan development. As the middle class moved more and more toward the edges of the city, farther and farther from the downtown, it necessarily had to depend more and more on the automobile to reach suburban shops and friends. No transit system could satisfy all the many paths of travel of the diffuse residential suburbs. A 1934 transit study showed that all the surface and subway traffic of the city had increased only 4.5 percent from 1912 to 1934.[11]

For a city which was starved for funds for so many social and welfare projects this vast 1916-1936 subway effort seems an enormously expensive failure. Too much was spent for the tunnels, stations, and elevated structures to gain so little traffic. Even the retail sector of the downtown failed to win much. The subways and elevateds did not substantially increase the volume of business at the downtown, nor did they succeed in holding middle-class customers. Rather, each year of the 1920's suburban shoppers made more and more use of outer retail centers, like 52nd Street and Market Street or the 69th Street Upper Darby stores located just across the city line at the outer end of the Market Street-West Philadelphia subway.

11. Mayor of Philadelphi *A Review of the Transit Situation in Philadelphia* (Philadelphia, 1929), 11-13; rhiladelphia Department of City Transit, *Passenger Traffic Survey* (Processed, 1934, Philadelphia Free Library), 6-10.

Altogether the transit effort of the twenties and early thirties constituted a costly misallocation of the city's scarce resources in favor of
the downtown and inner city. Such a misallocation, however, reflected the long tradition of the city. Philadelphians had since before
the Revolution conceived of their city as a place of business. Surely
no disgrace could accrue to a government which attempted to aid
some of its largest and many of its small businessmen in their private
pursuit of wealth.

WEST PHILADELPHIA, COMMUTER'S SUBURB

West Philadelphia was a modern suburb of downtown commuters, a
bedroom town. In 1860 it had been a handful of small villages,
farms, and estates of the wealthy; in 1930 its night-time population
numbered 412,000, a size comparable to all of Philadelphia before
the Civil War.

Within the structure of the Philadelphia metropolis the western district provided an open environment for those who were making their way successfully within the society—Negroes who had
achieved a steady living, Jews and Italians who, having prospered a
little, moved out of the south Philadelphia ghettos, and, most numerous of all, the great mass of Irish and old-stock Americans who
manned the stores and offices of the downtown. If the downtown
was the monument of the late industrial metropolis, the commuter
suburb was its base.[12]

West Philadelphia in the 1920's was not a pretty place, but it
offered its residents a narrow range of solid benefits: converted
rooms in big old houses, brand-new efficiency apartments, solid
twins with bay windows and ample porches, a few blocks of expensive detached houses, and miles upon miles of row-house domestic-
ity. Above all else row houses, pre-World War I rows without

12. William W. Weaver, *West Philadelphia: A Study of Natural Social Areas* (Philadelphia, 1930), 138-141. The concentrations of the top quartile of ethnic groups were
as follows: Negroes, wards 24, 44, 34; Russians, who must stand as proxies for Jews
since there is no official religious affiliation census, wards 24, 46; Irish, wards 34, 40,
44, 46; Industry groupings, Clothing, wards 24, 34; Professionals, wards 34, 40, 44, 46;
Wholesale and Retail, wards 24, 44, 34, 46; Hotels and Domestic, wards 24, 34; Iron
and Steel, Transport, Building Trades, ward 40. South of Market Street a preponderance of middle incomes gave the district the highest average income of any section of
the city; north of Market street the average reflected lower-middle class dominance,
Dewhurst and Tupper, "Social and Economic Character of Unemployment in Philadelphia, April, 1929," 44-45.

garages, post-war rows with garages in the alley or basement rear. With the least factories of any section of the city, short on stores because commuters and their wives shopped downtown, the residential tone of the district went unbroken except for the noise and bulk of the Market Street elevated. Beyond the district, outside the city limits to the west, stretched the newer and more fashionable suburbs of the railway, inter-urban, and automobile commuters.

TABLE XXI

TYPES OF STRUCTURES, BY DISTRICT,
1935

| | Percent of Structure Type in a District | | | |
	School	Retail	Wholesale	Factory
Center	17.0	41.0	65.8	30.1
Northeast	32.7	21.5	18.7	40.6
South	12.4	3.9	3.0	8.9
West	16.1	14.5	5.6	6.8
Northwest	21.8	19.1	6.9	13.6
	100.0%	100.0%	100.0%	100.0%
	Number of Structures			
	330	9,915	2,577	5,584

West Philadelphia, itself, had boomed in the immediate post-Civil War era, and again in the electric streetcar days of the 1890's. Its dense pattern of settlement, fields cut into blocks of narrow plots, had been established at the time when a slight patch of grass in front, or a small side and rear yard seemed a generous improvement over the old in-town rows which abutted the sidewalk. The automobile allowed a more generous allocation of land to each suburban family, but except in the very expensive streets of Ardmore, West Philadelphia continued in its streetcar-sized narrow row-house lots. The result in 1930, a compact grid of streets, almost fully built up, with forty to eighty persons per acre, and no room for later adjustments of streets or community facilities. At such density only the porches, front shrubs, and street trees identified the district as suburban. In any case, it was the relative newness of the houses, the convenience for commuting to work, and the neighborhood support for quiet, family privacy which made the district more attractive to its residents than the old intown districts or more distant mass suburbs.[13]

West Philadelphia and the downtown functioned as one system. The two made an expanded residence and work unit of unprecedented scale. The blocks and blocks of row-houses in West Philadelphia were as much a part of the downtown as the rows of mill worker's houses were part of the textile mills of the northeast. The structure of movement and discipline, however, differed from either the mill-town pattern or the ghetto pattern.

Prior to the Civil War, many middle-class families lived in the neighborhoods where they worked, and even those who lived in partial residential concentrations, like the Spring Garden and Penn Township commuters of the 1850's, lived close to, or in among the work places of others. In the modern industrial city, however, the middle-class commuter had earned a partial freedom from work by living in two separate worlds.

For the modern commuter the points of intense interaction and discipline came in two widely separated locations: in the offices, stores, and factories of the downtown, and in the isolated middle-class houses of the suburbs. The consequence of the new arrangement was the enlargement of the spatial freedom of the middle class. A by-product, like the income and ethnic residential segregation of the metropolis, was the easing of tensions between the two worlds by separating work and home.

One large fraction of the downtown worked in bureaucratic groups, and were thus as organized and disciplined as their contemporary factory workers. Another large fraction of the downtown commuters, however, still worked in small businesses or in individual professional roles as they had in the mid-nineteenth century. In either case, work conditions did not encourage an active supplementary group life in the same way that the irregular employment and variable hours of the factories encouraged association and neighboring among skilled workers.

The middle class in their jobs had learned some techniques of voluntary association, and the suburban parishes, clubs, and occa-

13. Weaver, *West Philadelphia*, 131.

sional reform associations testified to the latent abilities of the class. Nevertheless, since their jobs did not require unions or neighborhood clubs or associations, commuters used their new freedom for a more intense private family life. The newspaper and magazine advertisements for homes in the 1920's stressed the theme of a man's house as his castle. Scenes of escape from work and escape from the controls of society appealed to commuters, and they used their new spatial freedom that way. Instead of visiting with neighbors, the commuter sought recreation by automobile in the country or in shopping, eating in restaurants, or in going to movies and theatres in the downtown. His friendships, often built up for business contacts, scattered more widely over the suburban area than the distance described by the blocks about his home. By 1930 all that remained in active neighborhood contact with the isolated middle-class family were the primary schools, the grocery and drug stores, and the children on the block. Although the relative uniformity of class and income, and the presence of large numbers of churches and schools has often been interpreted as an indicator of strong community life in the suburbs, at least in the early twentieth century the suburbs seem to have been more an expression of freedom for the bourgeois family than a search for a new style of middle-class community.

The Northwest, Metropolitan Sector

The northwest can be summarized as a composite of the industrial northeast and the suburban west. The largest and most populous of all the five districts we have discussed, it was in the 1920's the fastest growing. It served the metropolis in two ways: its inner section was an excellent industrial location, while both its inner and outer sections offered some measure of open ethnic and racial occupancy. Jews and Negroes could settle in the inner section, Jews only in the outer.

By social and economic geography the northwest conformed to the metropolitan sector patterns observed by contemporary Chicago urbanists. The apex of the sector lay next to the downtown at Sixth and Vine streets. Its northeastern boundary was Sixth Street, its northwestern the Schuylkill River. Within this sector the social geography shifted according to the regular rules of American urban growth. Next to the downtown began a district of poverty, then came mills, working class and aging middle-class residences, then beyond Allegheney Avenue cheap new middle-class houses, acres of row houses and tiny detached singles and doubles, then ample streets of the *haut bourgeois,* and finally the estates and grounds of the aristocracy.[14]

Residentially the sector had grown easily from the eighteenth-century Quaker and German residential concentration on the north side of Market Street. Until the opening of the Broad Street subway in 1928, Ridge Avenue served as the axis of the sector's growth. This old road cut diagonally through Penn's street grid offering an easy line of expansion from the old town core. In the early nineteenth century downtown businessmen and shopkeepers followed its path building their homes on the hills of the inner northwest. By 1860 the Spring Garden-Penn Township Districts had become the city's first middle-class residential suburbs.[15]

Prior to 1860 the principal railroads of the city had also been built in the sector, between Ridge Avenue and the Schuylkill River. The railroads and the river brought foundries, locomotive building, and general machine work. By World War I a lattice of railroads and mills of all kinds made the inner northwest an important industrial segment of the metropolis. As a result, by 1930 it was a deposit of a century of metropolitan growth; its blocks of old houses, mills, churches, and public buildings stood, as they still do today, as an architectural history of the nineteenth century. More important to the Philadelphia metropolis, the inner northwest sector offered a place where lower-middle-class, working-class, and lower-class families of every ethnic and racial background could live, constrained only by their ability to pay the rent. The heterogeneity of the district contrasted favorably with the more narrow, exclusive, and prejudiced patterns of the industrial northeast.[16]

The outer section of the northwest had been building in the 1920's as the bourgeois vanguard of a crude urban tolerance. Despite rising twentieth-century prejudice against Jews and foreigners, their row houses, twins and small singles swept over the fields of es-

14. E. Digby Baltzell, *Philadelphia Gentlemen* (Glencoe, 1958), 176, 187-193.
15. Baltzell, *Philadelphia Gentlemen,* 277-291.
16. The openness of the northwest can be seen from a list of its concentrations. The concentrations of the low-income inner wards were: Clothing, ward 28; Hotels and Domestic, ward 32, 47; Bakeries, ward 15, 28; Russians, ward 28, 32; Negroes, ward 20, 47; Germans, ward 29.

tates in the northwest. Developers who sold impartially to all whites, drove truck farmers and wealthy clubmen before them.

In the decade 1920-1930 the northwest grew by 71,000. Most of the growth occurred at the end of the Broad Street transit line with the developments spreading out like the fan from the trunk of a palm tree. Germantown, Logan, Olney, Fern Rock, and Oak Lane filled with new homes.[17]

These new residents of the outer northwest were, more than any other group in the city, automobile and railroad commuters, (Table XXII), and in many other ways, too, the outer northwest presaged the patterns of the post-World War II city. As such the northwest offered two important warnings for the future. First, as in the growth of West Philadelphia, the subdivision methods of middle-

TABLE XXII

MODE OF JOURNEY TO WORK, BY DISTRICT, 1935

	Percent of a District's Workers Who					
	Walk	*Street-car*	*Subway Elevated*	*Auto*	*Bus, Rail, Other*	*At Home*
Center	40.5	41.6	1.1	3.4	1.4	12.0
Northeast	26.8	46.2	5.9	11.3	2.8	7.0
South	25.3	61.1	0.5	4.9	1.0	7.2
West	14.1	52.4	7.1	12.7	5.2	10.5
Northwest	18.1	43.1	7.7	17.0	7.6	6.5

Note:

The analysis was based on interviews of 348,098 "main wage earners" in Philadelphia families, W.P.A., *Philadelphia Housing Inventory*, 8-56. For district boundaries see Table XVIII.

17. Concentrations of residences in the top quartile of all wards of the city for the outer northwest were: Professions, ward 22, 38, 42; Wholesale and Retail, ward 22, 38, 42; Bakeries, ward 38, 42; Other Textiles, ward 21 (Manyunk), 38, 42; Hotels and Domestic, ward 22, 42; Paper and Printing, ward 21, 22, 42; Building Trades, ward 22, 42; Other Iron and Steel, ward 42; Russians, ward 42; Poles, ward 38, 21; Germans, ward 22, 38, 42; Irish, ward 22, 38, 42; Italians, ward 38. Also useful for the old industrial village overrun by suburban building, Joseph W. Miles and William H. Cooper, *A Historical Sketch of Roxborough, Manyunk, Wissahickon* (Philadelphia, 1940).

income building destroyed the physical amenities of the district, neither farm, nor estate, nor wild landscape survived. The grid siting of houses buried the land form. The strip layout of front-facing houses, each structure lined up parallel to the curb like a row of soldiers at attention, prohibited any satisfactory visual relationship between the houses and the natural objects of the area.

As a second warning of post-World War II conditions the northwest foretold that automobile suburbs would suffer as much as streetcar suburbs from lack of strong centers. The outer northwest had inherited the Broad Street and Germantown Avenue axes, and these developed in the 1920's into shopping strips just as older streets like Ridge Avenue, or South Second Street had before them. Except for the inherited eighteenth-century Germantown streets, the new shopping strips were visually as ugly, economically as cumbersome to shop at, and socially as useless for community centers as any that preceded them. Only by the accident of the survival of historic village centers would the post-World War II megalopolis achieve anything approaching adequate centers in its new regional dispersal.

10

The Industrial Metropolis
as an Inheritance

The Philadelphia of 1930 can be viewed as an important terminal event, the final settlement of the conflicts of the past century and one-half. Compared to the Philadelphia of the political Revolution, or the Philadelphia of the early Industrial Revolution, the twentieth-century metropolis was an extraordinarily peaceable kingdom. More than two million people of all sorts and backgrounds, and of the widest diversity of skills, interests, wealth, and power shared the narrow space that was Philadelphia and labored together in a crude harmony. It was a remarkable historical event.

The Philadelphia of 1930 can also be viewed as the typical inheritance of today's American cities. More than one-third of our citizens now live in metropolises of more than a million inhabitants. Their inheritance is the traditions, institutions, and structures of the industrial metropolis.

Looking back upon the Philadelphia of 1930 as an inheritance, one immediately senses its strength: its great productivity and its durable social order which enabled the city to survive both the Great Depression and World War II with little disruption of the everyday patterns of its citizen's lives. Its structures are still very much with us; we use its offices, stores, mills, houses and streets daily. Many of its institutions are ours, private firms and corporations, and most branches of the city and state governments. Since so much of the industrial metropolis still functions in our post-World War II city we are often led to assume that the present set of relationships which make up today's city derive from today's necessities. On the contrary, the industrial metropolis is our inheritance, not our creation. Two quite different Philadelphias previously stood where it stood. It was an event of a moment in history, just as our city now is. Its temporality should encourage us to consider today's urban relationships as by no means controlling the necessities of the future.

The quality which above all else characterizes our urban inheritance is privatism. By and large the productivity and social order of the metropolis flowed from private institutions and individual adjustments. So did its weaknesses. Privatism left the metropolis helpless to guarantee its citizens a satisfactory standard of living. Privatism encouraged the building of vast new sections of the city in a manner well below contemporary standards of good layout and construction. Privatism suffered and abetted a system of politics which was so weak it could not deal effectively with the economic, physical, and social events that determined the quality of life within the city. In short, the industrial metropolis of 1930, like the colonial town, and big city which had preceded it, was a private city and the public dimensions of urban life suffered accordingly.

PRIVATISM AND THE MALDISTRIBUTION OF INCOME

Reliance on private institutions and private wealth as the basic mode of social organization in the metropolis produced the notorious failing of the modern American city: Thousands of families lived below an adequate standard of food, clothing, housing, and employment in a metropolis of unprecedented wealth and productivity. There were just more poor people in Philadelphia in the 1920's than there needed to be.

Many charities, agencies of government, and individual investigators had reported on the manifestations of the maldistribution of income. For years the Octavia Hill Association had published accounts of Philadelphia slum housing; the University of Pennsylvania had commissioned W. E. Burghardt DuBois to study poverty among the city's Negroes; the City Planning Commission had become concerned over the decline in value and condition of buildings in the heart of Philadelphia; the Philadelphia Society for Organizing Charity had been swamped with applicants when it undertook to offer a little unemployment relief in 1922.[1]

The Industrial Relations Committee of the Philadelphia Chamber of Commerce, meeting in April 1929, a few months before the great crash, understood the city's unsolved economic problems well enough. Since in the private city a family's income depended upon employment there must be steady employment for all.

> It is the hope of your committee that American industry will rise to this responsibility and that Philadelphia businessmen will take a leading part in working out the means by which we may approach the ideal solution, namely, that every person who is honestly seeking should be able to find work that is suited to his capacities, under conditions that are reasonable; and that when he has to change from one job to another, it should be possible for him to do so without reducing himself and his family to living conditions that will deteriorate them.[2]

Thousands of families lived in conditions that "deteriorated them" in the 1920's in Philadelphia as they did in every other American city, but the city's businessmen had not risen to their responsibility, nor taken a leading part in doing much about it. On the contrary, some Philadelphia firms built plants outside the metropolis to escape the costs of maintaining their Philadelphia employees' higher wages and high living standards.[3]

In respect to the problems of full employment and the distribution of income Philadelphia faced the kind of political situation it had confronted in the early nineteenth century when it sought intercity canals and railroads. Since in neither case could the city

1. Harland B. Phillips, "A War on Philadelphia's Slums: Walter Vrooman and the Conference of Moral Workers, 1893," *Pennsylvania Magazine*, LXXVI (January, 1952), 47-62. The Octavia Hill Association's reports begin in 1895. The next big report is W. E. Burghardt DuBois, *The Philadelphia Negro (University of Pennsylvania, Series in Political Economy and Public Law 14*, Philadelphia, 1899), 164-196. The lack of progress in the twentieth century, report of the Planning Commission in, Mayor of Philadelphia, *Third Annual Report of Harry A. Mackey* (Philadelphia, 1931), 747; the failure of the Philadelphia system of private administration of public charity, Leah H. Feder, *Unemployment Relief in Periods of Depression, a Study of Measures Adopted in Certain American Cities 1857-1922* (New York, 1936), 308-314.

2. Philadelphia Chamber of Commerce, Industrial Relations Committee, *Program for Regularization of Employment and the Decrease of Unemployment in Philadelphia* (conference held April, 1929), 11.

3. C. Canby Balderson, *The Philadelphia Upholstery Weaving Industry* (Philadelphia, 1932), 18; the whole migration of textiles from Philadelphia between World Wars I and II can be similarly regarded, Gladys L. Palmer, *Philadelphia Workers in a Changing Economy* (Philadelphia, 1956), 43-44.

attain its ends only by its own efforts, the achievement of its goals
depended upon a united campaign before the state legislature and
U.S. Congress by Philadelphia's legislative representatives, its municipal corporation, and its business leaders. In the early nineteenth
century such united efforts had brought expensive improvements in
the Delaware River, canals to Baltimore and Pittsburgh, and later a
railroad to the West. In the twentieth century to improve the condition of its poor Philadelphia would have had to make common cause
with other large American cities. Indeed since all large cities then
suffered similar problems, coalitions for welfare legislation should
have been easier to form and maintain than they had been in the
nineteenth century when many cities and towns saw themselves as
competitors for transportation.

To be sure the devices of today's welfare economics were not
available in the 1920's, but a number of effective measures for alle-
viating poverty were well known, had been tried in Europe and
America, and had been urged upon the public by Progressives and
Socialists since before World War I. Such measures were: health
insurance, unemployment insurance, minimum wage and hour
regulation, flexible public works programming, and progressive taxation. Yet neither Philadelphia nor other large cities in America
sought national coalitions to alleviate common poverty.

The very internal organization of the industrial metropolis
foreclosed such a possibility. The privatism which had built the city
and ordered its population into separate work groups and into
income-segregated residential districts prevented any active public
concern for poverty or unemployment in times of prosperity. The
well-to-do of Philadelphia knew the regional and national scale of
business; it was the scope of their daily activity, and they knew that
this must be the scale of effective public measures. Their interests,
however, were not focused on the poor of Philadelphia. Rather, they
formed state and national coalitions to protect their tariff interests.
The downtown business leaders were concerned with local issues,
but they were also of no use for poverty and welfare issues. Their
interests were for real estate, traffic, and civic beautification. They,
like all the well-to-do of the metropolis, hid behind a screen of
Philadelphia's many private charities. The very committee of the
Chamber of Commerce which wrote the appeal to the city's business
leaders to save the city's families from the suffering of uncertain

employment had nothing practical to offer because it refused to consider national unemployment insurance!

Lacking leadership from the city's businessmen, with the poor confined to their own neighborhoods, and with unemployment striking only scattered workers at any given moment, the ordinary Philadelphian in the 1920's went about his personal affairs unconcerned. The vast majority of the city's families had learned to cope with the economic system on a personal basis, by friendships and aid from relatives. Thousands of families continued to suffer the pains and indignities of poverty; the slums went unmended, and the Bureau of Personal Assistance of the City of Philadelphia continued in its absurd task of separating the "worthy" from the "unworthy" poor.[4]

PRIVATISM AND THE BUILDING PROCESS

Like the city's inability to deal effectively with its standard-of-living problems, the building habits of Philadelphia in the twenties left later generations a legacy of failure. The fault also clearly lay with the tradition of privatism. Such a large share of land division and new construction remained in the hands of the private real estate market that despite very considerable efforts at municipal planning the city failed to cope successfully with the disorders it inherited in its old areas or the process of substandard building it faced in its areas of new growth.

The twentieth-century planning task required two things: first, a public institution or institutions that could make sure that land division, siting, and building at the growing edge of the city met the best standards of the day. Second, twentieth-century planning also required that public investments in the old sections of the city be not tied down to serving a small fraction of the city's interests. The industrial metropolis failed to create the necessary institutions to control the city's growth and to allocate the city's public investments effectively.

In Philadelphia, no less than in other large American cities, the early twentieth century was a period of active interest in city planning. Indeed, formal physical planning in most American cities began with this generation.

Since 1871 the Philadelphia Board of Surveyors of the munici-

4. Mayor of Philadelphia, *Third Annual Message of Harry A. Mackey*, 530.

pal corporation had been empowered to make general plans for the future development of the city, but it never had a large or ambitious enough staff to do any such planning. The day-to-day demands of real estate men, lawyers, engineers, and city offices for drawings of street alignments, grades, set-back lines, and approval of subdivision plots consumed all the small office's energies.[5]

Physical planning really began in Philadelphia in 1905 with the City Councils' acceptance of a citizens committee proposal to build the Fairmount Parkway boulevard connecting City Hall with a new art museum at the edge of the park. The proposal was a typical City Beautiful plan of the kind then sweeping the nation. Mayor John E. Rayburn enlarged upon this parkway effort by requesting that the Board of Survey conduct studies for downtown traffic improvement, and he also created a large committee of businessmen to work up plans for the city. Finally, the new 1919 Philadelphia municipal charter authorized the establishing of a regular planning commission. Intermittently ever since 1919, the Philadelphia municipal corporation has been engaged in city planning.[6]

Planning as then practiced by these municipal and businessmen's boards did not mean consciously allocating the city's scarce resources among the items of a comprehensive five or ten year plan. These planners did not endeavor to see that the new public and private investment in the city would conform to some overall program for housing, green space, public utilities, transport, municipal services, employment, and welfare. Rather planning in the early twentieth century was something carried on by a limited group of people to deal with a limited set of issues.

The people who planned, or who sat on planning commissions, were downtown merchants, utility, transit, and bank directors, real estate men, railroad and ocean transport carriers, and a few professionals (i.e. perennial Philadelphia board sitters, architects, and civil engineers). The issues that concerned these commissions matched

5. Mayor of Philadelphia, *First Annual Message of J. Hampton Moore* (Philadelphia, 1921), 237; Robert S. Glover, *Survey of the Housing Situation in Philadelphia* (University of Pennsylvania PhD Thesis, 1933), 80.

6. City of Philadelphia, *Philadelphia*, I (July, 1909), 4-7; Jacques Gréber, "Le Fairmount Parkway à Philadelphia," *La Vie Urbaine* (New Series, Jan-Mars, 1962), 1-18; City of Philadelphia, *Philadelphia*, IV ("Comprehensive Plans Number," March 11, 1911), 3-12; Werner Hegemann and Elbert Peets, *The American Vitruvius: an Architect's Handbook of Civic Art* (New York, 1922), 249-250, 259-260.

the commissioners: transit, the relief of traffic congestion by parkway and new downtown street construction, inter-city transportation improvements, especially terminals and wharves, and parks and parkway beautification. In the mid-twenties a concern for promoting the tourist trade was added to this list of interests.

By their personnel and their subject matter these first planning commissions continued the old American urban tradition of businessmen taking an active role in persuading the public and the municipal corporation to improve the commercial environment of the city. In this era the unique ingredient was the strong effort in behalf of the downtown and intracity transportation as opposed to the concerns for intercity business of the nineteenth century. Yet, despite the concentration of benefit on the downtown such was the strength of the tradition and its sanction of public support of business that a great deal of the planning commission's recommendations carried.

These early commissions had no public powers or budgets beyond the funds granted for studies and the publication of recommendations. Yet, to a remarkable extent their proposals became projects and were built: the Fairmount (now Benjamin Franklin) Parkway, the Schuylkill River Parkways, the Roosevelt Parkway in the northeast, the convention hall, the transit extension along Broad Street, and the Ridge Avenue loop, the Benjamin Franklin Bridge, and the wharf and terminal facilities of south Philadelphia.[7]

Except for the wharves and terminals, and perhaps the Roosevelt Parkway which was part of a state highway to New York City, all the projects in one way or another were downtown-oriented. All were to bring traffic to the downtown, to beautify it, and to raise or maintain downtown business property values. It was a remarkable effort, some of it, like the Fairmount Parkway and the transit extensions, involving massive municipal investments. The state helped with the bridge and road projects, the W.P.A. with the completion of the transit system, but the city and private funds financed the overwhelming fraction of the total outlay.

This effort, which might best be characterized as modernizing

7. Mayor of Philadelphia, *Third Annual Message of Harry A. Mackey* (Philadelphia, 1931), 747-9, lists current projects and shows the overlapping of personnel and personnel types with the early 1911 board of Mayor Reyburn and the later board of the Regional Plan of 1932.

the inner city, since it added facilities former generations would not have thought necessary or even conceived of, over-committed the municipal corporation to inner-city projects. It left too little funds, and too little energy, for other kinds of municipal enterprise, or for work in other sections of the city. For instance, increases in school attendance during the early twentieth century brought a crisis in school facilities. Despite a very heavy school-building program in the twenties overcrowding continued in many classrooms of the city.[8]

The City Beautiful aesthetic and the downtown interests of the planning boards also did not encompass a concern for the smaller clusters of the city. The two-dozen-odd shopping streets and retail clusters of the city badly needed modernizing if they were not to be destroyed by the automobile. Nothing was done for these lesser commercial areas, which were, for the majority of Philadelphians, their principal community centers.[9] Finally, the level of recreation, police, and health services of Philadelphia in the twenties was so low that the entire city could have benefited from more allocations in these directions. The heavy downtown commitment, however, like the municipal corporation's subscription to canal and railroad bonds in the early nineteenth century, was the inevitable consequence of Philadelphia's and America's tradition. The tradition held that the business of a city was business. In the 1920's the downtown was both the popular symbol of the "pep," and success of business; it was also the locus of business's political power.

Although the projects of the Philadelphia Planning Commissions took a very strong inner-city bias, the interest of some Philadelphia businessmen in transportation, utilities, and parks led them to follow these subjects to their full metropolitan scale. In 1923 a group of Philadelphia businessmen, both downtown-oriented merchants and bankers, and national corporations executives, joined

8. School crowding: "A Seat for Every Child," *Evening Bulletin* (October 26, 1923), editorial; Franklin D. Edmunds, *A Chronological List of the Public School Buildings of Philadelphia* (Philadelphia, 1934), 90-103; Board of Education, School district of Philadelphia, *Annual Report of the Superintendant of Public Schools* (Philadelphia, 1925), 11-21.

9. A map of retail locations in Philadelphia and some pictures of neighborhood stores appears in Malcolm J. Proudfoot, "City Retail Structure," *Economic Geography*, XIII (October, 1937), 425-428.

their opposites from Camden, Trenton, New Jersey, and Wilmington, Delaware, to establish a Tri-State Regional Planning Federation. The federation was a privately supported group established to study and make recommendations for land development, transportation, water supply, and parks for the entire region. The group raised $600,000, and published its recommendations for regional improvement in 1932. The project was carried on in the spirit of the 1909 Chicago plan. As in Chicago the federation had no public powers, it made recommendations and lobbied before state and county governments in its own behalf. The group did not propose a metropolitan government agency; rather it expected to continue as a federation of citizens' planning associations in each of the eleven counties of the three-state region.

The subject of the federation's plan was growth; its theme was the orderly programming of municipal and private investments according to a scheme which took into account the projected fifty-year growth of the region. The goal was conservation of land through an allocation among green space, housing, and industry. It was hoped that through planning, substantial savings to the metropolitan region could be effected by the coordination of some of the heavy capital investments in transportation, utilities, and water supply.[10]

Over and over again, in pictures, and in the text, *The Regional Plan* stressed the failure of the metropolis to control its own growth. The disorders noted were many: houses where highways, parks, and industries should be, barren, ugly subdivisions, traffic jams, heavy expenses in expanding utilities, transport and regional services, the failure to reserve adequate space for groupings of industry and stores.

The Regional Plan was written at the time when the Pennsylvania legislature had just authorized zoning ordinances in the state, and hopes ran high for the future benefits of the land use and building bulk classifications of common zoning procedures. These zoning laws were not novel in their regulations. Rather they enacted on a city-wide basis what had become common good practice in middle-income developments. The new zoning laws, by forbidding

10. Regional Planning Federation of the Philadelphia Tri-State District, *The Regional Plan* (Philadelphia, 1932), 1-22. A good discussion of the Chicago Plan, John W. Reps, *The Making of Urban America* (Princeton, 1965), 497-502.

industries in residential zones or apartments next to single family houses, enacted as law what had become by the twentieth century the norm for new residential areas.[11]

The Regional Plan, after recommending zoning ordinances to communities which did not yet have them, went on to observe that zoning could only prevent certain abuses; it could not ensure good building. *The Regional Plan* clearly stated that the key to achieving a satisfactory metropolitan development was good design of the new suburban communities. Such design meant: attention to the arrangement of streets to see that trips to stores, jobs, and houses would help make coherent communities; arrangement of house lots to preserve recreation space and to take advantage of the inherent beauties of the landscape; siting of houses on their lots to ensure a good final effect when all the lots had been built upon; hiring good architects for the design of the buildings themselves.

There can be no question but that these design objectives were obtainable in the 1920's and that the results would have proved more satisfactory both to their first occupants and to later generations than the mass suburbs then being built. The examples cited in *The Regional Plan* showed what could have been done with a different organization of the land subdivision and housing market: Radburn in Fair Lawn, New Jersey; Yorkship Village in Camden, New Jersey; French Village (McCallum street) in Chestnut Hill, Philadelphia. Yet because the businessmen of the regional plan commission and its authors were unwilling to confront the conflict between their goals of satisfactory metropolitan development and the daily product of private city building they had neither institution, law, nor technique to propose. Because of their unwillingness to disturb the private market in land they, like American city planners ever since, were helpless to prevent the continued destructive process of metropolitan building which their reports castigated.[12]

The problem of securing good design for the growing edge of the metropolis turned on the peculiar nature of the private building process. An ordinary city or suburban structure will stand at least sixty or a hundred years before being radically remodeled or torn

11. The hopes and limitations for zoning, Mayor of Philadelphia, *Third Annual Message of Harry A. Mackey* (Philadelphia, 1931), 775-776.

12. *The Regional Plan,* 378-412.

down. Thus, all new construction adds a long-lasting element to the metropolitan physical environment. Yet, each house and store must be designed and sold to meet the financial capabilities of the individual who first purchases it. According to the private building process, then, the capabilities of the large number of little home and store buyers set the future of the metropolis.

The industrial metropolis of the early twentieth century was built by a succession of thousands of bargains struck between two parties. On the one side the land owners and developers tried to maximize their profits on the sale of land for houses. On the other side the vast majority of working-class and middle-class home purchasers tried to become home owners without overstraining their limited financial capabilities. The only constraints on the bargaining between the two groups in the 1920's were the building and banking laws and the housing customs of the city. The building law of Philadelphia merely legislated what were long-ago minimal standards for structural safety, sanitation, and light and air. The banking laws of Pennsylvania allowed building and loan associations to lend money on both first and second mortgages, so that in Philadelphia one could attempt home ownership with almost no down-payment.

In the twenties many Philadelphians made the attempt at home ownership. In 1930 more than half the city's families owned their own houses for the first time in the city's history. The effort, however, proved more than many could sustain, and by World War II the Great Depression had reduced home ownership to just below the level of 1920.[13]

The surge to home ownership in the twenties clearly tells of the aspirations of Philadelphia's working-class and middle-class families. Yet their incomes tell how the building of the metropolis had to be tailored. The important figures for the twenties were: 48.3 percent of all Philadelphia families earned less than $2,000 per year and thus could not enter the new housing market either as purchasers or renters; next, 39.2 percent of Philadelphia's families earned $2,000 to $4,000 per year. These were the customers for mass suburban

13. Philadelphia, Bureau of Building Inspection, *The Building Code* (January, 1930), 103-104; David T. Rowlands, *Two Decades of Building and Loan Associations in Pennsylvania* (Philadelphia, 1940), 24-5; Henry M. Muller, *Urban Home Ownership; a Socio-Economic Analysis with Emphasis on Philadelphia* (Philadelphia, 1947), 78.

housing. Two thirds of the residential construction of the twenties was designed, built, and sold for this income range.[14]

The result—miles and miles of grid streets filled with narrow lots and six-room row houses. These structures varied from their 1880 predecessors only by the addition of a front porch, a tiny front yard, and a basement garage connected to a paved, rear, service alley. Fancy detailing and elaborate brickwork and fixtures dressed up the standard model to give the salesmen some talking points. The results were equivalent to six-unit flats, two families, and detached singles then being run up by the thousands all over America. The only unique Philadelphia quality was the continuation of the row-house style in the twentieth century when all other cities save Baltimore had turned to detached dwellings.

The developers of Philadelphia followed the American builder's tradition of giving as much structure as they could. The profit lay in pinching on the land. The new construction of the 1920's, thus, meant a good deal of structure set on a disastrous land plan. Not one of the rules of good design was followed: the grid streets did not make visually or socially coherent communities, the narrow lots destroyed the inherited beauty of the land, the façade of the houses, once all the lots were filled, was ugly and endless, and the land so cramped with structures that no recreation space existed and no space was left for future development of the suburbs. In later years streets could be widened, sewers laid, new schools erected, stores and offices and factories moved into the area only with the greatest difficulty and expense. Because the land was so crowded with structures at one moment in time, modernization could only be achieved by the enormously cumbersome, disruptive, and expensive method of urban renewal. The painful irony of the private building process was that at the very moment the building was going on developers knew how to build better, and their customers aspired to more.

In the early twentieth century Philadelphia nourished some of the nation's best examples of suburban design. Local architects had carried out a very successful revival of historical English and colonial American styles and they had worked out a very attractive free

14. Robert S. Glover, Jr., *A Survey of the Housing Situation in Philadelphia* (University of Pennsylvania Master's Thesis, based on the Philadelphia Housing Association's materials, 1933, deposited at School of Fine Arts Library), 64-7.

style using local stone and traditional design elements. In the expensive sections of the city, and on the Main Line, there stood a full range of good architecture, well suited for mass adaptation. There were small Tudor and colonial detached houses of brick and stone, groupings of English "cottages," arranged in forms which would later be imitated by post-World War II garden apartments, and there was even a fine example of a high-rise apartment house in Germantown next to the city park (foot of McCallum street). Architectural magazines and writers of the period featured such work, and it has been imitated widely in expensive building ever since.[15]

The private real estate market was so organized that it had no way to join this architectural design skill to the mass demand for housing. Radburns and French Villages cost more than grid streets of row houses; especially they cost the profit on the land. In the twenties the developer's profit could only be maximized at the expense of building a substandard new city. The substandard habit persists to this very day.

Thus the industrial metropolis passed on its legacy of building failure. Vast public effort had been expended in modernizing the downtown at the very moment when the city of the next century was being built below the capabilities of contemporary knowledge and standards. This destructive tradition could only have been overcome if Philadelphia had imitated contemporary European cities, set up its own land development and housing institutions, and used the profit it would realize on land at the growing edge of the city to build for the mass of Philadelphians according to the best standards of the day. The traditions of privatism, however, forbade the city to take the measures necessary to control its own growth. According to the tradition of the private city the municipality could rehabilitate by transit, park, street, and school investments what had already been built, but it could not become an entrepreneur in its

15. Examples of Philadelphia styles which could have been adapted for mass suburbs, George H. Edgell, *The American Architecture of To-day* (New York, 1928), 98-101, 113-119; A. Lawrence Kocher, "The Country House, Are We Developing an American Style?" *Architectural Record*, LX (November, 1926), 388, 403-417. A discussion of alternatives to the row house and street grid site design, especially based on lessons of the U.S. Housing Corporation's World War I designs, Frank C. Brown, "Low Rental Housing," *Architectural Record*, LXV (May, 1924), 405-415, LXVI (September, 1924), 206-212, LXVI (October, 1924), 353-367.

own right, no matter what the later public costs of the private real estate market might be.

PRIVATISM AND POLITICAL FAILURE

In the end the failure of the industrial metropolis was political. Although much of urban life is inescapably public the genius of Philadelphia in the 1920's lay not in its public institutions but in its containment of masses of people in thousands of private settings. The single-generation family, the private company's work group, and the income-segregated neighborhood were the metropolis' basic units, and they were the secret of its productivity and social peace. These same units, however, when they confronted the traditional forms of American municipal politics did not produce a creative competition.

By the twentieth century Philadelphia politics had become highly stylized. Three groups of leaders competed for control of public offices: reformers, locally oriented professionals, and state and nationally oriented professionals.

Since the middle of the nineteenth century Philadelphia's wealthy lawyers and businessmen took only an occasional interest in local politics unless they had an immediate interest in downtown business or real estate. When most business leaders did take an interest they were cast in that peculiar modern role of "reformer." The peculiarity of this role consisted in its turning participation in government into a philanthropic activity. These wealthy lawyers and businessmen carefully defined themselves as amateurs, helping out for a brief time, as if the municipal corporation were ordinarily someone else's affair, the governing institution of someone else's city.[16]

Others did indeed regard the municipal corporation and local government as their own affair, worthy of full-time attention. These were the professional politicians, men whose interests and actions had set the terms of political competition since the Civil War. The professional politicians can be divided into two groups—the locally oriented, and the state and federally oriented. The former sought to create power in organizing the wards and districts of Philadelphia in order to control Philadelphia city and county offices and to benefit

16. The pattern of reform politics in the twenties is nicely characterized in a contemporary novel by Francis Biddle, *The Llanfear Pattern* (New York, 1927), Ch. 18.

from the private business done with these governments; the latter, working from a base outside the city, sought to control the blocks of Philadelphia votes in order to gain power in state and federal political competition. The most conscientious research would be required to arrive at a judicious estimate of which of these two groups of professional political leaders did the most damage to the city of Philadelphia.

Since the early nineteenth century the presence of neighborhood militia and firehouse gangs had made it possible for local politicians to maintain a continuous ward organization rather than having to assemble their followers afresh at each election. The professional politician, however, paid for the use of these gangs. The price was intensive work serving the needs and prejudices of his low-income wards. In the twentieth century the south Philadelphia machine of Congressman William S. Vare and his brothers continued this demanding tradition. Their machine was the core of the Republican organization of Philadelphia, and in alliance with leaders from other inner wards of the city it could deliver the largest single block of votes at any election for any candidate.

Three brothers, Edwin, George, and William, had built the machine. It had been slow and arduous work. Their power had come slowly, earned with years of petty services to south Philadelphians and encouraged by the support of shifting coalitions with Republican factions outside the city. In 1922 only William, the youngest, still lived.

William had been born December 4, 1867, the son of a south Philadelphia truck farmer. His was a Methodist family of English and old Massachusetts immigration. William's career advanced much less rapidly than would have been the normal pace for a contemporary college graduate. He quit school and the farm chores at twelve to go to work as a cash boy in Wanamaker's store. Then in 1883, when he was sixteen years old, his political career began. In that year he went out to work for one of his brothers who peddled stove oil through the streets of south Philadelphia. On this job, and subsequent jobs as a produce peddler, William learned the streets and neighborhoods of his political base. Parades were William's special delight throughout his lifetime, and he began this pleasure when he was eighteen by organizing a mummer's club for the New Year's Day parades.

In the mid-eighties his brothers successfully seized control of south Philadelphia's Ward One Republican Organization. In 1886, when he turned twenty-one, William's district elected him representative to the Ward One Republican Committee.[17]

From 1890 to 1926 the Vare brothers held a succession of city, county, and state elective offices. Edwin and William both served terms in Congress as representatives of south Philadelphia. In addition, for many years the Vares obtained lucrative building contracts from the city and ran the municipal trash and garbage routes in their southern and central wards.

This machine linked several interest groupings: those seeking the non-civil-service jobs in the city and county government, and those seeking recommendations to civil service positions; those who wished favorable representation before municipal officials, and the city's magistrate courts; and those with private business with the municipal and county government or whose business depended on local custom. William Vare's leading backers were a coal dealer and an owner of a fleet of taxis.[18]

A decayed version of Philadelphia's old equal-opportunity tradition covered this cluster of interests with an umbrella of familiar rhetoric. "Service" was William Vare's personal slogan. To show the machine's readiness to better the common citizen's lot, its candidates promised anything and everything that had popular appeal, whether it was a high school stadium, the return of the five-cent fare, better traffic conditions, more efficient government, and of course, lower taxes. Vare candidates tended to promise everything, but they also had the locally oriented organization's bias for making these promises on a ward-by-ward basis. One rule, however, could not be breached. The root of the Vare's power grew in the south Philadelphia ethnic ghettos, and like Boss Martin Lomasney in Boston, the Vares maintained a crude ethnic peace in their districts. One candidate for mayor had to be repudiated when he compared south Philadelphia to the slums of Moscow.[19]

17. William S. Vare, *My Forty Years in Politics* (Philadelphia, 1933), 37-43, 47-55.

18. Sixty-ninth Congress, First Session, *Report of the Special Committee Investigating Expenditures in Senatorial and General Elections*, Pt. I (Washington, 1926), 451-452, 493.

19. The Vare Machine, William F. Vare, *Forty Years*, espec. 29-30, 118-119. The county offices were the most numerous non-civil service positions since the major departments of the city all had civil service since 1905. In 1920, exclusive of the school department, there were 15,372 city and county positions. Of these 12,817 were civil

The peak of William's career came in 1926 when he was elected to the United States Senate from Pennsylvania. The Senate, however, refused to seat him. The Vares had a very unpleasant reputation for dishonest election practices, false voter registration, illegal accompaniment of voters into the voting booths, purchase of votes from poor citizens, the use of paid repeat voters, ballot-box stuffing, and false counting. None of the brothers had ever been convicted of such crimes, but Philadelphia elections were conducted amidst charges of such practices, and an occasional offender was arrested and convicted. After three years of investigation and delay Vare was denied his seat in the U.S. Senate on the ground that he had spent too lavishly in the Republican primary. The conclusion was an improper one since his rivals, Senator George W. Pepper, and Governor Gifford Pinchot, had each declared larger expenditures, and Pepper had surely spent the most. Partisan pressure and the Vares' unsavory reputation can only account for William's failure to be seated.[20]

In any case, after almost forty years of power and effort the Vares could boast of very little constructive results for Philadelphia or Philadelphians. As congressmen the brothers had, of course, supported the south Philadelphia Navy Yard, and as city councilors they had encouraged all sorts of public works measures for south Philadelphia wards. William, although by no means a leader in these movements, had been instrumental in guiding the final bills through the Pennsylvania legislature for workmen's compensation, child labor, hours of labor for women, Mother's Assistance welfare payments, and the constitutional amendment giving women the

---

service posts, 2,555 were non-civil service. The largest city departments were Public Safety 6,754 employees, Public Works 3,239 employees, Public Health 1,890 employees. Mayor of Philadelphia, *First Annual Message of J. Hampton Moore* (Philadelphia, 1921), 873-876. Court and criminal service groups, Spencer Ervin, *The Magistrates Courts of Philadelphia* (Philadelphia, 1931), 105-107; Law Association of Philadelphia, *Report on the Crimes Survey Committee* (Philadelphia, 1926), 450-453; Fred D. Baldwin, "Smedley D. Butler and Prohibition Enforcement in Philadelphia 1924-1925," *Pennsylvania Magazine*, LXXXIV (July, 1960), 352-368; election promises *Philadelphia Evening Bulletin*, August 18, 1923, September 12, 1927; ward-by-ward promises, September 8, 1923.

20. Common newspaper voting fraud charges, *Philadelphia Evening Bulletin*, October 29, 1919, August 30, 1923, August 31, 1923, September 21, 1927, November 9, 1927. The hearing on the primary centered on corrupt practices in Pittsburgh, Sixty-ninth Congress, First Session, *Report of the Special Committee. . . ,* 35-36, 91-136, 268, 451-458, 492-508.

vote. Also he had unsuccessfully sponsored old-age pension measures.[21]

Finally, in 1905 William Vare had responded favorably to requests of school reformers to help pass a new state school law as a Republican organization measure. The event was an interesting one since it showed that the machine separated school from county and city issues. In this case the Vares supported for the educational system the very kinds of reforms they often fought against in municipal and county government. This incident also showed the irresistible power in the American urban tradition of any reform which united the business community with a strong equalitarian campaign.

The 1905 school law created for the cities and towns of Pennsylvania a modern, centralized, bureaucratic management of schools. In Philadelphia power was taken from the forty-two sectional school boards out in the wards and placed in the hands of a small Board of Education and a strong superintendent of schools. The Board of Education continued, as in the past, to be appointed by the judges of the Courts of Common Pleas, so presumably the Board remained as amenable to political organization pressure as did the judges the Republican organization nominated. An orderly eligible list for teacher appointments was to be established.

Altogether the school reform of 1905 resembled the attempts to get identifiable responsibility and expert, executive management that were later embodied in a series of anti-machine programs: in Mayor Blakenberg's reforms of 1912-1916, the new Philadelphia charter of 1919, and the Pennsylvania Administrative Code of 1923. The Vares however, did not object to the changes. Apparently their machine did not depend upon school jobs and school business for its power. Also the 1905 school reform was linked in the public mind with the drive to make high school education easily available to all Philadelphia children who wanted it. Uniform, centralized, professional management had become tied with the proposals for industrial and commercial high schools for the non-college-bound student. The big district high school, serving all classes and talents of children resulted, and in the process of achieving this equalitarian uniformity the old elite college preparatory Central High School was destroyed. As always with American municipal institutions, the possibility of

21. Vare, *Forty Years*, 22, 131.

serving all the publics of the city, rich and poor, with a variety of institutions, instead of restricting the system to a few dreary uniform ones, proved to be beyond the capabilities of the Board of Education and the citizens of Philadelphia.[22]

The state and federally based professional politicians proved no more useful to the city than the Vares, who were, after all, to some extent their product. The line of descent of leadership in Pennsylvania Republican politics ran from the Camerons, the father Simon, (1867-1877) and the son Donald (1877-1887) to Matthew S. Quay (1887-1911), to Boise Penrose (1911-1921). In the 1920's Joseph R. Grundy of the Pennsylvania Manufacturers Association and the Mellons of the Gulf Oil Corporation of Pittsburgh disputed control of the state party with William Vare. The entire list of Republican state leaders had been an able, unscrupulous group whose power rested on uniting party service to business with business financial support of the party. In the years since the Civil War they had succeeded in driving the Democratic Party into an ever narrower compass so that from 1895 to 1935 Pennsylvania politics were Republican politics.

The power and success of the state Republican rule proved a great misfortune to Philadelphia since it sharply narrowed the issues of political competition. The state party's goals and methods became the focus of all Pennsylvania politics. The party was the subject of campaigns, not the problems of Pennsylvania's economy and institutions. In the twentieth century two issues overshadowed all the rest: honesty in government, and big-business domination of government. The first issue should not have been a major concern in a well-led democratic society. The second issue prevented the state from dealing with the difficult and important matters of social welfare and economic development, which became more and more serious as the twentieth century advanced.

The polarities of state politics repeated themselves in Philadelphia. In Pennsylvania in the 1920's political conflict paired coal companies with their unions, electric utilities with the Public Service Commission, and the traditions of politicians' patchwork office

22. Vare, *Forty Years*, 63-64; Public Education Association of Philadelphia, *Twenty-fourth Annual Report* (Philadelphia, 1905), 5, 31-34; William H. Cornog, *School of the Republic, 1893-1943* (Philadelphia, 1952), 224-232; Donald W. Disbrow, "Reform in Philadelphia under Mayor Blankenburg, 1912-1916," *Pennsylvania History*, XXVII (October, 1960), 379-396.

practice with the state administrative code. In Philadelphia similar pairs appeared between textile manufacturers and their unions, the Philadelphia Transit Company and the municipal corporation; regular city employees and the experts. Although splits in Republican machine leadership twice allowed the independent Republican Gifford Pinchot to be elected governor (1923-1927, 1931-1935) these dualities consumed most of his energies. The state and federal Republican leadership was so conservative that it could not see the important economic development issues in Pinchot's power studies, although his program could have aided Pennsylvania's growth as well as keeping the utilities prosperous. No more did Governor Pinchot, or other Republican leaders, see the enormous state expenditure on roads over the years from the Sproul Bill of 1911 to the Great Depression as an extraordinary public effort to be allocated with as much care as electric power. Nor did the state Republican leaders sponsor the economic and social legislation necessary to alleviate the disorders of poverty which affected Philadelphia and large sections of Pennsylvania. Rather, after a decade of opposition they blocked state relief measures in the early 1930's when one-quarter of Pennsylvania's workers were unemployed. Finally, the whole negative attitude toward government which characterized the Republican state and federal leadership encouraged a least-cost, low-quality orientation toward all public institutions and programs whether they were police departments or schools, hospitals or highways.[23]

Lacking a state or local Republican Organization leadership which could define contemporary problems in terms which led to public action, and given the issues of honesty and business domination which the leaders did create, Philadelphia's politics became a highly stylized activity. The elections of the 1920's repeated a contest between Republican organization coalitions and loosely joined opposition groups. The opposition might be styled modernizers.

The nature of this contest between the organization and the modernizers can be observed in the primary elections for Republican candidate for Mayor of Philadelphia. The organization's coali-

23. Sylvester K. Stevens, *Pennsylvania, Birthplace of a Nation* (New York, 1964), 264-282; Wayland S. Dunaway, *A History of Pennsylvania* (Englewood, 1948), 456, 479; Gifford Pinchot, "Giant Power," *The Survey*, LI (March, 1924), 561-562 and balance of this month's issue on power.

tions began with the Vares' south Philadelphia machine and its allies in the inner, poor, wards of the city. Ward leaders in west Philadelphia and in the northeast and northwest joined after considerable bargaining among local and state Republican leaders. These coalitions did not always come together easily. In 1911 a conflict between the Vares' faction and Boise Penrose, the state leader, allowed an independent mayor, Rudolph Blankenberg, to be elected for a term (1912-1916). A similar conflict gave Congressman J. Hampton Moore the mayorality in 1919. Throughout the early twentieth century the Republican organization candidates won or failed for mayor on the popular appeal and strength of a politically and economically conservative, locally based, local-serving, personal party organization.

Aligned against this organization stood a vague grouping of people who have been variously styled as reformers, progressives, and cosmopolitans. At the time they called themselves independent Republicans. They seemed to have been, in large measure, a new group of middle and upper-income voters who knew something of the world beyond their neighborhood and city, who responded to appeals for business-like, but not expensive, performance of municipal services, reduction of the municipal debt, civil service, use of experts, honesty in voting and administration, and the prosecution of some new projects like transit, high schools, or a municipal convention hall. In short, the opposition to the organization were modernizers, people who voted to make the city more like the Philadelphia they knew; it should conduct its business like a downtown office or a modern factory or store and it should offer its services at a level of quality which matched that of the new sections of the city.[24]

A tabulation of the votes for Republican organization candidate for mayor in the primaries of 1919, 1923 and 1927 clearly

24. Samuel P. Hays, "The Social Analysis of American Political History 1880-1920," *Political Science Quarterly*, LXXX (September, 1965), 373-394; Vare, *Forty Years*, 117-119. Voting participation, measured by the number of votes cast in the Republican primaries for mayor as a percentage of the estimated ward population did not show any strong differences between the core wards where the less well-to-do lived and the ring wards of the suburbanites. The core percentage of voters to population was 16.1 percent (1919), 19.1 percent (1923), 20.6 percent (1927); the ring 17.5 percent (1919), 16.0 percent (1923), 20.3 percent (1927). These variations can be explained by the attractiveness of the candidates to the core or ring voters (Table XXIII).

shows the distribution of the organization and modernizing voters. Each of the four major districts of Philadelphia can be divided into core and ring, the core wards being those of least new construction in the twenties, the ring wards being the growing edge of the city. This core-and-ring division is thus a division between those districts which the middle and upper-working class were leaving in the twenties and those districts which they sought out. In all elections and in all districts of the city, save south Philadelphia in 1923, the old core wards voted most heavily for the organization candidate for mayor, the new ring wards voted most heavily for the independent candidates. Moreover, the difference in voting proportions between the core and ring increased steadily from 1919 to 1927, indicating that the cleavage between organization and modernizers was growing sharper, as indeed, were the physical and social conditions of their two worlds (Table XXIII).

TABLE XXIII

REPUBLICAN PRIMARY ELECTIONS FOR MAYOR 1919-1927,
VOTE FOR THE "ORGANIZATION'S" CANDIDATE
BY RING AND CORE

Ring Wards of	Percentage of District's Total Vote		
	1919	1923	1927
Northeast	46.7	76.7	37.9
South	43.5	91.3	66.2
West	42.1	71.6	51.4
Northwest	38.5	66.2	36.5
Ring	41.8	71.1	42.9
Core	53.7	84.2	68.0
All City	49.8	80.1	58.1

Source:
Calculated from election returns published in the *Philadelphia Evening Bulletin,* October 10, 1919, September 19, 1923, September 22, 1927.

This polarity of voters, expressed in Philadelphia in the twenties as the conflict between the organization and the modernizers, perpetrated the city's long political tradition. Like the American Revolutionary conflict between the radicals and the merchants, or the early industrial debate between the Democrats and the nativists, it reflected the private structure and orientation of the city, not its public problems. The unwillingness and inability of Philadelphia's citizens in all periods to conceive of democratic regulation of their private economic affairs prevented the political conflicts from defining the problems of the city in a way suitable for public action.

During the Revolution the radicals had not understood the regional and international basis of Philadelphia's economy; its merchants, in turn, failed to appreciate a democratic society's need to guarantee its citizens a fair distribution of a limited food supply.

In the early industrial era the highly charged equalitarian conflicts for worker and ethnic representation in government obscured the very changes of industrialization which unsettled the city's everyday life.

In the twentieth century the economically and politically conservative debate between Republican organization followers and the modernizers mirrored the growing class segregation of the city, but it utterly avoided dealing with the mounting social welfare and economic and physical development issues which constituted both the disorders and the potential of the metropolis.

From first to last, the structure of Philadelphia had been such that, with the exception of the brief and creative union of equalitarian goals and business leadership in the early nineteenth century, no powerful group had been created in the city which understood the city as a whole and who wanted to deal with it as a public environment of a democratic society. In 1930 Philadelphia, like all large American cities, stood as a monument to the tradition of the private city.

Bibliography of Recent Philadelphia Books

When the *Private City* was first published in 1968 it appeared at a time of rising interest in the history of American cities. Since that year American urban history has continued to grow and to branch out so that it has become a far-reaching historical endeavor.

Philadelphia's history is at the forefront of this scholarly advance. Today it is one of the most studied American cities. The prominence of the city's urban design and preservation programs make it a leader in American city planning and architecture. At the same time the Philadelphia History Data Bank of the University of Pennsylvania, and the many urban studies of Temple University have fostered numerous historical projects. (A complete bibliography of the work of the Philadelphia Social History Project and a description of its computer tapes can be obtained from the Center for Greater Philadelphia, University of Pennsylvania, International House, 3701 Chestnut St., Philadelphia, Pennsylvania, 19104.)

Today there is a rich library of Philadelphia books. The following selection of books, most published since 1968, is offered as an aid to readers who wish to explore this recent literature. A special effort has been made to include books and studies that chronicle the post World War II rebuilding of the city.

SOME WAYS OF CONTINUING

Readers vary a great deal in the ways they advance upon a subject: some like to sniff about, others to work systematically. For myself, I find that pictures often stimulate my imagination and lead me into fresh ways of thinking. A photograph of a wooden washtub, or a picture of boys and girls sitting in rows tending a bank of machines will often help me comprehend important changes in urban living. Three social historians from Temple University, Fredric M. Miller, Morris J. Vogel, and Allen F. Davis have assembled a fine selection of photographs and woven them into a very informative narrative of the city. Their *Still Philadelphia: A Photographic History, 1890–1940* is a good place to start. It could be followed by books illustrating earlier eras: Robert F. Looney's *Old Philadelphia in Early Photographs, 1839–1914* and Nicholas B. Wainwright's *Philadelphia in the Romantic Age of Lithography.*

On other occasions I find the best way to study a city is to get out and to look at it. Philadelphia has numerous guides to help the walker and the driver. My favorites are John Andrew Gallery, ed., *Philadelphia Architecture*, and the earlier book by Richard Saul Wurman, *Man-Made Philadelphia.* The constructions of urban renewal will be seen everywhere as you walk about the inner city, and a tour will necessarily lead to questions about the renewal process itself. The best materials for studying these questions are the speeches by former mayor Clark and his planner Edmund Bacon. Bacon's 1975 speech is particularly moving since it came from the man in charge. He said that Philadelphia's urban renewal program took the wrong approach to housing and that it should have developed procedures for block-by-block neighborhood control of improvements. Both the Clark and the Bacon speeches appear in Stanley Newman, ed., *The Politics of Utopia: Towards America's Third Century.* A strong attack on urban renewal as a federal and municipal subsidy to wealthy individuals and institutions appears in Ken Kimnik, *Redevelopment in Philadelphia: Who Pays? Who Benefits?*

If walking about and urban renewal lead you to contemporary politics, then two books offer good entry: Peter Binzen, *Who Runs Philadelphia?* and Henry S. Resnick, *Turning on the System: War in the Philadelphia Schools.*

At present only one third of all Philadelphians live in the city of Philadelphia itself. Most now dwell in the dispersed metropolitan region. There is an excellent history of the region as a whole written for a metropolitan planning agency: Joseph Oberman and Stephen F. Kozakowski, *History of Development in the Delaware Valley Region.* Some of this material also appears in the more readily available book by Peter O. Muller, Kenneth C. Meyer, and Roman A. Cybriwsky, *Metropolitan Philadelphia: A Study of Conflicts and Social Cleavages.* So far, however, very little has been written on either the history or current experiences of the new metropolitan form. The best social study is Herbert J. Gans, *The Levittowners.* The 1982 edition of this book includes a new preface in which Gans discusses his more recent evaluation of suburban life. There is additional Philadelphia information in Peter O. Muller's *Contemporary Suburban America.*

Most of the writing on the region is economic in orientation, like the reports of Anita A. Summers and Thomas F. Luce, *Economic Report on the Philadelphia Metropolitan Area, 1985,* and *Economic Development within the Philadelphia Metropolitan Area,* but for the early decades of industrialization there exists a nice trio of books: Diane Lindstrom, *Economic Development in the Philadelphia Region 1810–1850,* which can be read with Anthony F. C. Wallace, *Rockdale: The Growth of an American Village in the Early Industrial Revolution* and Philip Scranton, *Proprietary Capitalism: The Textile Manufacture at Philadelphia, 1800–1885.*

For transportation history the most informed and stimulating book is Charles W. Cheape, *Moving the Masses: Urban Public Transit in New York, Boston, and Philadelphia, 1880–1912.*

For those who like a chronological approach to urban history Russell F. Weigley has edited a comprehensive volume on the city from earliest days to the present, *Philadelphia: A Three Hundred Year History,* which offers the reader a place to begin with any period of interest. Recent scholarship then follows with a series of books giving entry to the major periods of the city's history: Richard S. and Mary Maples Dunn, *The World of William Penn*; Gary Nash, *The Urban Crucible: Social Change, Political Consciousness, and the Origins of the American Revolution*; Theodore Hershberg ed., *Philadelphia: Work, Space, Family, and Group Experience in the Nineteenth Century*; Bruce Laurie, *Class and Culture: The Working People of Philadelphia, 1800–1851*; Edward Digby Baltzell, *Puritan Boston and Quaker Philadelphia*; and John A. Lukacs, *Philadelphia: Patricians and Philistines, 1900–1950.*

These period histories can be followed by the ethnic and racial histories of Allen F. Davis and Mark H. Haller, *The Peoples of Philadelphia: A History of Ethnic Groups and Lower Class Life, 1790–1940*; Caroline Golab, *Immigrant Destinations*; and Roger Lane, *Roots of Violence in Black Philadelphia, 1860–1900.*

VIEWS AND PICTURE BOOKS

Albrecht, Harry P. *Broad Street Station, Pennsylvania Railroad, Philadelphia, 1881–1952.* Clifton Heights, Pa.: Harry P. Albrecht, 1972.

Cecelia Beaux: Portrait of an Artist: An Exhibition. Philadelphia: Pennsylvania Academy of Fine Arts, 1974.

George Robert Bonfield: Philadelphia Marine Painter, 1805–1898. Philadelphia: Philadelphia Maritime Museum, 1978.

Davis, Myra Tolmach. *Samuel Yellin: American Master of Wrought Iron, 1885–1940.* Washington D. C.: The Dimock Gallery, The George Washington University, 1971.

Susan Macdowell Eakins, 1851–1938. Philadelphia: Pennsylvania Academy of the Fine Arts, 1973.

Etting, Gloria Braggiotti. *Philadelphia, The Intimate City.* New York: Viking Press, 1968.

Fabian, Monroe H. *Mr. Sully, Portrait Painter: The Works of Thomas Sully (1783–1872).* Washington D.C.: published for the National Portrait Gallery by the Smithsonian Institution, 1983.

Fairmount Park Art Association. *Sculpture of a City: Philadelphia's Treasures in Bronze and Stone.* New York: Walker Publishing Co., 1974.

———. *Philadelphia's Treasures in Art and Stone.* New York: Walker Publishing Co., 1976.

Ferber, Linda S. *William Trost Richards: American Landscape and Marine Painter, 1883–1905.* Brooklyn, N.Y.: Brooklyn Museum, 1973.

———. *Tokens of a Friendship: Miniature Watercolors by William T. Richards.* New York: Metropolitan Museum of Art, 1982.

Finkel, Kenneth, ed. *Nineteenth Century Philadelphia: Two Hundred and Fourteen Historic Prints from the Library Company of Philadelphia.* New York: Dover Publishing Inc., 1980.

———. *Nineteenth Century Photography in Philadelphia: 250 Historic Prints from the Library Company of Philadelphia.* New York: Dover Publications; Philadelphia: Library Company of Philadelphia, 1980.

Goodrich, Lloyd. *Thomas Eakins.* Cambridge: published for the National Gallery of Art by the Harvard University Press, 1982.

Goodyear, Frank H., Jr. *Thomas Doughty, 1793–1856: An American Pioneer in Landscape Painting.* Philadelphia: Pennsylvania Academy of the Fine Arts, 1973.

Hayes, John P. *Philadelphia in Color.* New York: Hastings, 1983.

Huber, Christine Jones. *The Pennsylvania Academy and Its Women, 1850–1920.* Philadelphia: Pennsylvania Academy of the Fine Arts, 1974.

Johns, Elizabeth. *Thomas Eakins, the Heroism of Modern Life.* Princeton, N.J.: Princeton University Press, 1983.

Lee, Jean Gordon. *Philadelphia and the China Trade, 1784–1844.* Philadelphia: Philadelphia Museum of Art, 1984.

Looney, Robert F., compiler. *Old Philadelphia in Early Photographs, 1839–1914: Two Hundred and Fifteen Prints from the Collection of the Free Library of Philadelphia.* New York: Dover Publishing Inc., 1976.

———, ed. *Philadelphia Printmaking: American Prints Before 1860: A Conference, Held April 5, 6, 7, 1973.* West Chester, Pa.: Tinicum Press, 1976.

Miller, Fredric M., Morris J. Vogel and Allen F. Davis. *Still Philadelphia: A Photographic History, 1890–1940.* Philadelphia: Temple University Press, 1983.

Miller, Lillian B., ed. *The Selected Papers of Charles Willson Peale and His Family*. New Haven: published for the National Portrait Gallery, Smithsonian Institution, by Yale University Press, 1983.

Milley, John C., ed. *Treasures of Independence: Independence National Historical Park and Its Collections*. New York: Mayflower Books, 1980.

Parrington, Michael. *Archaeology at Sansom Street, Area F. Independence National Historical Park, Philadelphia, Pa. 1979*. Philadelphia: Museum Institute for Conservation Archaeology, University of Pennsylvania Museum, 1980.

Richardson, Edgar P., et al. *Charles Willson Peale and His World*. New York: H. N. Abrams, 1983.

William Rush, American Sculptor. Philadelphia: Pennsylvania Academy of the Fine Arts, 1982.

Sellers, Charles Coleman. *Charles Willson Peale with Patron and Populace; a Supplement to Portraits and Miniatures by Charles Willson Peale, with a Survey of his Work in Other Genres*. Transactions of the American Philosophical Society, vol. 59, pt. 3. Philadelphia: American Philosophical Society, 1969.

————. *Mr. Peale's Museum: Charles Willson Peale and the First Popular Museum of Natural Science and Art*. New York: W. W. Norton, 1980.

Sellin, David. *The First Pose*. New York: Norton, 1976.

Sewall, Darrel, ed. *Philadelphia: Three Centuries of American Art*. Philadelphia: Philadelphia Museum of Art, 1976.

————. *Thomas Eakins: Artist of Philadelphia*. Philadelphia: Philadelphia Museum of Art, 1982.

Smith, Philip Chadwick Foster. *Philadelphia-on-the-River*. Philadelphia Maritime Museum Publications. Philadelphia: University of Pennsylvania Press, 1986.

Snyder, Martin P. *City of Independence: Views of Philadelphia before 1800*. New York: Praeger Publishers, 1975.

Teitelman, S. Robert. *Birch's Views of Philadelphia: A Reduced Facsimile of "The City of Philadelphia. . . . As It Appeared in the Year 1800" with Photographs of the Sites in 1960 and 1982*. Philadelphia: The Free Library of Philadelphia, 1982; University of Pennsylvania Press, 1983.

Wainwright, Nicholas B. *Philadelphia in the Romantic Age of Lithography*. Philadelphia: Pennsylvania Historical Society, 1970.

Watson, Howard N. *Philadelphia Watercolors*. Barre, Mass.: Barre Publishers, 1971.

Wilmerding, John. *Important Information Inside: The Art of John F. Peto and the Idea of Still-Life Painting in Nineteenth Century America*. Washington, D. C.: National Gallery of Art, 1983.

Wolamin, Barbara A. *Arthur B. Carles (1882–1952): Painting with Color*. Philadelphia: Pennsylvania Academy of the Fine Arts, 1983.

GUIDES

Alotta, Robert I. *Street Names of Philadelphia*. Philadelphia: Temple University Press, 1975.

Anderson, Susan H. *The Most Spendid Carpet*. Philadelphia: National Park Service, 1978.

Appleman, Madelyn, and Patricia Goodwin, eds. *Enjoy Philadelphia: Philadelphia Magazine's Guide*. Philadelphia: Philadelphia Magazine, 1976.

Curson, Julie P. *A Guide's Guide to Philadelphia*. Philadelphia: Curson House, 1978.

Eizen, Lisa. *Subject Index to the Photograph Collection of the Philadelphia City Archives*. Philadelphia: Department of Records, 1976.

Gales, Ruth L. *Bicentennial Philadelphia: A Family Guide to the City and Countryside*. Philadelphia: Lippincott, 1974.

Gallery, John Andrew, ed. *Philadelphia Architecture: A Guide to the City*. Cambridge: M. I. T. Press, 1984.

Hogarth, Paul. *Paul Hogarth's Walking Tours of Old Philadelphia: Through Independence Square, Society Hill, Southwark, and Washington Square*. Barre, Mass.: Barre Publishing, 1976.

Holloway, Lisabeth M. *Philadelphia Resources in the History of the Health Sciences*. Philadelphia: published by the author, 1975.

Klein, Esther M. *Fairmount Park, A History and Guidebook: World's Largest Landscaped Municipal Park: Official Directory of the Fairmount Park Commission*. Bryn Mawr, Pa.: Harcum Junior College Press, 1974.

Levitt, Joy D. *A Guide to Jewish Philadelphia and Suburbs*. Philadelphia: Jewish Campus Activities Board, 1979.

Long, Christina, and Dorel Shannon. *The Women's Guide to Philadelphia*. Philadelphia: Prestegord Publishers, 1983.

Marion, John Francis. *Walking Tours of Historic Philadelphia*. Rev. ed. Philadelphia: ISHI Publications, 1984.

————. *Philadelphia Medica, Being a Guide to the City's Historical Places of Health Interest*. Harrisburg, Pa.: Smith Kline Corp., 1975.

Milgrim, Shirley. *Pathways to Independence: Discovering Independence National Historic Park*. New York: Chatham Press, 1975.

Newmann, Libby. *A City Sketched: Guide to the Art and History of Philadelphia*. Philadelphia: University City Science Center and the University of Pennsylvania, 1976.

Roth, Arnold. *Disproportionate Map of Points of Literary Interest in Philadelphia*. Philadelphia: Philadelphia Free Library, 1979.

Teitelman, Edward, and Richard W. Longstreth. *Architecture in Philadelphia: A Guide*. Cambridge: M. I. T. Press, 1974.

Wicks, Judith, ed. *Philadelphia Resource Guide: Access to Information for Individual and Community Growth*. Philadelphia: Synapse, 1982.

Wolf, Edwin, II, and Marie Elena Korey, eds. *Quarter of a Millenium: The Library Company of Philadelphia, 1731–1981: A Selection of Books, Manuscripts, Maps, Drawings, and Paintings*. Philadelphia: the Company, 1981.

Wurman, Richard Saul. *Man-Made Philadelphia: A Guide to Its Physical and Cultural Environment*. Cambridge: M. I. T. Press, 1972.

ARCHITECTURE

Burke, Bobbye, Otto Sperr, Hugh J. McCauley, and Trina Vaux. *Historic Ritten-house: A Philadelphia Neighborhood*. Philadelphia: University of Pennsylvania Press, 1985.

Dallett, Francis James. *An Architectural View of Washington Square, Philadelphia*. Philadelphia: Butler and Tanner, 1968.

Detweiler, Willard S., Jr. *Chestnut Hill: An Architectural History*. Philadelphia: published by the author, 1969.

Drawing Toward Building: Philadelphia Architectural Graphics, 1732–1984. Philadelphia: Pennsylvania Academy of the Fine Arts. University of Pennsylvania Press, 1986.

Eisenhart, Luther P., ed. *Historic Philadelphia: From the Founding until the Early Nineteenth Century, Twenty-Seven Papers Dealing with Its People and Its Buildings*. Transactions of the American Philosophical Society, vol. 43, pt. 1. Philadelphia: American Philosophical Society, 1980.

Environmental Research Group. *South Philadelphia Historic Sites Survey: Final Report, Phase I*. 2 vols. submitted to the Pennsylvania Historical Museum Commission. Philadelphia: ERG, 1980.

Feaver, Jane. *Seventeenth Century Survivors: Pre–1700 Buildings in the Five County Philadelphia Area*. Philadelphia: Colonial Society of Philadelphia, 1982.

Garvan, Anthony N. B., et al. *Mutual Assurance Company for Insuring Houses from Loss by Fire, Philadelphia. The Architectural Surveys, 1784–1794*. Philadelphia: Mutual Assurance Co., 1976.

Greene, Jerome A. *Historic Structure Report, Historical Data Section, Area F. Independence National Historical Park, Pennsylvania*. Denver: Denver Service Center, National Park Service, 1974.

Greiff, Constance M. *John Notman, Architect, 1810–1865*. Philadelphia: Athenaeum of Philadelphia, 1979.

Harbeson, William P., et al. *Philadelphia Architecture in the Nineteenth Century*. 2nd rev. ed. by Theodore B. White. Philadelphia: Art Alliance Press, 1973.

Hemenway, Paul T. M. *I'd Rather Be In (Center City) Philadelphia: An Examination of Apartment Growth and Development in Philadelphia's Central Business District*. Philadelphia: Temple University School of Communications and Theatre, 1980.

Historic American Engineering Record. *Rehabilitation, Fairmount Waterworks, 1978: Conservation and Recreation in a National Historic Landmark*. Washington D.C.: United States Department of the Interior, Heritage Conservation and Recreation Service, Historic American Engineering Record, 1979.

Latrobe, Benjamin Henry. *The Correspondence and Miscellaneous Papers of Benjamin Henry Latrobe*. Edited by John C. Van Horne and Lee W. Formwalt. New Haven: Yale University Press, 1984.

———. *The Engineering Drawings of Benjamin Henry Latrobe*. Edited by David H. Stapleton. New Haven: Yale University Press, 1980.

———. *The Journals of Benjamin Henry Latrobe, 1799–1820: From Philadelphia to New Orleans*. Edited by Edward C. Carter II, John C. Van Horne, and Lee W. Formwalt. New Haven: Yale University Press, 1980.

Liggett, Barbara. *Archaeology at New Market*. Philadelphia: Athenaeum, 1978.

Maass, John. *The Glorious Enterprise: The Centennial Exhibition of 1876 and J. H. Schwarzmann, Architect-in-Chief*. Watkins Glen, N.Y.: Institute for the Study of Universal History through the Arts and Sciences/American Life Foundation, 1973.

Manton, John C. *Victorian Roxborough: An Architectural History*. Philadelphia: J. C. Manton, Historical Research, 1983.

Mitchell, Ehrman B., and Romaldo Giurgola. *Mitchell/Giurgola Architects*. New York: Rizzoli, 1983.

John Milner Associates. *Adaptive Reuse Feasibility Study for the Historic Fairmount Waterworks, Philadelphia, Pennsylvania*. West Chester, Pa.: John Milner Associates, 1981.

O'Gorman, James F., et al. *The Architecture of Frank Furness*. Philadelphia: Philadelphia Museum of Art, 1973. Rev. 1987. University of Pennsylvania Press, distr.

Ronner, Heinz, et al. *Louis I. Kahn: Complete Works: 1935–1974* Boulder, Colorado: Westview Press, 1977.

Santostefano, Piero. *Le Mackley Houses di Kastner e Stonorov. . . .* Roma: Officina, 1982.

Snyder, June Avery, and Martin P. Snyder. *The Story of the Naomi Wood Collection and the Woodford Mansion in Philadelphia's Fairmount Park*. Wayne, Pa.: Haverford House, 1981.

Stern, Robert A. M. *George Howe: Toward A Modern American Architecture*. New Haven: Yale University Press, 1975.

Tatman, Sandra L., and Roger W. Moss. *Biographical Dictionary of Philadelphia Architects, 1700–1930*. Boston: G. K. Hall, 1985.

Tatum, George B. *Philadelphia Georgian: The City House of Samuel Powel and Some of Its Eighteenth Century Neighbors*. Middletown, Conn.: Wesleyan University Press, 1976.

Uhlfelder, Eric. *Center City Philadelphia: The Elements of Style*. Philadelphia: University of Pennsylvania Press, 1984.

Webster, Richard J. *Philadelphia Preserved: A Catalogue of the Historic American Buildings Survey*. Rev. ed. Philadelphia: Temple University Press, 1981.

White, Theophilus Ballou. *Fairmount, Philadelphia's Park: A History*. Philadelphia: Art Alliance Press, 1975.

———, ed. *Paul Philippe Cret: Architect and Teacher*. Philadelphia: Art Alliance Press, 1973.

Wilson, George. *Yesterday's Philadelphia*. Historic Cities Series, no. 13. Miami: E. A. Seeman, 1975.

Yarnel, Elizabeth B. *Addison Hutton: Quaker Architect 1834–1916*. Philadelphia: Art Alliance Press, 1974.

CITY PLANNING AND URBAN DESIGN

Andrade, Stephen, and R. Duane Perry. *Hunting Park West Development Plan: Report.* Philadelphia: Philadelphia City Planning Commission, 1981.

Bacon, Edmund N. *Design of Cities.* New York: Viking Press, 1967.

Berry, David, and Robert E. Coughlin. *Land and Landscape in the Philadelphia Region: 2025 (Discussion Paper Series #95).* Philadelphia: Regional Science Research Institute, 1977.

Census of Population and Housing, 1980. Neighborhood Statistics Program. Narrative Profiles. Philadelphia, Pa. Washington, D.C.: U.S. Department of Commerce, Bureau of the Census, 1984 (?).

The City of Philadelphia: An Urban Strategy / The City of Philadelphia, Frank L. Rizzo, Mayor. Submitted by the City to the White House and the Interagency Coordinating Council in Response to the President's National Urban Policy. Philadelphia: Office of the Mayor, 1978.

DACP Associates. *Philadelphia Riverwalk: Planning and Design Standards.* Philadelphia: Philadelphia City Planning Commission, 1983.

Delaware Valley Regional Planning Commission. *Alternative Futures for the Delaware Valley: Report on the 2000 Sketch Planning Process.* Philadelphia: the Commission, 1976.

Garz, Sandra L. et al. *Housing in Philadelphia: Trends Influencing Philadelphia's Housing Market.* Philadelphia: Philadelphia City Planning Commission, 1977.

Isard, Walter, and Thomas Langford. *Regional Input-Output Study: Recollections, Reflections, and Diverse Notes on the Philadelphia Experience.* Cambridge: M. I. T. Press, 1971.

Kilimnik, Ken. *Redevelopment in Philadelphia: Who Pays? Who Benefits?* Philadelphia: Community Involvement Council, 1975.

Leonardo, Joseph J. *Review of the Eastwick Urban Renewal Plan.* Philadelphia: Philadelphia City Planning Commission, 1982.

Longacre, Maryann T., Horace H. Allen, Jr. et al. *Industrial Area Profile: Report.* Philadelphia: Philadelphia City Planning Commission, 1981.

National Urban Recreation Study: Philadelphia, Wilmington, Trenton. Denver: Denver Service Center, National Park Service, 1977.

Newman, Stanley Simeon ed. *The Politics of Utopia: Towards America's Third Century: A Series of Community Oriented Lectures and Discussions on Philadelphia's Future as an Urban Center, April 28–May 23, 1975.* Philadelphia: Political Science Department, Temple University, 1975.

Pellachia, Elba Cenal, et al. *13th and Callowhill Industrial District Followup.* Philadelphia: Philadelphia City Planning Commission, 1981.

Philadelphia City Planning Commission. *Amendments to Center City Redevelopment Area Plan.* Philadelphia: the Commission, 1971.

———. *Population and Housing Trends, 1970 Census, Philadelphia and Its Metropolitan Area.* Philadelphia: the Commission, 1971.

———. *Upper Roxborough Open Space Plan.* Philadelphia: the Commission, 1972.

———. *Socio-Economic Characteristics, 1960 & 1970, Philadelphia Census Tracts.* Philadelphia: the Commission, 1973.

———. *Philadelphia: A City of Neighborhoods.* Philadelphia: the Commission, 1976.

———. *Wissahickon Watershed Development Guide.* Philadelphia: the Commission, 1976.

———. *Equal Opportunity in Housing in Philadelphia.* Philadelphia: the Commission, 1978.

———. *Housing and Socio-Economic Inventory.* Philadelphia: the Commission, 1979.

———. *Old City Philadelphia.* Philadelphia: the Commission, 1979(?).

———. *Academy East Study: Working Paper 1, Areawide Inventory.* Philadelphia: the Commission, 1980.

———. *City of Philadelphia Capital Program—1981/1986.* Philadelphia: the Commission, 1980.

———. *Target Industries: Analysis.* Philadelphia: the Commission, 1980.

———. *1980 Census, Special Population Summary for Philadelphia Census Tracts.* Philadelphia: the Commission, 1981.

———. *Central Riverfront Plan.* Philadelphia: the Commission, 1982.

———. *Convention Center Site Study: Draft for Review.* Philadelphia: the Commission, 1982.

———. *Economic and Social Indicators for Philadelphia Census Tracts, 1980.* Philadelphia: the Commission, 1982.

———. *Enterprise Zones in Pennsylvania.* Philadelphia: the Commission, 1982.

———. *South Delaware Waterfront District Plan.* Philadelphia: the Commission, 1982(?).

———. *Waterfront Industry Analysis.* Philadelphia: the Commission, 1983.

———. *Population and Housing Characteristics.* Philadelphia: the Commission, 1983.

———. *Community Development Strategies for New Housing Areas in North Philadelphia.* Philadelphia: the Commission, 1984.

———. *Philadelphia's Plan for River Recreation.* Philadelphia, the Commission, 1984.

———. *Socio-Economic Characteristics for Philadelphia Census Tracts 1980 & 1970.* Philadelphia: the Commission, 1984.

———. *Plan for Philadelphia Riverfronts.* Philadelphia: the Commission, 1985.

———. *Center City Plan, 1985.* Forthcoming.

———. *Proposed Interim Changes to Center City Zoning Districts.* Philadelphia: the Commission, 1985.

Philadelphia—Past, Present, and Future: A Century IV Project of the Center for Philadelphia Studies, School of Public and Urban Policy, University of Pennsylvania. Philadelphia: Center for Philadelphia Studies, 1981.

Philadelphia, Pennsylvania Metropolitan Area . . . Today: ULI 1981 Fall Meeting Project Brochure. Compiled by Carla S. Crane et al. in cooperation with the ULI Fall Meeting Local Arrangments Committee. Washington, D.C.: Urban Land Institute, 1981.

Philadelphia Port Corporation. *Ports of Philadelphia: Waterfront Facilities.* Philadelphia: 1971 or 1972.

Promises to Keep: A Social Survey of an Urban Renewal Area: Grays Ferry, Philadelphia, Pennsylvania. Washington, D.C.: Trans Century Corporation, 1969. (A social survey prepared for the Redevelopment Authority of Philadelphia.)

Venturi and Rauch et al. *Old City Study.* Philadelphia: Philadelphia City Planning Commission, 1978.

Venturi, Rauch, and Scott Brown. *Fairmount Park: Master Plan Proposal.* Philadelphia: s.n., 1982.

Zoning Maps of the City of Philadelphia. Philadelphia: The Legal Intelligencer, 1973.

Histories
General

Baltzell, Edward Digby. *Philadelphia Gentlemen: The Making of a National Upper Class.* Glencoe, Ill.: Free Press, 1958. [repr. University of Pennsylvania Press, 1979.]

————. *Puritan Boston and Quaker Philadelphia: Two Protestant Ethics and the Spirit of Class Authority and Leadership.* New York: Free Press, 1979.

Burke, John J. *The Writer in Philadelphia, 1682–1982.* Philadelphia: Saint Joseph's University Press, 1981.

Bussy, R. Kenneth, ed. *Philadelphia's Publishers and Printers: An Informal History.* Philadelphia: Philadelphia Book Clinic, 1980.

Clark, Dennis, ed. *Philadelphia 1776–2076: A Three-Hundred Year View.* Port Washington, N.Y.: Kennikat Press, 1975.

Cochran, Thomas C. *Pennsylvania: A Bicentennial History.* New York: Norton, 1978.

Daly, John, and Allen Weinberg. *Descriptive Inventory of the Archives of the City of Philadelphia.* Philadelphia: Department of Records, 1970.

Passing Through: Letters and Documents Written in Philadelphia by Famous Visitors. Charlottesville, Va.: University Press of Virginia, 1983.

Philadelphia: A Medical Panorama of 200 Years, 1776–1976. Bicentennial Edition. Philadelphia: Philadelphia County Medical Society. [1977]

Siegel, Adrienne, ed. *Philadelphia: A Chronological and Documentary History 1651–1970.* Dobbs Ferry, N.Y.: Oceana Publications, 1975.

Weigley, Russell F., et al. *Philadelphia: A Three Hundred Year History.* New York: Norton, 1982.

Wolf, Edwin, II. *Philadelphia, Portrait of an American City: A Bicentennial History.* Harrisburg, Pa.: Stackpole Books, 1975.

————. *"At the Instance of Benjamin Franklin": A Brief History of the Library Company of Philadelphia, 1731–1976.* Philadelphia: The Library Company of Philadelphia, 1976.

Seventeenth and Eighteenth Centuries

Alexander, John K. *Render Them Submissive: Responses to Poverty in Philadelphia 1760–1800.* Amherst, Mass.: University of Massachusetts Press, 1980.

Costa Pereira Furtado do Mendonca, Hippolyto José da. *Diario da Minha Viagem para Filadelfia, 1797–1799*. Porto Allegre: Livre Sulina Editora, 1974.

Dunn, Mary Maples, and Richard S. Dunn, eds. *The Papers of William Penn*. Philadelphia: University of Pennsylvania Press, 1981–1987.

Dunn, Richard S., and Mary Maples Dunn, eds. *The World of William Penn*. Philadelphia: University of Pennsylvania Press, 1986.

Foner, Eric. *Tom Paine and Revolutionary America*. New York: Oxford University Press, 1976.

Gifford, Edward S. *The American Revolution in the Delaware Valley*. Philadelphia: Pennsylvania Society of the Sons of the Revolution, 1976.

Hunt, James Barton. *The Crowd and the American Revolution: A Study of Urban Political Violence in Boston and Philadelphia 1763–1776*. Ann Arbor, Mich.: University Microfilms, 1974.

Jackson, John W. *The Delaware Bay and River Defenses of Philadelphia 1777–1778*. Philadelphia: Philadelphia Maritime Museum, 1977.

———. *With the British Army in Philadelphia 1777–1778*. San Rafael, Calif.: Presidio Press, 1979.

Kantrow, Louise. *The Demographic History of a Colonial Aristocracy: A Philadelphia Case Study*. Ann Arbor, Mich.: University Microfilms, 1978.

Kelley, Joseph J. *Life and Times in Colonial Philadelphia*. Harrisburg, Pa.: Stackpole Books, 1973.

Lucas, Stephen E. *Portents of Rebellion: Rhetoric and Revolution in Philadelphia 1765–1776*. Philadelphia: Temple University Press, 1976.

Miller, Richard G. *Philadelphia: the Federalist City: A Study in Urban Politics 1789–1801*. Port Washington, N. Y.: Kennikat Press, 1976.

Nash, Gary. *The Urban Crucible: Social Change, Political Consciousness, and the Origins of the American Revolution*. Cambridge: Harvard University Press, 1979.

Olton, Charles S. *Artisans for Independence: Philadelphia Mechanics and the American Revolution*. Syracuse: Syracuse University Press, 1975.

Ryerson, Richard Allen, *The Revolution is Now Begun: The Radical Committees of Philadelphia, 1765–1776*. Philadelphia: University of Pennsylvania Press, 1978.

Smith, Samuel Stelle. *Fight for the Delaware 1777*. Monmouth Beach, N.J.: Philip Freneau Press, 1970.

Thompson, Ray. *Benedict Arnold in Philadelphia*. Fort Washington, Pa.: Bicentennial Press, 1975.

Wright, Esmond. *Franklin of Philadelphia*. Cambridge: Harvard University Press, 1986.

Nineteenth Century

Adams, Donald R. *Finance and Enterprise in Early America: A Study of Stephen Girard's Bank, 1812–1831*. Philadelphia: University of Pennsylvania Press, 1978.

Baatz, Simon. *Venerate the Plough: A History of the Philadelphia Society for Promoting Agriculture, 1785–1885*. Philadelphia: the Society, 1985.

Bell, Marion, L. *Crusade in the City: Revivalism in Nineteenth-Century Phila-delphia*. Lewisburg, Pa.: Bucknell University Press, 1977.

Brown, Dee Alexander. *The Year of the Century: 1876*. New York: Scribner, 1976.

Clement, Priscilla F. *Welfare and the Poor in the Nineteenth Century City: Phila-delphia 1800–1854*. Cranbury, N.J.: Fairleigh Dickinson University Press, 1985.

Cope, Thomas P. *Philadelphia Merchant: The Diary of Thomas P. Cope, 1800–1851*. Edited by Eliza Cope Harrison. South Bend, Ind.: Gateway Editions, 1978.

Davis, Susan G. *Parades and Power: Street Theatre in Nineteenth-Century Phila-delphia*. Philadelphia: Temple University Press, 1986.

Feldberg, Michael. *The Philadelphia Riots of 1844: A Study of Ethnic Conflict*. Westport, Conn.: Greenwood Press, 1975.

————. *The Turbulent Era: Riot and Disorder in Jacksonian America*. New York: Oxford University Press, 1980.

Fisher, Sydney George. *A Philadelphia Perspective: The Diary of Sydney George Fisher Covering the Years 1834–1871*. Philadelphia: Historical Society of Pennsylvania, 1967.

Hershberg, Theodore ed. *Philadelphia: Work, Space, Family, and Group Experi-ence in the Nineteenth Century: Essays Toward an Interdisciplinary History of the City*. New York: Oxford University Press, 1981.

Johnson, David Ralph. *Policing the Urban Underworld: The Impact of Crime on the Development of the American Police 1800–1887*. Philadelphia: Temple University Press, 1979.

Lane, Roger. *Violent Death in the City: Suicide, Accident, and Murder in Nine-teenth-Century Philadelphia*. Cambridge: Harvard University Press, 1979.

Laurie, Bruce. *Class and Culture: The Working People of Philadelphia, 1800–1851*. Philadelphia: Temple University Press, 1980.

Martin, Donald J. *The Philadelphia Police 1840–1860: The Founding of a Modern Law Enforcement Agency*. Philadelphia: University of Pennsylvania, Human Resources Center, Institute for Environmental Studies, 1969.

Mease, James. *The Picture of Philadelphia*. New York: Arno Press, 1970; reprint of the 1811 edition.

Miller, Lillian B., et al. *1876: The Centennial Year*. Indianapolis: Indiana His-torical Society, 1973.

Nicolai, Richard R. *Centennial Philadelphia*. Bryn Mawr, Pa.: Bryn Mawr Press, 1976.

Penrose, Maryly Barton. *"Heads of Families" Index, 1850 Federal Census, City of Philadelphia*. 2nd rev. ed. Franklin Park, N.J.: Liberty Bell Associates, 1974.

————. *Philadelphia Marriages and Obituaries (1857–1860), Philadelphia Satur-day Bulletin*. Franklin Park, N.J.: Liberty Bell Associates, 1974.

Philadelphia Board of Guardians of the Poor. *The Almshouse Experience: Col-lected Reports*. New York: Arno Press, 1971.

Seltzer, Maurice. *Autobiography of a Creek: The Pennypack: A Creek's Adventure with History*. Jenkintown, Pa.: Tri-County Press, 1980.

Sinclair, Bruce. *Philadelphia's Philosopher Mechanics: A History of the Franklin Institute 1824–1865*. Baltimore: Johns Hopkins University Press, 1974.

Whiteman, Maxwell. *Gentlemen in Crisis: The First Century of the Union League of Philadelphia 1862–1962*. Philadelphia: the League, 1975.

Twentieth Century

Blumberg, Leonard, Thomas E. Shipley, and Irving W. Shandler. *Skid Row and Its Alternatives: Research and Recommendations from Philadelphia*. Philadelphia: Temple University Press, 1973.

Coughlin, Robert E., et al. *Distribution of Social Service Facilities within the City of Philadelphia*. Discussion Paper Series, no. 93. Philadelphia: Regional Science Research Institute, 1967, 1976.

Cutler, William G., III, and Howard Gillette, Jr. *The Divided Metropolis: Social and Spatial Dimensions of Philadelphia, 1800–1975*. Westport, Conn.: Greenwood Press, 1980.

Gans, Herbert J. *The Levittowners: Ways of Life and Politics in a New Suburban Community*. New York: Pantheon, 1967.

Grieff, Constance M. *Independence: The Creation of a National Park*. Philadelphia: University of Pennsylvania Press, 1987.

Jaipaul. *Anthology of Human Relations Resources*. Philadelphia: Ethnic Heritage Affairs Institute, 1977.

Lewis, Allen. *This Date in Philadelphia Phillies History: A Day-By-Day Listing of Events in the History of the Philadelphia National League Baseball Club*. New York: Stein and Day, 1979.

Lukacs, John A. *Philadelphia: Patricians and Philistines, 1900–1950*. New York: Farrar, Straus and Giroux, 1981.

Lyons, Paul. *Philadelphia Communists 1936–1956*. Philadelphia: Temple University Press, 1982.

Muller, Peter O. *Contemporary Suburban America*. Englewood Cliffs, N.J.: Prentice-Hall, 1981.

Muller, Peter O., Kenneth C. Meyer, and Roman A. Cybriwsky. *Metropolitan Philadelphia: A Study of Conflicts and Social Cleavages*. Cambridge: Ballinger Publishing Co., 1976.

Phalen, Dale. *Samuel Fels of Philadelphia*. Philadelphia: Samuel S. Fels Fund, 1969.

Philadelphia Magazine. *The Improper Philadelphians: A Dossier of Investigative Reporting from Philadelphia Magazine*. New York: Weybright and Talley, 1970.

Visco, Anthony F. *The Sixty-Year History of Frankford High School, 1910–1970*. Philadelphia: Alumni Association of Franklin High School, 1973.

Welch, Charles E. *Oh! Dem Golden Slippers*. New York: Nelson, 1970.

Wolpert, Julian. *The Metropolitan Philadelphia Philanthropy Study: Final Report*. Philadelphia: University of Pennsylvania, Philanthropy Study Office, Regional Science Department, 1980.

Municipal Politics

Ashford, Douglas E., ed. *National Resources and Urban Policy.* New York: Methuen, 1980.

Binzen, Peter. *Who Runs Philadelphia?* Philadelphia: Bulletin Co., 1980.

Civic Organization Survey Steering Committee, Philadelphia. *Strenthening Civic Organizations in Philadelphia: A Report of the Civic Organization Survey Steering Committee.* Philadelphia: the Committee, 1978.

Comey, Dennis J. *The Waterfront Peacemaker.* Philadelphia: St. Joseph's University Press, 1983.

Committee of Seventy, City Governance Project. *Charter Revisions: A Review.* Philadelphia: Committee of Seventy, 1979.

Daughen, Joseph R. and Peter Binzen. *The Cop Who Would Be King.* Boston: Little-Brown, 1977.

Elazar, Daniel Judah. *Studying the Civil Community: A Guide for Mapping Local Political Systems.* Philadelphia: Temple University Press, 1970.

Ershkowitz, Miriam, ed. *Black Politics in Philadelphia.* New York: Basic Books, 1973.

Gitell, Marilyn, and T. Edward Hollander. *Six Urban School Districts: A Comparative Study of Educational Response.* New York: Praeger, 1968.

Kotler, Milton. *Neighborhood Government: The Local Foundations of Political Life.* Indianapolis: Bobbs-Merrill Co., 1969.

Levy, Paul R. *Queen Village: The Eclipse of a Community.* Public Papers in the Humanities, no. 2. Philadelphia: Institute for the Study of Civic Values, 1972.

Levy, Paul R., and Dennis McGrath. *Selective Resurgence: Corporate Strategy for the Urban Northeast.* Philadelphia: Institute for the Study of Civic Values, 1980.

Moldovsky, Joel. *The Best Defense.* New York: Macmillan, 1975.

Petshek, Kirk R. *The Challenge of Urban Reform: Policies and Programs in Philadelphia.* Philadelphia: Temple University Press, 1973.

Resnik, Henry S. *Turning on the System: War in the Philadelphia Schools.* New York: Pantheon Books, 1970.

Rogers, David. *The Management of Big Cities: Interest Groups and Social Change Strategies.* Beverly Hills, Calif.: Sage Publications, 1971.

Rubenstein, Jonathan. *City Police.* New York: Farrar, Straus and Giroux, 1973.

Ruchelman, Leonard I. *Police Politics: A Comparative Study of Three Cities.* Cambridge: Ballinger, 1974.

Salter, John T. *Boss Rule: Portraits in City Politics.* New York: Arno Press, 1974.

Weiler, Conrad. *Philadelphia: Neighborhood, Authority, and The Urban Crisis.* New York: Praeger, 1974.

The Economy

Adams, Carolyn Teich. *The Constrained City, Philadelphia Past Present and Future #20.* Philadelphia: University of Pennsylvania, Center for Philadelphia Studies, 1982.

Adams, Donald R., Jr. *Wage Rates in Philadelphia, 1790–1830*. New York: Arno Press, 1975.

Glickman, Norman J. *An Econometric Forcasting Model for the Philadelphia Region*. Discussion Paper Series, no. 39. Philadelphia: Regional Science Research Institute, 1970.

———. *Economic Analysis of Regional Systems: Explorations in Model Building and Policy Analysis*. New York: Academic Press, 1977.

Goldstein, Jonathan. *Philadelphia and the China Trade, 1682–1846, Commercial, Cultural, and Attitudinal Effects*. University Park, Pa.: Penn State University Press, 1978.

Green, James W. *Residential Sales Monitoring System*. Philadelphia: Philadelphia City Planning Commission, 1984.

Hochheiser, Sheldon. *Rohm & Haas: History of a Chemical Company*. Philadelphia: University of Pennsylvania Press, 1986.

Leif, Alfred. *Family Business: A Century in the Life and Times of Strawbridge and Clothier*. New York: McGraw-Hill, 1968.

Lindstrom, Diane. *Economic Development in the Philadelphia Region 1810–1850*. New York: Columbia University Press, 1978.

Nelson, Daniel. *A Checklist of Writings on the Economic History of the Greater Philadelphia-Wilmington Region*. Wilmington, Del.: Eleutherian Mills Historical Library, 1968.

Oberman, Joseph, and Stephen F. Kozakowski. *History of Development in the Delaware Valley Region*. Year 2000 Plan Report No. 1. Philadelphia: Delaware Valley Regional Planning Commission, 1976.

Philadelphia Export Directory: A Guide to International Trade for the Greater Delaware Valley. Philadelphia: University of Pennsylvania, Philadelphia Export Network, Wharton Applied Research Center, 1984.

Powell, Howard Benjamin. *Philadelphia's First Fuel Crisis: Jacob Cist and the Developing Market for Pennsylvania Anthracite*. University Park, Pa.: Penn State University Press, 1978.

Rubin, Michael, and Theodore Hershberg. *Greater Philadelphia as an Advanced Services Center: An Assessment of Trends and the Strategic Positioning of the Region in the National Shift to a Service-Based Economy*. Philadelphia: University of Pennsylvania, Center for Greater Philadelphia, 1983.

Scranton, Philip. *Proprietary Capitalism: The Textile Manufacture at Philadelphia, 1800–1885*. Philadelphia: Temple University Press, 1984.

Scranton, Philip, and Walter Licht. *Work Sights: Industrial Philadelphia, 1890–1950*. Philadelphia: Temple University Press, 1986.

Summers, Anita A., and Thomas F. Luce. *Economic Report on the Philadelphia Metropolitan Area, 1985*. Philadelphia: University of Pennsylvania Press, 1985.

———. *Economic Development Within the Philadelphia Metropolitan Area*. Philadelphia: University of Pennsylvania Press, 1987.

RACE AND ETHNICITY

Binzen, Peter. *Whitetown, U.S.A.* New York: Random House, 1970.

Bodnar, John E. ed. *The Ethnic Experience in Philadelphia*. Lewisburg, Pa.: Bucknell University Press, 1973.

Brown, Ira. *The Negro in Pennsylvania History*. Gettysburg, Pa.: Pennsylvania Historical Association, 1970.

Clark, Dennis J. *The Irish in Philadelphia: Ten Generations of Urban Experience*. Philadelphia: Temple University Press, 1973.

———. *The Irish Relations: Trials of an Immigrant Tradition*. Rutherford, N.J.: Fairleigh Dickinson University Press, 1982.

Corson, Ruth A. *Continuity and Change: 75th Anniversary Exhibit, the Federation of Jewish Agencies of Greater Philadelphia, the Museum of the Philadelphia Civic Center, November 1, 1976*. Philadelphia: The Federation of Jewish Agencies of Greater Philadelphia, 1976.

Davis, Allen F., and Mark H. Haller, eds. *The Peoples of Philadelphia: A History of Ethnic Groups and Lower-Class Life, 1790–1940*. Philadelphia: Temple University Press, 1973.

Filby, William P., ed. *Philadelphia Naturalization Records 1789–1880: Index to Records of Aliens' Declaration of Intention and/or Oaths of Allegiance*. Detroit: Gale, 1982.

Frankel, Barbara. *Childbirth in the Ghetto: Folk Beliefs of Negro Women in a North Philadelphia Hospital Ward*. San Francisco: R & E Research Associates, 1977.

Franklin, Vincent P. *The Education of Black Philadelphia: The Social and Educational History of a Minority Community, 1900–1950*. Philadelphia: University of Pennsylvania Press, 1979.

Friedman, Murray, and Daniel J. Elazar, *Moving Up: Ethnic Succession America; With a Case History from the Philadelphia School System*. New York: Institute on Pluralism and Group Identity, 1976.

Friedman, Murray, ed. *Jewish Life in Philadelphia, 1830–1940*. Philadelphia: Institute for the Study of Human Issues, 1983.

Golab, Caroline. *Immigrant Destinations*. Philadelphia: Temple University Press, 1977.

Juliani, Richard N. *The Social Organization of Immigration: The Italians in Philadelphia*. New York: Arno Press, 1980.

Keene, Joseph P., and Spencer E. Sewell. *A Residential Survey of the Spanish Speaking Community, Model Cities Area of Philadelphia, Pennsylvania*. Philadelphia: s.n., 1974.

Lane, Roger. *Roots of Violence in Black Philadelphia, 1860–1900*. Cambridge: Harvard University Press, 1986.

Lapsansky, Emma Jones. *Before the Model City: An Historical Exploration of North Philadelphia*. Philadelphia: Philadelphia Historical Commission, 1968.

Ley, David. *The Black Inner City as Frontier Outpost: Images and Behavior of a Philadelphia Neighborhood*. Washington, D.C.: Association of American Geographers, 1974.

Morgan, Kathryn L. *Children of Strangers: The Stories of a Black Family*. Philadelphia: Temple University Press, 1980.

Nelson, H. Viscount. *The Philadelphia NAACP: Epitome of Middle Class Consciousness.* Los Angeles: Center for Afro-American Studies, University of California, 1972.

Richter, William Benson. *North of Society Hill and Other Stories.* North Quincy, Mass.: Christopher Publishing House, 1970.

Smith, Robert C. *In and Out of Town.* Boston: Brandon Press, 1970.

Varady, David P. *Ethnic Minorities in Urban Areas: A Case Study of Racially Changing Communities.* Hingham, Mass.: M. Nijhoff, 1979.

Ward, David. *Cities and Immigrants: A Geography of Change in Nineteenth-Century America.* New York: Oxford University Press, 1971.

RELIGION

Bacon, Margaret Hope. *Quiet Rebels: The Story of the Quakers in America.* New York: Basic Books, 1969.

———. *Let This Life Speak: The Legacy of Henry Joel Cadbury.* Philadelphia: University of Pennsylvania Press, 1987.

Benjamin, Philip S. *The Philadelphia Quakers in the Industrial Age, 1865–1920.* Philadelphia: Temple University Press, 1976.

Clark, Dennis J. *Proud Past: Catholic Laypeople of Philadelphia.* Philadelphia: Catholic Philopatrian Literary Society, 1976.

Connelly, James F. *St. Charles Seminary, Philadelphia: A History of the Theological Seminary of Saint Charles Borromeo, Overbrook, Philadelphia, Pennsylvania, 1832–1979.* Philadelphia, the Seminary, [1979?].

Donaghy, Thomas J. *Philadelphia's Finest: A History of Education in the Catholic Archdiocese, 1692–1970.* Philadelphia: American Catholic Historical Association, 1972.

Der Heilige aus dem Böhmerwald: Johannes Nepomuk Neumann, Bischof in Philadelphia. Königsten im Taunus: Sudetendeutsches Priesterwerk, 1979.

Klein, Esther M. *Guide Book to Jewish Philadelphia: History, Landmarks, and Donors of the Jewish Community for the Life of Philadelphia, 1703–1965.* Philadelphia: Philadelphia Jewish Times Institute, 1965.

Marietta, Jack D. *Reformation of American Quakerism, 1748–1783.* Philadelphia: University of Pennsylvania Press, 1984.

Moore, John W. ed. *Friends in the Delaware Valley: Philadelphia's Yearly Meeting, 1681–1981.* Haverford, Pa.: Friends Historical Association, 1981.

Naven, Lindsay B. *A Guide to the Philadelphia Jewish Archives Center.* Philadelphia: Jewish Archives Center, 1977.

Neumann, John Neomucene, Saint. *Autobiography of Saint John Neumann, C. S. S. R., Fourth Bishop of Philadelphia.* Boston: St. Paul Editions, 1977.

Teske, Robert Thomas. *Votive Offerings Among Greek Philadelphians.* New York: Arno Press, 1980.

Williams, Richard E. *Called and Chosen: The Story of Mother Rebecca Jackson of the Philadelphia Shakers.* Metuchen, N.J.: Scarecrow Press, 1981.

Wolf, Edwin II, and Maxwell Whiteman. *History of the Jews in Philadelphia: From Colonial Times to the Age of Jackson.* Philadelphia: Jewish Publication Society of America, 1975.

TRANSPORTATION

Beetle, George. *Investigations of Camden–Philadelphia Trunkline Capacities for Discrete Levels of Improvement: Delaware River Port Authority*. Philadelphia: published by the author, 1978.

Boorse, J. W. *Philadelphia in Motion: A Nostalgic View of How Philadelphians Travelled, 1902–1940*. Bryn Mawr, Pa.: Bryn Mawr Press, 1976.

Boyce, David E., et al. *Impact of Rapid Transit on Suburban Residential Property Values and Land Development: Analysis of the Philadelphia-Lindenwold High-Speed Line*. Philadelphia: University of Pennsylvania, Wharton School, Regional Science Department, 1972.

Cheape, Charles W. *Moving the Masses: Urban Public Transit in New York, Boston, and Philadelphia, 1880–1912*. Cambridge: Harvard University Press, 1980.

Cox, Harold E. *Utility Cars of Philadelphia, 1892–1971*. Forty Fort, Pa.: published by the author, 1972.

———. *Philadelphia Car Routes*. Forty Fort, Pa.: published by the author, 1982.

DeGraw, Ronald. *The Red Arrow: A History of One of the Most Successful Suburban Transit Companies in the World*. Haverford, Pa.: Haverford Press, 1972.

Draper, Sarah. *Once Upon the Main Line*. New York: Carlton, 1980.

Gannett, Fleming, Corddry, and Carpenter. *Technical Studies Report for the Mass Transportation Development Program of the Delaware River Port Authority: Final Report*. Philadelphia: Delaware River Port Authority, 1975.

Gannon, Colin Allan. *The Impact of Rail Transit Systems on Commercial Office Development: The Case of the Philadelphia-Lindenwold Speedline*. Philadelphia: University of Pennsylvania, Transportation Studies Center; Springfield, Va.: Distributed by National Technical Information Service, 1972.

Penn Jersey Transportation Study. *PJ Papers*. 1–24, Philadelphia, 1961–1965.

———. *PJ Reports*. 1–3, Philadelphia, 1964–1965.

———. *PJ Technical Reports*. 1–3, Philadelphia, 1961–1965.

A Planning Program for PJD; A Proposed Comprehensive Regional Planning Program for the Philadelphia, Camden, Trenton, Wilmington Urban Region Including a Continuing Transportation Planning Process. Prepared for the Penn Jersey Transportation Study by the Institute for Urban Studies, University of Pennsylvania and the Operations Research Group, Case Institute of Technology, Philadelphia, 1963.

Philadelphia Maritime Museum. *Philadelphia: Port of History, 1609–1837*. Philadelphia: the Museum, 1976.

Rosenberger, Homer T. *The Philadelphia and Erie Railroad: Its Place in American Economic History*. Potomac, Md.: Fox Hills Press, 1975.

Sechler, Robert P. *Speed Lines to City and Suburbs: A Summary of Rapid Transit Development in Metropolitan Philadelphia from 1879 to 1974*. Drexel Hill, Pa.: published by the author, 1975.

Thompson Associates. *Philadelphia International Airport: Master Plan, Prepared for City of Philadelphia, Department of Commerce, Division of Aviation.* White Plains, N. Y.: Arnold W. Thompson Associates, 1975.

Vuchic, Vukan R., et al. *General Operations Plan for the SEPTA Regional High Speed System: Report for the Southeastern Pennsylvania Transportation Authority (SEPTA).* Philadelphia: Prepared by the University of Pennsylvania, 1984.

Notes to Tables in Text

TABLE I

Historians have customarily used the population figure of 40,000 for Philadelphia and environs at the eve of the American Revolution. This is the figure used by Bridenbaugh in his *Cities in Revolt* (New York, 1955), 216, and upon this estimate rests Philadelphia's claim to be the second city in the British Empire. A very careful study of the tax records and constables returns will support at most an estimate of 23,739 for urban Philadelphia (the city plus the Liberties and Southwark).

This calculation of 23,739 fits well with the 1790 U.S. Census [Bureau of the Census, *Heads of Families at the First Census of the United States Taken in the Year 1790*, vol. *Pennsylvania* (Washington, 1908), 10] which reported urban Philadelphia to have 44,096 inhabitants. Such an estimated growth of 79 percent from a population of 23,739 in 1775 to a population of 44,096 in 1790 would also be consistent with General Cornwallis' enumeration. He had a census made in 1777 in which there were returned 5,470 structures of all kinds for urban Philadelphia and 21,767 inhabitants. His census did not include men over sixty years of age, and of course, it took place when an unknown number of persons, perhaps several thousand, had fled the city to escape the British occupation. His census and a 1779 tax list was used by Stella H. Sutherland, *Population Distribution in Colonial America* (New York, 1936), 167.

The large 40,000 estimate for Philadelphia's population in 1775 seems to be based upon an extrapolation of Mease's unexplainably high 1769 population estimate of 28,042 for urban Philadelphia and upon Captain Montresor's 1777 statement of 45,000 inhabitants for the same area. All estimates previous to the one given in Table I, above, appear in Evarts B. Greene and Virginia D. Harrington, *American Population before the Federal Census of 1790* (New York, 1932), 117-120.

Statistical research on eighteenth-century Philadelphia was begun using 1774 sources and all the data of this chapter are for 1774 except this Table I. Unique record opportunities determined the use of the year 1775 for a population estimate. In the construction of Table I all persons who were twenty years and older were counted as adults as was the custom of taxation in the 1770's. Also, all persons recorded as married were counted automatically as adults. The source of this estimate for the wards of the City of Philadelphia was the 1775 Constables Returns of the City of Philadelphia, dated October 27 to November 17, 1775, now deposited in the Archives Division, Department of Records, City of Philadelphia.

This estimate is of the "maximum population" because of the method of handling those listed on the Constable's returns as "inmates." If a man was listed as an inmate in a household he was considered to be married and his hypothecated wife and he were both added to the estimate unless there were further information. In approximately 150 cases otherwise unidentifiable males were discovered to be unmarried because they were so identified by an April 1775 Philadelphia County Duplicate Tax List, also in the Archives of the City of Philadelphia, and in these cases the men were entered in the estimate as single.

Since there are no extant constables' returns for the Northern Liberties and Southwark for 1775, a different method had to be employed to estimate the population of these adjacent districts than that used for the city itself. A count was made of all occupied structures listed in the Seventeenth Eighteen Penny Provincial Tax List for 1774, now in possession of the Pennsylvania Historical and Museum Commission in Harrisburg. The count gave 527 occupied structures for East Northern Liberties, 396 for West Northern Liberties, and 694 for Southwark. Next, the 1775 ratio of persons to structures previously determined for the city of Philadelphia of 4.44 persons per structure (16,560 persons to 3,723 occupied structures) was used to estimate the population of the districts. It is this crude estimate which is given in Table I.

TABLE II

This index of Dissimilarity is offered to give the reader some measure by which he can compare the intensity of residential clustering in Philadelphia in 1774 to clustering in 1860 and clustering in 1930. The index was constructed entirely from ward data since this was the only small-area data available in all three periods. First, the proportions of any group (laborers, foreign-born Irish or whatever) to the total population of each ward were calculated. Next the proportion of the group to the total population of the city was calculated. Then, the index was computed. The index measures the degree to which the group in question clustered in some wards in higher proportions than its proportion to the total population of the city. It is a measure of the variation of the ward-by-ward distribution of the residential addresses of one group as compared to the residential addresses of all others in the city. If the index number were 0, then in each ward of the city the group in question would be distributed in precisely its proportion to the entire city's population. If the index number were 100 the group would be entirely concentrated in its ward, or wards, and present in no others.

The index has some weaknesses as it approaches its extremes, especially being unable to distinguish a 100 percent concentration in one ward from a 100 percent concentration in more than one ward. No such cases occurred in Philadelphia in any of the three periods studied. Indeed, the necessity to calculate the proportions of any group in question for each ward forewarns the user against any extreme case. Finally since the indexes given in this book were all constructed from large-area, ward data, the values may be a bit lower than they would be had small-area data been used. For a full explanation of the Index of Dissimilarity and other methods of measuring clustering see Karl E. and Alma F. Taeuber, *Negroes in Cities* (Chicago, 1965), 203-4, 223-238.

This analysis of the location of urban Philadelphia's population by occupation and industrial category, by homeownership, and by German surnames was derived from successive series of computations based on three record sources.

First, the ward-by-ward listings of the population by occupation was based on the Philadelphia County Duplicate Tax List of April 8, 1774, which gave taxpaying householders and/or taxpaying adult inmates of houses by household. Any persons who appeared on this list without an occupation who were listed as having a specific one in the Transcript of the Assessment of the Seventeenth Eighteen Penny Provincial Tax, Philadelphia County, of April 8, 1774 were assigned that occupation.

Next, to arrive at as complete an estimate of homeowners and houses as possible the Transcript was used as a base. This information was supplemented for taxpayers who were renters, and renters who were not taxpayers, on April 8, 1774, by searching the Duplicate Tax List and the Constables Returns of the City of Philadelphia October 27, 1775.

Occupations for 116 renters who were not taxpayers, and for 121 taxpayers, all of whom lived in the same houses on October 27, 1775, as they had on April 8, 1774, were tabulated from the Constables Returns. Additionally, some occupations were made more specific, i.e., "turpentine distiller" instead of just "distiller."

This process increased the identified occupations of Philadelphia residents from the 2,014 previously available in the published *Pennsylvania Archives* to 4,264, as well as increasing the reliability of the listing. These occupations were then classified according to the industrial groupings of the 1930 U.S. Census so that comparison would be possible from 1774 to 1860 to 1930. The German surnames were determined by consulting the Index of I. Daniel Rupp, *A Collection of Upwards of Thirty Thousand Names of German, Swiss, Dutch, French, and Other Immigrants in Pennsylvania* (2nd. ed., Baltimore, 1965).

The 1860 data for this table were obtained from two sources. The birthplace information came from a transcription of the original schedules of the Eighth Census, Philadelphia County. The industrial groups information was derived by classifying a sample from *McElroy's Philadelphia Directory, 1860* according to the industrial classification scheme of the U.S. Census of 1930.

After the Directory sample was taken an opportunity presented itself for taking an occupation sample from the 1860 Census. This second sample was taken and used in the comparative tables of the work structure of Philadelphia 1774, 1860, 1930. Its principal difference from the Directory sample lies in its inclusion of many more female occupations, domestics, housekeepers, seamstresses, tailoresses, and the male and female factory operatives. Since there is no satisfactory way to compare the mixed male and female listings of the 1860 Census to the almost all male listings of the 1774 tax records, the Directory sample has been used for all the 1860 analytical tables.

In many cities street directories are more convenient to research than Census schedules. For that reason a comparison of the two samples is given for major occupations (those with 51 or more persons in the sample). The Census sample had 3,548 members who could be classified by industries, the Directory sample had 4,280 who could be similarly classified.

Occupation	Census Sample	Directory Sample
Blacksmith	1.13%	1.47%
Butcher	0.28	1.29
Cabinetmaker	0.79	1.50
Carpenter	2.93	3.49
Clerk	3.44	6.61
Cordwainer	1.47	0.37
Grocer	0.93	2.22
Laborer	8.09	10.33
Liquor	0.39	1.75
Machinist	1.38	1.92
Operative	2.17	0.07
Shoemaker	2.71	1.52
Tailor	2.00	2.85
Tobacco	0.42	0.77
Weaver	2.40	2.73
Major Occupations	30.53%	42.02%
Other Occupations	69.47%	57.98%

TABLE III

This summary of the statistics of the Middle Ward is based on an attempt to reconstruct the block-by-block, house-by-house settlement pattern of the ward on April 8, 1774. First, to set the geography of the ward the Constable's Returns of October 27, 1775, were consulted. These returns listed the householder, the house landlord, the ground landlord, and if the property were vacant gave a description of the property and noted whether it was a commercial structure or a dwelling. Grant M. Simon, "Map of Part of Old Philadelphia," in *Historic Philadelphia (Transactions of the American Philosophical Society*, XLIII, Pt. 1, 1953) also proved useful.

Given these references, the reconstruction of the ward was built from the Philadelphia County Duplicate Tax List of April 8, 1774, which provided the most complete list available of taxpayers. The Duplicate List was broken down into households and showed the rate-paying inmates of households as well as heads of households. The Seventeenth Eighteen Penny Provincial Tax List of April 8, 1774, gave information on home ownership, house or store rents, ground rents, the number of indentured servants and the number of slaves owned by resident taxpayers. This same Tax List gave the rents or assessed rental value of all the real property of the ward.

The total population listed for 1774 is 284 less than the estimate of maximum population in 1775 given in Table I and some of the sub-categories also vary from those given in Table I. The ward did gain a little population during the eighteen-month interval between the 1774 tax list upon which Table III is based and the 1775 Constables returns upon which Table I is based. The amount of growth is unknown. Also, the 1774 Middle Ward population is smaller than that given in Table I because of some variations in the sources. The 1774 tax list does not enumerate hired servants unless they were also taxpayers. Children listed as under two years of age in 1775 were not included in this 1774 estimate. Finally, an indeterminate number of persons who were not taxed do not appear on the 1774 list: single men who had been apprenticed within the last six months, some female hired servants, infant and aged slaves, and female relatives of the householder.

TABLE VI

All the boroughs and districts of Philadelphia County joined into one consolidated city in 1854. In order to approximate the spread of dense settlement out from the core city of Philadelphia the boroughs and districts of Philadelphia County have been considered "urban" and hence listed on this table only when they attained a population of 5,000 or more. Pennsylvania Economy League, *Penjerdel Governmental Studies, Monograph #2* (Philadelphia, mimeographed, 1962), C-69; *Eighth Census: 1860*, I, *Population*, 431-2.

TABLE VII

1. The core is the original municipality of Philadelphia, 1860 wards 5-10; the ring is the eighteen outer wards. The location of the Negroes was given in *Ninth Census*, I, *Population*, 254; the location of the foreign born was determined by transcribing the original Eighth Census schedules at the National Archives, Washington, D.C. The error in the transcription was less than 1.0%. The location of the occupations was determined from a sample of *McElroy's Street Directory*, 1860.

2. The ring wards are, Northeast 23, 35, 41; South 48; West 34, 46, 40; Northwest 38, 21, 22, 42; the Core is the thirty-seven inner wards of the city. All figures calculated from unpublished tract statistics of the Fifteenth Census, 1930.

3. The owning families plus the renting families do not quite add to 100.0% because there were 3,497 families who were listed as renting but did not specify their rental group. *Fifteenth Census: 1930, Population, Families*, IV, 1162-1163.

TABLE VIII

The percentage of a ward's residents engaged in manufacturing was taken from the occupations listed in the 1860 *McElroy's Directory* sample. The male employment by ward was taken from the *Eighth Census: 1860* III, *Manufactures*, 536; the male population of each ward fifteen years and older was estimated by using the age and sex proportions of the *Seventh Census: 1850 Population*, 154-5 in conjunction with the total ward population for the ward given in the *Eighth Census*, I, *Population*, 431-2. Owing to the crudity of this method it doesn't seem reasonable to project a flow of male workers when the differences are less than 10 percent.

TABLE IX

It seems reasonable to assume that a group organization of work prevailed in those lines whose average number of persons per establishment was over twenty.

A major line of manufacturing is one which employed one thousand or more persons in the city of Philadelphia. Office help are included with the mill hands, supervisors, owners, and employers. Many children are omitted in 1860 in those lines, like cigar making, which were dominated by small shops. Philadelphia Board of Trade, *Manufactures of Philadelphia* (Phila., 1861), 5-18.

TABLE XI

It was necessary to use a sample of 1,126 names drawn at random from *McElroy's Philadelphia Directory of 1840* because the Sixth U.S. Census did not return people by their occupations. The estimation of the location of persons by occupation was further handicapped by the lack of any complete address listing of Philadelphia streets prior to the house numbering reform of January 1, 1857 (Scharf & Westcott, *History of Philadelphia*, I, 725). Therefore the city was divided up into approximate address districts and the sample from the directory distributed as follows. *South,* all addresses south of Spruce street, not including Spruce, and all addresses with street numbers of south 200 or higher, and the villages of Passyunk and Moyamensing. This district is equivalent to 1860 wards 1-4, and part of 5. *Old City,* all addresses from Vine to Spruce, inclusive, Delaware to Schuylkill rivers, and all street numbers 1-150 north and south. This district is equivalent to 1860 wards 6-10 and part of 5. *Northeast,* all addresses north of Vine, east of 6th street and in the far north east of Germantown avenue; all street numbers 200 north or higher, and the villages of Frankford, Kensington, Northern Liberties, Old York, West Kensington. Equivalent to 1860 wards 11, 12, 16-19, 23. *Northwest,* all addresses north of Vine and west of 6th street, not including 6th, and all street numbers 200 north and higher, and the villages of Germantown, Fairmount, Penn Township, Francisville, Ridge, and Bush Hill. Equivalent to 1860 wards 13-15, 20, 22. *Not located,* 195 addresses from the sample. These addresses lay in the completely uncertain area north and south of the old city, the house numbers 150-199 north and 150-199 south; east and west streets on the north that ran through both the northeast and northwest where no identifying intersection was given; addresses of streets whose names were repeated in different sections of the city; West Philadelphia across the Schuylkill river; addresses that couldn't be located within the districts set forth for analysis.

The results of this table seem in conformity with the findings for a decade earlier presented by William S. Hastings, "Philadelphia Microcosm," *Pennsylvania Magazine*, XCI (April, 1967), 164-180.

TABLE XII

The figures of the table include all foreign born Irish, from both Northern and Southern Ireland. They were transcribed from the original schedules of the Eighth Census. In the transcribing a slight error occurred; there were 559 more foreign born Irish on the schedules than have been copied for ward analysis above.

TABLE XIV

A major line of manufacturing is one which employed one thousand or more persons in the city of Philadelphia. Office help are included with the mill hands, supervisors, owners, and employers. *Fifteenth Census: 1930, Manufactures,* III, 466-7.

Table XV

See Table II for an explanation of this index. The source for 1860 was a random sample drawn from *McElroy's Philadelphia Directory, 1860.* Foreign born 1930, and the industrial categories of 1930 were taken from unpublished ward data of the Fifteenth Census; the rental information *Fifteenth Census: 1930, Families,* IV (Washington, 1933), 1162-3.

Table XVIII

The districts of this WPA study were slightly different than those adopted for analysis elsewhere in this book. The "Center" is larger than the "Downtown"; it includes the Downtown wards 5-10 and wards 11-13 of the Northeast, 14-15 of the Northwest, and 2-4, and 30 of the South.

"Crowded" accommodations mean accommodations of more than one person per room.

Works Progress Administration, *Philadelphia Housing Inventory* (processed, Philadelphia, 1936, Fine Arts Library, University of Pennsylvania), 44-156.

Table XX

This origin and destination estimate was based on an average of daily traffic surveyed from October 14-November 18, 1912. The total fares were 1,238,000 exclusive of transfers. *Philadelphia Traffic Commissioner's Report,* I (Philadelphia, 1913), 74-77.

Table XXI

For district boundaries see notes to Table XVIII; source, W.P.A., *Philadelphia Housing Inventory,* 44-156.

Index

Abolition, 1840 riots on, 130-134
Academy of Natural Sciences in private higher education, 119
American Philosophical Society in private higher education, 119
Artisans, 1860, industrialization and, 64-78
Associations clubs and, 1860, 61, 62

Baird, Mathew, 85
Baldwin, Matthias W., as generalized businessman, 82, 85
Bossism, 1860, 86-91
Breck, Samuel, in development of public schools, 117
Building, pattern of, community life and, 54, 56
Broome, Edwin C., in expansion of school system, 122
Brown, David Paul, in dedication of Pennsylvania Hall, 133
Bryant and Stratton Business College in private higher education, 120
Building, process of, privatism and, 1900–, 205-214
Building, public, 1860, 54
Building, types of, 1935, *195*
Business, benefit to, in city planning, 206, 207, 208
  city, ties to national business of, 64
  generalized, examples of, 80, 81, 82
  specialization in, 1860, 79, 80

Cadwalader, John, Revolutionary supplies controversy and, 40, 41
  in 1844 rioting against Catholics, 149
Carriages, manufacture of, 1860, 71
Catholics, rioting against, 1844, 148-151. *See also* Irish Catholics.
City, colonial, Middle Ward of, constitution of, 14, 15, *15*, 16, 17
  occupations in, *18*
  development of, privatism and, 4
  1860, area of, 53
  civic goals of, 99, 100
  1900–, social order of, work groups and, 169
  transition to, 1830-1860, 49, 50
City Normal School, in public higher education, 119
Civic affairs, specialized businessmen and, 85, 86

Clothing industry, 1860, specialization in, 69
Clubs, 1860, 61, 62
Coal heavers, organization of, 1860, 75
Coffee houses, 1770, social life and, 20
Communications, 1770, patterns of, 17, 18, 19, 20
Community, changes in, transition to city and, 49, 50
  life of, building patterns and, 54, 56
Community, 1770, 10, 11, 13, 14
Commuting, family life and, 196, 197
  1860, patterns of, 59, 60, *60*, 61
Conrad, Robert T., in political contest with Richard Vaux, 95
Consolidation, city, in development of police force, 1840-1860, 152-157
  results of, 102
Constitution, state, Revolutionary War, establishment of, 29
Cooke, Jay, as specialized businessman, 83, 84, 85
Cope, Thomas Pym, as generalized businessman, 80, 81, 82
  in waterworks campaign, 104
Corporation, municipal, history of, 100-102
Crittenden Commercial College in private higher education, 120

Deane, Silas, in Revolutionary supplies controversy, 32-36
Democracy, Revolutionary, privatism and, 45
Democrats in 1850 consolidation of city, 152, 153, 154, 155, 156
Depression 1837, labor movement and, 76
  race riot in, 132, 133, 134
  rioting and, 137-141
Downtown, description of, 185-194
  development of, 188
Drinker, Henry, Jr., in waterworks campaign, 104

Economic activity, 1860 housing and, 52, 53
Education, higher, private, 119, 120
  See also Schools.
Elections, reforms in, effects of, 101
  1835 riot and, 130
Enterprise, individual, 1770, 6, 7

253